WILLIAM SHAKESPEARE was born in Stratford-upon-Avon in April, 1564, and his birth is traditionally celebrated on April 23. The facts of his life, known from surviving documents, are sparse. He was one of eight children born to John Shakespeare, a merchant of some standing in his community. William probably went to the King's New School in Stratford, but he had no university education. In November 1582, at the age of eighteen, he married Anne Hathaway, eight years his senior, who was pregnant with their first child, Susanna. She was born on May 26, 1583. Twins, a boy, Hamnet (who would die at age eleven), and a girl, Judith, were born in 1585. By 1592 Shakespeare had gone to London, working as an actor and already known as a playwright. A rival dramatist, Robert Greene, referred to him as "an upstart crow, beautified with our feathers." Shakespeare became a principal shareholder and playwright of the successful acting troupe the Lord Chamberlain's men (later, under James I, called the King's men). In 1599 the Lord Chamberlain's men built and occupied the Globe Theatre in Southwark near the Thames River. Here many of Shakespeare's plays were performed by the most famous actors of his time, including Richard Burbage, Will Kempe, and Robert Armin. In addition to his 37 plays, Shakespeare had a hand in others, including *Sir Thomas More* and *The Two Noble Kinsmen*, and he wrote poems, including *Venus and Adonis* and *The Rape of Lucrece*. His 154 sonnets were published, probably without his authorization, in 1609. In 1611 or 1612 he gave up his lodgings in London and devoted more and more of his time to retirement in Stratford, though he continued writing such plays as *The Tempest* and *Henry VIII* until about 1613. He died on April 23, 1616, and was buried in Holy Trinity Church, Stratford. No collected edition of his plays was published during his lifetime, but in 1623 two members of his acting company, John Heminges and Henry Condell, published the great collection now called the First Folio.

Bantam Shakespeare
The Complete Works—29 Volumes
Edited by David Bevington
With forewords by Joseph Papp on the plays

The Poems: Venus and Adonis, The Rape of Lucrece, The
Phoenix and Turtle, A Lover's Complaint,
the Sonnets

Antony and Cleopatra	*The Merchant of Venice*
As You Like It	*A Midsummer Night's Dream*
The Comedy of Errors	*Much Ado about Nothing*
Hamlet	*Othello*
Henry IV, Part One	*Richard II*
Henry IV, Part Two	*Richard III*
Henry V	*Romeo and Juliet*
Julius Caesar	*The Taming of the Shrew*
King Lear	*The Tempest*
Macbeth	*Twelfth Night*

Together in one volume:

Henry VI, Parts One, Two, and Three
King John and Henry VIII
Measure for Measure, All's Well that Ends Well, and
Troilus and Cressida
Three Early Comedies: Love's Labor's Lost, The Two
Gentlemen of Verona, The Merry
Wives of Windsor
Three Classical Tragedies: Titus Andronicus, Timon
of Athens, Coriolanus
The Late Romances: Pericles, Cymbeline, The Winter's
Tale, The Tempest

Two collections:

Four Comedies: The Taming of the Shrew, A Midsummer
Night's Dream, The Merchant of Venice,
Twelfth Night
Four Tragedies: Hamlet, Othello, King Lear, Macbeth

William Shakespeare

HENRY IV, PART TWO

Edited by
David Bevington

David Scott Kastan,
James Hammersmith,
and Robert Kean Turner,
Associate Editors

With a Foreword by
Joseph Papp

BANTAM BOOKS
TORONTO / NEW YORK / LONDON / SYDNEY / AUCKLAND

HENRY IV, PART TWO

A Bantam Book / published by arrangement
with Scott, Foresman and Company

PRINTING HISTORY
Scott, Foresman edition published / January 1980
Bantam edition, with newly edited text and substantially revised,
edited, and amplified notes, introductions, and other
materials, published / February 1988
Valuable advice on staging matters has been
provided by Richard Hosley.
Collations checked by Eric Rasmussen.
Additional editorial assistance by Claire McEachern.

Library of Congress Cataloging-in-Publication Data

Shakespeare, William, 1564–1616.
  [King Henry IV. Part 2]
  Henry IV. Part two / William Shakespeare; edited by David
Bevington; David Scott Kastan, James Hammersmith, and Robert Kean
Turner, associate editors; with a foreword by Joseph Papp.
    p. cm.—(A Bantam classic)
  "Bantam edition, with newly edited text and substantially revised,
edited, and amplified notes, introductions, and other materials"—
—T.p. verso.
  Bibliography: p.
  ISBN 0-553-21294-X (pbk.)
  1. Henry IV, King of England, 1367–1413—Drama. I. Bevington,
David M. II. Title.
PR2811.A2B48 1988
822.3'3—dc19
                                      87–24098
                                       CIP

Published simultaneously in the United States and Canada

Bantam Books are published by Bantam Books, a division of Bantam
Doubleday Dell Publishing Group, Inc. Its trademark, consisting of the
words "Bantam Books" and the portrayal of a rooster, is Registered in
U.S. Patent and Trademark Office and in other countries. Marca Regis-
trada. Bantam Books, 666 Fifth Avenue, New York, New York 10103.

PRINTED IN THE UNITED STATES OF AMERICA

O   0 9 8 7 6 5 4 3 2 1

Contents

Foreword

It's hard to imagine, but Shakespeare wrote all of his plays with a quill pen, a goose feather whose hard end had to be sharpened frequently. How many times did he scrape the dull end to a point with his knife, dip it into the inkwell, and bring up, dripping wet, those wonderful words and ideas that are known all over the world?

In the age of word processors, typewriters, and ballpoint pens, we have almost forgotten the meaning of the word "blot." Yet when I went to school, in the 1930s, my classmates and I knew all too well what an inkblot from the metal-tipped pens we used would do to a nice clean page of a test paper, and we groaned whenever a splotch fell across the sheet. Most of us finished the school day with ink-stained fingers; those who were less careful also went home with ink-stained shirts, which were almost impossible to get clean.

When I think about how long it took me to write the simplest composition with a metal-tipped pen and ink, I can only marvel at how many plays Shakespeare scratched out with his goose-feather quill pen, year after year. Imagine him walking down one of the narrow cobblestoned streets of London, or perhaps drinking a pint of beer in his local alehouse. Suddenly his mind catches fire with an idea, or a sentence, or a previously elusive phrase. He is burning with impatience to write it down—but because he doesn't have a ballpoint pen or even a pencil in his pocket, he has to keep the idea in his head until he can get to his quill and parchment.

He rushes back to his lodgings on Silver Street, ignoring the vendors hawking brooms, the coaches clattering by, the piteous wails of beggars and prisoners. Bounding up the stairs, he snatches his quill and starts to write furiously, not even bothering to light a candle against the dusk. "To be, or not to be," he scrawls, "that is the—." But the quill point has gone dull, the letters have fattened out illegibly, and in the middle of writing one of the most famous passages in the history of dramatic literature, Shakespeare has to stop to sharpen his pen.

Taking a deep breath, he lights a candle now that it's dark, sits down, and begins again. By the time the candle has burned out and the noisy apprentices of his French Huguenot landlord have quieted down, Shakespeare has finished Act 3 of *Hamlet* with scarcely a blot.

Early the next morning, he hurries through the fog of a London summer morning to the rooms of his colleague Richard Burbage, the actor for whom the role of Hamlet is being written. He finds Burbage asleep and snoring loudly, sprawled across his straw mattress. Not only had the actor performed in *Henry V* the previous afternoon, but he had then gone out carousing all night with some friends who had come to the performance.

Shakespeare shakes his friend awake, until, bleary-eyed, Burbage sits up in his bed. "Dammit, Will," he grumbles, "can't you let an honest man sleep?" But the playwright, his eyes shining and the words tumbling out of his mouth, says, "Shut up and listen—tell me what you think of *this*!"

He begins to read to the still half-asleep Burbage, pacing around the room as he speaks. ". . . Whether 'tis nobler in the mind to suffer the slings and arrows of outrageous fortune—"

Burbage interrupts, suddenly wide awake, "That's excellent, very good, 'the slings and arrows of outrageous fortune,' yes, I think it will work quite well. . . ." He takes the parchment from Shakespeare and murmurs the lines to himself, slowly at first but with growing excitement.

The sun is just coming up, and the words of one of Shakespeare's most famous soliloquies are being uttered for the first time by the first actor ever to bring Hamlet to life. It must have been an exhilarating moment.

Shakespeare wrote most of his plays to be performed live by the actor Richard Burbage and the rest of the Lord Chamberlain's men (later the King's men). Today, however, our first encounter with the plays is usually in the form of the printed word. And there is no question that reading Shakespeare for the first time isn't easy. His plays aren't comic books or magazines or the dime-store detective novels I read when I was young. A lot of his sentences are complex. Many of his words are no longer used in our everyday speech. His profound thoughts are often condensed into poetry, which is not as straightforward as prose.

Yet when you hear the words spoken aloud, a lot of the language may strike you as unexpectedly modern. For Shakespeare's plays, like any dramatic work, weren't really meant to be read; they were meant to be spoken, seen, and performed. It's amazing how lines that are so troublesome in print can flow so naturally and easily when spoken.

I think it was precisely this music that first fascinated me. When I was growing up, Shakespeare was a stranger to me. I had no particular interest in him, for I was from a different cultural tradition. It never occurred to me that his plays might be more than just something to "get through" in school, like science or math or the physical education requirement we had to fulfill. My passions then were movies, radio, and vaudeville—certainly not Elizabethan drama.

I was, however, fascinated by words and language. Because I grew up in a home where Yiddish was spoken, and English was only a second language, I was acutely sensitive to the musical sounds of different languages and had an ear for lilt and cadence and rhythm in the spoken word. And so I loved reciting poems and speeches even as a very young child. In first grade I learned lots of short nature verses— "Who has seen the wind?," one of them began. My first foray into drama was playing the role of Scrooge in Charles Dickens's *A Christmas Carol* when I was eight years old. I liked summoning all the scorn and coldness I possessed and putting them into the words, "Bah, humbug!"

From there I moved on to longer and more famous poems and other works by writers of the 1930s. Then, in junior high school, I made my first acquaintance with Shakespeare through his play *Julius Caesar*. Our teacher, Miss McKay, assigned the class a passage to memorize from the opening scene of the play, the one that begins "Wherefore rejoice? What conquest brings he home?" The passage seemed so wonderfully theatrical and alive to me, and the experience of memorizing and reciting it was so much fun, that I went on to memorize another speech from the play on my own.

I chose Mark Antony's address to the crowd in Act 3,

scene 2, which struck me then as incredibly high drama.
Even today, when I speak the words, I feel the same thrill I
did that first time. There is the strong and athletic Antony
descending from the raised pulpit where he has been speaking, right into the midst of a crowded Roman square. Hold-
ing the torn and bloody cloak of the murdered Julius
Caesar in his hand, he begins to speak to the people of
Rome:

> If you have tears, prepare to shed them now.
> You all do know this mantle. I remember
> The first time ever Caesar put it on;
> 'Twas on a summer's evening in his tent,
> That day he overcame the Nervii.
> Look, in this place ran Cassius' dagger through.
> See what a rent the envious Casca made.
> Through this the well-belovèd Brutus stabbed,
> And as he plucked his cursèd steel away,
> Mark how the blood of Caesar followed it,
> As rushing out of doors to be resolved
> If Brutus so unkindly knocked or no;
> For Brutus, as you know, was Caesar's angel.
> Judge, O you gods, how dearly Caesar loved him!
> This was the most unkindest cut of all . . .

I'm not sure now that I even knew Shakespeare had written a lot of other plays, or that he was considered "timeless," "universal," or "classic"—but I knew a good speech
when I heard one, and I found the splendid rhythms of
Antony's rhetoric as exciting as anything I'd ever come
across.

Fifty years later, I still feel that way. Hearing good actors
speak Shakespeare gracefully and naturally is a wonderful
experience, unlike any other I know. There's a satisfying
fullness to the spoken word that the printed page just can't
convey. This is why seeing the plays of Shakespeare performed live in a theater is the best way to appreciate them.
If you can't do that, listening to sound recordings or watch-
ing film versions of the plays is the next best thing.

But if you do start with the printed word, use the play as a
script. Be an actor yourself and say the lines out loud. Don't
worry too much at first about words you don't immediately
understand. Look them up in the footnotes or a dictionary,

but don't spend too much time on this. It is more profitable
(and fun) to get the sense of a passage and sing it out. Speak
naturally, almost as if you were talking to a friend, but be
sure to enunciate the words properly. You'll be surprised at
how much you understand simply by speaking the speech
"trippingly on the tongue," as Hamlet advises the Players.

You might start, as I once did, with a speech from *Julius
Caesar*, in which the tribune (city official) Marullus scolds
the commoners for transferring their loyalties so quickly
from the defeated and murdered general Pompey to the
newly victorious Julius Caesar:

> Wherefore rejoice? What conquest brings he home?
> What tributaries follow him to Rome
> To grace in captive bonds his chariot wheels?
> You blocks, you stones, you worse than senseless
>   things!
> O you hard hearts, you cruel men of Rome,
> Knew you not Pompey? Many a time and oft
> Have you climbed up to walls and battlements,
> To towers and windows, yea, to chimney tops,
> Your infants in your arms, and there have sat
> The livelong day, with patient expectation,
> To see great Pompey pass the streets of Rome.

With the exception of one or two words like "wherefore"
(which means "why," not "where"), "tributaries" (which
means "captives"), and "patient expectation" (which
means patient waiting), the meaning and emotions of this
speech can be easily understood.

From here you can go on to dialogues or other more chal-
lenging scenes. Although you may stumble over unaccustomed phrases or unfamiliar words at first, and even fall
flat when you're crossing some particularly rocky passages, pick yourself up and stay with it. Remember that it
takes time to feel at home with anything new. Soon you'll
come to recognize Shakespeare's unique sense of humor
and way of saying things as easily as you recognize a
friend's laughter.

And then it will just be a matter of choosing which one of
Shakespeare's plays you want to tackle next. As a true fan
of his, you'll find that you're constantly learning from his
plays. It's a journey of discovery that you can continue for

the rest of your life. For no matter how many times you read or see a particular play, there will always be something new there that you won't have noticed before.

Why do so many thousands of people get hooked on Shakespeare and develop a habit that lasts a lifetime? What can he really say to us today, in a world filled with inventions and problems he never could have imagined? And how do you get past his special language and difficult sentence structure to understand him?

The best way to answer these questions is to go see a live production. You might not know much about Shakespeare, or much about the theater, but when you watch actors performing one of his plays on the stage, it will soon become clear to you why people get so excited about a playwright who lived hundreds of years ago.

For the story—what's happening in the play—is the most accessible part of Shakespeare. In *A Midsummer Night's Dream*, for example, you can immediately understand the situation: a girl is chasing a guy who's chasing a girl who's chasing another guy. No wonder *A Midsummer Night's Dream* is one of the most popular of Shakespeare's plays: it's about one of the world's most popular pastimes—falling in love.

But the course of true love never did run smooth, as the young suitor Lysander says. Often in Shakespeare's comedies the girl whom the guy loves doesn't love him back, or she loves him but he loves someone else. In *The Two Gentlemen of Verona*, Julia loves Proteus, Proteus loves Sylvia, and Sylvia loves Valentine, who is Proteus's best friend. In the end, of course, true love prevails, but not without lots of complications along the way.

For in all of his plays—comedies, histories, and tragedies—Shakespeare is showing you human nature. His characters act and react in the most extraordinary ways—and sometimes in the most incomprehensible ways. People are always trying to find motivations for what a character does. They ask, "Why does Iago want to destroy Othello?"

The answer, to me, is very simple—because that's the way Iago is. That's just his nature. Shakespeare doesn't explain his characters; he sets them in motion—and away they go. He doesn't worry about whether they're likable or not. He's interested in interesting people, and his most fascinating characters are those who are unpredictable. If you lean back in your chair early on in one of his plays, thinking you've figured out what Iago or Shylock (in *The Merchant of Venice*) is up to, don't be too sure—because that great judge of human nature, Shakespeare, will surprise you every time.

He is just as wily in the way he structures a play. In *Macbeth*, a comic scene is suddenly introduced just after the bloodiest and most treacherous slaughter imaginable, of a guest and king by his host and subject, when in comes a drunk porter who has to go to the bathroom. Shakespeare is tickling your emotions by bringing a stand-up comic on-stage right on the heels of a savage murder.

It has taken me thirty years to understand even some of these things, and so I'm not suggesting that Shakespeare is immediately understandable. I've gotten to know him not through theory but through practice, the practice of the *living* Shakespeare—the playwright of the theater.

Of course the plays are a great achievement of dramatic literature, and they should be studied and analyzed in schools and universities. But you must always remember, when reading all the words *about* the playwright and his plays, that *Shakespeare's* words came first and that in the end there is nothing greater than a single actor on the stage speaking the lines of Shakespeare.

Everything important that I know about Shakespeare comes from the practical business of producing and directing his plays in the theater. The task of classifying, criticizing, and editing Shakespeare's printed works I happily leave to others. For me, his plays really do live on the stage, not on the page. That is what he wrote them for and that is how they are best appreciated.

Although Shakespeare lived and wrote hundreds of years ago, his name rolls off my tongue as if he were my brother. As a producer and director, I feel that there is a professional relationship between us that spans the centuries. As a human being, I feel that Shakespeare has enriched my understanding of life immeasurably. I hope you'll let him do the same for you.

❖

In *Henry IV, Part Two,* Shakespeare begins putting distance between us and the Falstaff we knew and loved in *Part One,* preparing us for Hal's rejection of the fat man at the end of the play:

> I know thee not, old man. Fall to thy prayers.
> How ill white hairs becomes a fool and jester!
> I have long dreamt of such a kind of man,
> So surfeit-swelled, so old, and so profane,
> But being awaked, I do despise my dream. . . .
> Presume not that I am the thing I was,
> For God doth know, so shall the world perceive,
> That I have turned away my former self;
> So will I those that kept me company.

In a sense this rejection comes as no surprise, for throughout the play there has been a subtle and gradual shift in how we perceive Falstaff—we don't like him as much, especially when he's not with Hal. The old geniality seems a little sharper now, and a tone of bitterness or cynicism has crept in with it. Falstaff has lost some of the humorous spontaneity and improvisational ability he entertained us with in *Part One.* For example, in the first part, Shakespeare let him conduct his money-making impressment of soldiers offstage; here we see it directly onstage, where it shows a side of Falstaff that's not entirely attractive. Shakespeare is deliberately drawing away from his popular creation, and taking the audience with him.

To buffer us against the blow of losing Falstaff, he introduces a new character—Master Shallow, country justice. Shallow is so gentle, warm, and human that he immediately endears himself to us. We like him; his friends and servants like him; even the late *New York Times* critic Brooks Atkinson, when asked what Shakespearean role he'd most like to play, smiled and said, "Justice Shallow." But Shakespeare has Falstaff speak derogatorily of Shallow and pick him out as the victim of his next swindling operation. We don't want to see Falstaff cheat Shallow or abuse his friendship—and it gives us mixed feelings when he does. And that's exactly what Shakespeare is after.

Shakespeare doesn't stop there; he's determined to turn our sympathies away from Falstaff. He gives the fat knight a cynical soliloquy at the end of Act 3 that is in striking contrast to the friendliness of Shallow's farewell: "Sir John, the Lord bless you! God prosper your affairs! God send us peace! At your return, visit our house; let our old acquaintance be renewed. Peradventure I will with ye to the court." The ensuing speech shows a very tough Falstaff, openly contemptuous of someone he thinks beneath him, someone whose prosperity he seems to resent—"And now is this Vice's dagger become a squire. . . . And now has he land and beefs." He concludes, "I see no reason in the law of nature but I may snap at him. Let time shape, and there an end." The bitter language and the blatant opportunism shock us—is this the Falstaff that is not only witty in himself, but "the cause that wit is in other men"? What has happened?

Yet we still have a place in our hearts for Falstaff, and Shakespeare knows it. The playwright shows how sensitive he is to the audience in his Epilogue, in which he apologizes should the play have proved to be displeasing. He promises more Falstaff, and plugs his next play, *Henry V:* "If you be not too much cloyed with fat meat, our humble author will continue the story, with Sir John in it, and make you merry with fair Katharine of France. Where, for anything I know, Falstaff shall die of a sweat, unless already 'a be killed with your hard opinions." Shakespeare barely keeps his promise, since Falstaff doesn't appear in person in *Henry V,* but only in the words of Mistress Quickly, who describes his death: "his nose was as sharp as a pen, and 'a babbled of green fields."

JOSEPH PAPP

JOSEPH PAPP GRATEFULLY ACKNOWLEDGES THE HELP OF ELIZABETH KIRKLAND IN PREPARING THIS FOREWORD.

HENRY IV, PART TWO

Introduction

Shakespeare wrote *2 Henry IV* quite soon after *1 Henry IV*, perhaps in 1597, partly no doubt to capitalize on the enormous theatrical success of Falstaff, partly to finish the story of Falstaff's rejection. In writing *2 Henry IV*, Shakespeare drew on materials similar to those used for *I Henry IV*, notably Raphael Holinshed's *Chronicles* (1587) and the anonymous play *The Famous Victories of Henry V* (1583–1588). Moreover, he undertook to write a play that structurally is much like its predecessor, revealing more similarity between these plays than one can find elsewhere in Shakespeare. Even the three *Henry VI* plays do not reiterate structural patterns to the same degree. Is Shakespeare repeating himself, rewriting the earlier play, and if so why? Is *2 Henry IV* essentially a way of giving audiences more of what they had found so entertaining in the earlier play, or is it a way of reflecting on new and troublesome issues only partially raised in *1 Henry IV*?

The structural pattern runs as follows. In both plays, Shakespeare alternates between scenes of political seriousness and scenes of comic irresponsibility, juxtaposing a rebellion in the land with a rebellion in the King's own family. In *1 Henry IV* we move from a council of war (1.1) to a planning of the robbery at Gad's Hill (1.2). The scenes comment on each other by their nearness and by their mutual concern with lawlessness. Similarly in *2 Henry IV* we are at first introduced to a political rebellion in the north of England, after which we encounter Falstaff and Prince Hal's page. In both plays Act 2 scene 2 shows us Hal with Poins, setting up a future meeting to embarrass Falstaff by means of a plot, and in both plays Act 2 scene 4 is a long, centrally located scene at the tavern involving Hal and Falstaff in a contest of wits devised to expose Falstaff as a resourceful liar. The festivities in both scenes are brought to an end by a knocking at the door. (The act-scene divisions are probably not Shakespeare's, for they do not appear in the early quartos of either play; nevertheless, the structural location of these scenes is similar.) Between these linked scenes of

comic action, we turn in both plays to the rebel camp of the
Percys for a discussion of military planning against King
Henry (2.3). In both plays Falstaff goes off supposedly to
fight against the rebels but instead manages to abuse his
authority as recruiting officer and to garner undeserved
honors, either through wounding the dead Hotspur in the
leg or through capturing Coleville of the Dale with the aid
of an inflated reputation. The battle scenes are punctuated
by Falstaff's wry soliloquies; his disputation on wine
in *2 Henry IV* (4.3.88–123) serves a function like that of
his better-known catechism on honor in *1 Henry IV*
(5.1.129–140). Both plays introduce a confrontation between Hal and his father; the son is penitent for his way-
wardness, the father lectures on statecraft, and the prodigal
son is recovered into kingly grace. Prince Hal goes on thereafter to win public honor and to prove himself his father's
true son. Even the rejection of Falstaff, with which the second play ends, finds its counterpart in *1 Henry IV* in Hal's
impatience with Falstaff during the battle of Shrewsbury,
his elegy over the seemingly dead body of his onetime companion, and his resolve to be henceforth a prince.

These resemblances, and still others, are further high-
lighted when we realize that Shakespeare continues to use
in his second play the structural device of foils, or paired
characters around Hal who help define alternative models
of conduct. The father is, as before, an awesome figure of
authority, one whose sternness Hal never fully adopts and
yet one whose public role as king Hal must inherit. Falstaff,
as before, offers himself as a companion in revelry, dissipation, and joie de vivre, and must be rejected even though
much of what he says offers insight into the coldness of
King Henry and especially of Hal's dutiful brother Prince
John. Yet the chief purpose of these recapitulations is to
suggest profound differences. *2 Henry IV* does not simply
go over familiar material. Repeatedly, the similarities of situation reveal how much Hal has still to learn, how much
Falstaff has changed, and how much more complicated the
political process is than it first appeared. The foil relationships in this play focus less on honor, as in *1 Henry IV,* than
on two related matters: rumor or reputation, and justice.

Rumor begins the play—quite literally, since Rumor is
presented to us in allegorized form as portrayed by Virgil,

painted full of tongues, spreading false information about
the battle of Shrewsbury just ended. Rumor takes particular delight in its most cruel trick of all, raising false hopes
and then dashing them. In the scene following at the Percys'
household, we see rumor as it manifests itself in the real
world of men, beguiling Northumberland with the "news"
of his son Hotspur's triumph only to disappoint him afterward with the stark truth of defeat and death. What is the
function of the uncharacteristic allegory at the start of this
play? It serves first to establish a new dispiriting tone. The
rebels are in disarray, their cause in jeopardy. Hotspur is
dead, and with him has died the bright honor of his cause.
His kinsmen, always more Machiavellian than he, are now
warier than ever. Northumberland is persuaded, in a later
scene, to prevaricate to his allies and withdraw to Scotland
when they most need his support, waiting to come in on
their side only when he can be sure of success. The atmo-
sphere of realpolitik and of dealing in false appearances is
a consequence of a world governed by rumor. The rebels'
case is never as attractive in this play as in *1 Henry IV*; Hotspur's idealism and chivalry are sorely missed.

Rumor has profound consequences for the King's side as
well, and for Falstaff and Prince Hal. Falstaff rides on false
reputation through the early scenes of *2 Henry IV*. He
evades arrest at the hands of the Lord Chief Justice because
of his presumed deeds at Shrewsbury, deeds that we know
to be illusory. His day's service at Shrewsbury "hath a little
gilded over" his "night's exploit on Gad's Hill," as the Lord
Chief Justice reluctantly concedes (1.2.147–148). His reputation makes possible his capture of Coleville of the Dale at
Gaultree Forest, even though by this time Falstaff's reputation is clearly beginning to wear thin.

Conversely, Hal discovers that his reputation for prodi-
gality will not leave him. Hal begins to realize that despite
the fact that the King has severed Falstaff from him
(1.2.201–202), so that Hal scarcely knows of Falstaff's
whereabouts until he agrees to a kind of reunion for old
times' sake at the tavern, everyone assumes the worst of
Hal and expects his future reign to be one of continual riot.
He himself characterizes his visit to the tavern, in order to
see Falstaff again, as a base "transformation" like those
Ovidian portrayals of Jove in lowly human disguise. Talking

with Poins in 2.2.1–44, Hal professes to be "exceeding weary" of the "disgrace" it is in him to remember all his vile companions, including Poins, and he sardonically congratulates his companion on thinking like everyone else when Poins assumes that any weeping on Hal's part for his father's death would be no more than princely hypocrisy. "Let the end try the man," says Hal, in what should be a plain notice of his reformation, but no one credits him with sincerity. When his father does take to his deathbed, surrounded by hushed courtiers, Hal, until now notably absent from court, enters with exaggerated offhandedness as though eschewing the show of mourning he knows cannot be believed in him. His taking the crown from the pillow of his seemingly dead father strikes King Henry and his courtiers as one last confirmation of Hal's desire to supplant his father, and indeed we too are forced to wonder at Hal's imprudence. (The patricidal overtones in one of Shakespeare's sources, *The Famous Victories of Henry V,* are much more overt than those in Shakespeare's play.)

The structural recapitulations of *2 Henry IV,* then, in which Hal first jests with Falstaff at the tavern and afterward confronts his father at court, are no mere repetitions; they stress the dreary fact that a reputation for riotous conduct persists, that the father's embracing of his son has lapsed into renewed distrust, that "reformation" is not the simple process Hal once supposed. Reformation is first a matter of improving one's own conduct, but it is also a matter of improving one's image. This is not a happy revelation to a young man impatient of ceremony and public display, but it is the way of the world and an integral part of any successful kingship. King Henry's last advice to Hal, in fact, once they have been reconciled anew, concerns the manipulation of appearances in the name of statecraft; the father urges the son to resolve civil strife by going to war against some foreign enemy. He must "busy giddy minds / With foreign quarrels" (4.5.213–214). Hal will adopt this stratagem in *Henry V* by warring against the French. Meantime, in *2 Henry IV,* he must overcome his reputation not only with his father but with the Lord Chief Justice, the nobles of the court, and his brother John. Not until the play's end do they believe other than that Hal will turn riot loose in his kingdom. The intransigent nature of false "rumor" or reputation does much to explain why the new king must reject Falstaff so publicly and so sharply. He has in fact already rejected Falstaff in the sense of leaving him, but no one has taken the point—least of all Falstaff, who now presses in upon the new king with hopes of reward and license to act as he pleases. "The laws of England are at my commandment," he exults (5.3.138–139). Only a public repudiation can meet the demands of kingship by making full use of the act's symbolic value. Hal must reject Falstaff not only in his heart but in the view of his nation. It is a distasteful act, perhaps to him as to us, but is made necessary by the political exigencies of the moment.

The play's concern with justice emerges in the first confrontation between the Lord Chief Justice and Falstaff (1.2.54–226). The one represents law, the other license. Who is to represent and administer the law in Henry V's reign? The Lord Chief Justice is a firm and austere figure, a deputy or substitute for the father-king, one who has presumed to imprison Hal for resisting his authority. This Lord Chief Justice does not expect to remain in office once the new king is crowned; like other serious characters in the play, and ourselves as well, he longs for reassurance in the troubled times of civil war and change of administration under a monarchy. In contrast to this somewhat awesome parental figure, Falstaff offers hedonism and irresponsibility. His wit is in a sense no less engaging than in *1 Henry IV*. His scenes with Shallow and Silence, as they choose soldiers for the upcoming campaign or prepare for the golden time they anticipate, are as funny as the best of Falstaff. The pairing of the Lord Chief Justice and Falstaff as foils might suggest at first that one is lacking where the other is strong, and that Hal must steer between extremes.

Yet this play does not give us a genuine debate on justice like that on honor in *1 Henry IV*, where Falstaff's comments on honor strike home because of Hotspur's fanaticism. The Lord Chief Justice of this play is essentially in the right, however austere, and Falstaff is essentially in the wrong, however funny. The Lord Chief Justice sees through Falstaff and patiently bides his time. Falstaff's excesses are more pronounced than in the earlier play. We see him with Doll Tearsheet, a whore, in maudlin, drunken conversation. He is associated with images of disease—gout, the pox or syphilis, consumption, lameness—and of purging. His lying is not as consistently clever as before. Hal recalls the brilliant lie about the Gad's Hill robbery and credits Falstaff with having seen through the Prince's trick on that occasion (2.4.305–307), but in the second tavern scene Falstaff can only mutter incoherently that he had no idea that Hal was behind him in disguise listening to his foulmouthed reproaches. Falstaff's rioting with Pistol disturbs the peace, and in such brawls homicides occur necessitating arrest and punishment (5.4). When Falstaff appears with the diminutive page, as in scene 2, we are forcefully reminded of the grossness of his body, though he too laughs at this. His mooching off Mistress Quickly and his breach of promise of marriage to her, though hinted at in the earlier play, are much more open here; the humor is keen, but we cannot forget that Falstaff is victimizing a woman. Lawsuits and arrests are more prominent in this play than in its predecessor. Falstaff's abuse of authority to recruit soldiers, about which he discourses wittily in the earlier play, is here fully shown both in its hilarity and in its lawless consequences.

Falstaff's new companions, Pistol, Doll, and then Justice Shallow and Justice Silence, sharpen our perception of Falstaff's increasingly flagrant lawlessness. Shallow and Silence are, by their very profession, counterparts to the Lord Chief Justice. In their complacent interest in their own prosperity ("How a good yoke of bullocks at Stamford fair?" 3.2.39), in their countenancing of influence peddling by their subordinates (5.1.37–52), and in Shallow's foxy aspirations to deceive Falstaff before Falstaff can deceive him, these pillars of rural respectability reveal how far injustice has permeated the English countryside. They are fit companions for Falstaff when he hears the news of his rejection and are suitably victimized by Falstaff's inability to repay a loan that Justice Shallow has advanced to him from motives of self-interest. These old men, myopically recollecting the jolly days of their youth, accentuate Falstaff's physical frailty and aging. Falstaff mocks the stories of their escapades, but he too, as he confesses to Doll over his drink, is old. The necessary course of justice is made plain by the structural configurations of the play. Falstaff and his companions seek lawlessness and must be rebuked; the Lord Chief Justice, who fears rejection, must instead be embraced by Hal explicitly as a father figure ("You shall be as a father to my youth," 5.2.118) in order to reaffirm public decency. The Lord Chief Justice is to bear "the balance and the sword" (l. 103) as emblems of justice and its stern role in maintaining order; Falstaff is dismissed as "The tutor and the feeder of my riots" (5.5.62). These necessities are plain, even though they do not answer the emotionally complicated issue of Hal's (and our) fondness for the companion of his youth.

Hal's brother Prince John of Lancaster is another opposite to Falstaff. Here the contrast is less prejudicial to Falstaff. Prince John takes charge of his ailing father's wars, and engineers a surrender of the rebels at Gaultree Forest that is a triumph of equivocation and double-dealing. It also saves the nation from further civil conflict, at least for the time being, and establishes the peace that Hal inherits and turns to his advantage against France. What are we to make of what has been called (by Paul Jorgensen, *PMLA*, 1961) John's "dastardly treachery"? It seems all too much in keeping with the realpolitik that has characterized the conduct of both sides heretofore, and may thus be said to be a suitable conclusion. The dismaying "revolution of the times" (3.1.46) brings with it the cooling of friendships and the recollection of dire prophecies from the days of Richard II. The only justification possible for what John does is that it succeeds. It surely lacks the glory and honor attendant on the conflict of Hal and Hotspur in *1 Henry IV*. Not coincidentally, Hal is far away from Gaultree Forest when this dismal surrender is brought about. Prince John is a master at knowing how to "construe the times to their necessities" (4.1.104). His acts scarcely represent justice any more than honor. "Is this proceeding just and honorable?" ask the betrayed rebels, and are answered merely "Is your assembly so?" (4.2.110–111). The end justifies the means. Falstaff's observations at Prince John's expense therefore have a point. John is, as Falstaff characterizes him, "sober-blooded"; he drinks no wine and relies not on valor but on sagacity. Falstaff hopes that Hal will prove more valiant, tempering "the cold blood he did naturally inherit of his father" (4.3.88–117) with the imbibing of sherry and other pleasures learned from Falstaff. Whatever the merits of drinking as an inducement to courage, we do perceive that

Prince John is too much his father's son, and that Hal will avoid this cold extreme in his quest for a kingly identity that is both symbol and substance.

Hal has thus learned something from Falstaff, if only as a caution against extremes, and partly for this reason his rejection of Falstaff must come as a shock no matter how inevitable. Hal may well appear to dwindle in the process, for he has given up a good deal of his private self to adopt the public role thrust upon him. He accepts that public role not unwillingly but may also perceive that he does so at some cost to himself—and to Falstaff. His terms of rejection are not wholly ungenerous—he allows the possibility of Falstaff's returning to court if he reforms, and makes financial allowance so that Falstaff will have no need to continue in crime—but the finality of the action remains stunning. We are left with a broken Falstaff, on his way to the Fleet prison by order of the Lord Chief Justice, trying to deceive himself into believing that all will be well. Hal and England have turned in a new direction; a war against the French is clearly in prospect already, one that will absorb the energies of the new king and his father's erstwhile political enemies as well. The emergence of Hal into his public role is complete.

Henry IV, Part Two
in Performance

2 Henry IV has not enjoyed the popularity onstage of
1 Henry IV, despite the continuing presence of Falstaff. Perhaps audiences have felt uncomfortable with a Falstaff who
is visibly older, more disreputable, surrounded by such
companions as Pistol, Doll Tearsheet, and Justice Shallow,
and at last rejected by King Henry V; or perhaps producers
have been unwilling to offer a play with no dignified wom-
en's roles; or perhaps (especially in the eighteenth and nineteenth centuries) audiences have been reluctant to see their
heroic Henry do such a mean-spirited thing as rejecting his
old companion. No doubt it is a darker and more disillusioned play than *1 Henry IV.*

Still, *2 Henry IV* has had significant stage successes.
Thomas Betterton, playing Falstaff, apparently did well
with a revival about 1704 at the theater in Lincoln's Inn
Fields, London, albeit in a much-changed version that cut
Rumor's prologue and the Northumberland–Lady Percy
scenes, and ended with material added from the early part
of *Henry V* to provide a less dispiriting conclusion than that
found in Shakespeare's *2 Henry IV.* In similarly rearranged
form the play was again well received in 1720 at the Theatre
Royal, Drury Lane, with Barton Booth as Henry IV, John
Mills as Falstaff, and Robert Wilks as Hal; and the play was
revived with some regularity through the rest of the eighteenth and early nineteenth centuries. A production at
Drury Lane in 1736 advertised itself as "Written by Shakespeare, in which will be restored scenes, soliloquies, and
other circumstances, originally in the part of Falstaff,
which have been for many years omitted." Two years later
the rival theater at Covent Garden also produced "the genuine play of Shakespeare, and not that altered by Mr. Betterton." Nonetheless, Betterton's version was not entirely
displaced from the stage, and clearly the success of productions of *2 Henry IV* depended less on the acting text than on
the skill of the actor playing Falstaff. James Quin, John
Henderson, and George Frederick Cooke were among those

who ensured that the play, in whatever version, continued in the repertory.

Though David Garrick produced *2 Henry IV* and acted the King, first in 1758, during the period of his management at Drury Lane, he had no great success with the play, in large part because he lacked an actor to play Falstaff with the ebullience the role demands. Perhaps for the same reason, John Philip Kemble's production of *2 Henry IV* at Covent Garden in 1804 introduced new pageantry and spectacle to refocus attention on the King. An essay of that year admired this strategy, claiming that Kemble "in giving the scene all the splendor the chamber of a monarch requires, and his person all the elegance of costume, shows a desire to render stage exhibitions as perfect as possible for public gratification." The final scene introduced the arrest of Falstaff before the reconciliation of Henry V with the Lord Chief Justice so that the play could end with a triumphant restoration of order.

Covent Garden's production of *2 Henry IV* in 1821 illustrates the extent to which the play could be rewritten to accommodate audiences' desire to see King Henry and the English monarchy in an attractive light. The show was designed, in fact, as a way of celebrating the accession to the throne in that year of King George IV. To that end the theater managers, who included Charles Kemble, staged a spectacular coronation procession for Henry V in a stage replica of Westminster Abbey, its galleries and aisles filled with noble spectators. The procession led off with the King's herb-woman, six strewers of flowers, the Dean's Beadle of Westminster, the High Constable of Westminster, drums and trumpets, chaplains, sheriffs and aldermen of London, Masters in Chancery, the King's Sergeant and Attorney General, judges, the Lord Chief Justice, a choir singing the coronation anthem, and many more. The King then followed under the royal canopy, escorted by two bishops, train bearers, mace bearers, and halberdiers. The critic for *John Bull* objected to the inclusion of the Yeomen of the Guard, on the grounds that they had not in fact been established until the reign of Henry VII, but admitted that "a more splendid pageant never graced a theatre." The production, extravagant and unwieldy by today's standards, merely amplified the realistic attention to detail and glorification of English royalty of Kemble's version seventeen years earlier.

The production also cut and rearranged scenes to minimize the unpleasantness of Shakespeare's conclusion. A reordering of events enabled audiences to hear the reassuring news of Henry V's accession even before his appearance as king. Gone were the arrests of Mistress Quickly and Doll Tearsheet (5.4), with their reminder of the disreputable past that Prince Hal had once known in the company of Falstaff. The rejection of Falstaff could scarcely be left out, but any negative effect it might have had on the spectators' view of King Henry was, as in Kemble's text of 1804, neutralized by a subsequent upbeat ending: the King was reconciled to his Lord Chief Justice and no mention was made of the Lord Chief Justice's imprisonment of Falstaff and Shallow (5.5.99 ff.). Clearly the actor-managers of this age were intent on presenting Henry as the future king, no longer encumbered by his association with a thoroughly dissipated Falstaff. Predictably, the spectacular production, starring William Charles Macready as the King and Charles Kemble as Hal, was a great success, and for its performance on July 19, the coronation day itself, the theater was opened free to the public.

Royalty obviously approved of *2 Henry IV* as it was acted in the nineteenth century, and when Samuel Phelps was asked to give a command performance before Queen Victoria at Windsor Castle in January of 1853, he chose *2 Henry IV*. This was his first production of the play; his own theater at Sadler's Wells had to wait until March for a performance. Phelps revived the play at Sadler's Wells in 1861. His unusually versatile doubling of the parts of King Henry IV and Shallow earned him warm praise. The *Morning Advertiser* spoke for others when it congratulated Phelps on his "plasticity of imagination" that was able to "conceive and represent mankind in all its varied and varying phases."

Although the two parts of *Henry IV* were performed on consecutive nights on at least eight occasions prior to 1750, only rarely during the later eighteenth and the nineteenth centuries were the two parts of *Henry IV* produced within a week of one another. The twentieth century, then, has discovered anew the value of exploring the emotional and po-

litical transformations of these and other historical plays
when they are played in sequence. Frank Benson was the
first to present a "cycle" of history plays, in 1901 and then
again in 1906, at Stratford-upon-Avon. He omitted
1 Henry IV, sad to say, but included *2 Henry IV* as a necessary link to *Henry V*. And in 1905 he did produce both
Henry IV plays as part of a season that included all four
plays of the second tetralogy—that is, *Richard II* through
Henry V. Barry Jackson seems to have been the first to
present *1* and *2 Henry IV* on a single day, April 23 (Shakespeare's birthday), in 1921, at the Birmingham Repertory
Theatre. The two parts were paired again on Shakespeare's
birthday at Stratford-upon-Avon in 1932; Edward, the
Prince of Wales, flew over from Windsor in his private
plane for the occasion. Orson Welles put together parts of
Henry IV and *Henry V* into a single dramatic presentation,
Five Kings, at Philadelphia in 1939; and Welles's 1965 film,
called *Chimes at Midnight* (in England) or *Falstaff* (in the
United States), with Welles himself as Falstaff and Jeanne
Moreau implausibly cast as Doll Tearsheet, included parts
of both plays down through the rejection of Falstaff. More
recent productions in sequence include Terry Hands's di-
rection of all three "Hal" plays, *1* and *2 Henry IV* and
Henry V, at Stratford-upon-Avon in 1975 and Michael
Bogdanov's three-play "Hal" series at the Old Vic in 1987.

   Inevitably, the rejection of Falstaff is the touchstone of
every version of the play. To fulfill his destiny as Henry V,
Hal must repudiate his dissolute friend, but it is in how he
does it that productions reveal their moral center. John
Burrell's Old Vic *2 Henry IV* in 1945 at London's New Theatre, with Ralph Richardson as Falstaff and Laurence Oli-
vier as Shallow, tried to subordinate the pressures of
history to the humanity of the play's comic energies. Nevertheless, when in Act 5 the newly crowned Henry V arro-
gantly cut off Falstaff's last attempted joke with his curt
"Reply not to me with a fool-born jest," Falstaff was
crushed by the betrayal. In Gerald Freedman's 1968 New
York Shakespeare Festival production, both Hal and Falstaff were distraught by the event, however inevitable it
must have seemed to them both: Sam Waterston as Hal
turned away from his erstwhile companion in pain, while
Stacy Keach as Falstaff knelt before the new King, in the

words of *The New York Times*, "as though he would never rise again." Conversely, in 1951 at Stratford-upon-Avon, Michael Redgrave directed a production that made Hal's rejection of Anthony Quayle's opportunistic Falstaff seem necessary and right, while in Douglas Seale's *2 Henry IV* in 1955 at the Old Vic, the rejection of a coarse and self-serving Falstaff was even less lamentable. The range of theatrical possibilities arising from the complex mixture of love and rejection give the play an intensity of vision that no single production can exhaust.

Theatrical explorations of the complexities of *2 Henry IV* have been enhanced in recent years by a search for balance and multiplicity of points of view, qualities that can only be increased by the staging of the *Henry* plays in sequence. When Terry Hands directed the three "Hal" plays in 1975 at Stratford-upon-Avon, he focused on the development of Hal from Prince to King. Alan Howard's Hal revealed how fully he had learned the lessons of kingship as he stood in golden armor before a ragged Falstaff and pronounced the inevitable verdict. He spoke dispassionately, almost charitably; as critic Robert Speaight wrote, what the king said was "spoken *about* Falstaff rather than *at* him." A dead tree stood in the background of the dazzling vision of Henry's kingship as mute commentary on what lay in the future. In Trevor Nunn's production at London's Barbican Theatre in 1982, Hal stepped out of the coronation procession to address Falstaff with obvious strain, and then resumed his emotionless, public persona, revealing the terrible human cost of his crown. In Michael Bogdanov's modern-dress "Hal" trilogy, the opening offering of the new English Shakespeare Company (at the Old Vic, 1987, after a fall 1986 national tour), Michael Pennington played a shrewd and secure Hal who coolly snubbed Falstaff (John Woodvine) in his mature awareness of Falstaff's irrelevance to the historical world Hal had just inherited.

Any production of *2 Henry IV* that does not willfully cut and rearrange its scenes in the manner of Betterton or Kemble must take account of the play's dark humor and disillusionment. The alternations back and forth between court and tavern, as in *1 Henry IV*, provide contrasting theatrical worlds of political manipulation and festive dissipation; but whereas in *1 Henry IV* the tavern world is (for a

time at least) one of release and nearly magical inver-
sion, the corresponding world in *2 Henry IV* is more disillusioned from the start. No longer is there any joyous
playacting and exchanging of roles between Hal and Falstaff, and virtually no badinage. Falstaff presides over a
kingdom populated by swaggerers, cheats, and whores, or
venal country justices and their cunning servants. The political world, too, is largely governed (until the very last)
by the likes of Prince John, maker of deceitful promises at
Gaultree Forest. The Royal Shakespeare Company's production at Stratford-upon-Avon in 1964, directed by Peter
Hall, John Barton, and Clifford Williams, was well attuned
to the iconoclastic vision called for in the play's contrasts:
Hugh Griffith as Falstaff reveled in his debauchery in a way
that vividly offset the coldly political behavior of Prince
John. Such a Brechtian interpretation necessarily found
less patriotic inspiration in the final emergence of Henry V
than, for example, did the lavish triumphal processions of
the Covent Garden production in 1821. But productions will
always in some way respond to their historical moment,
and the wide variance of successful interpretations in the
stage history of this complex and unsettling play reveals its
ability to speak powerfully to different needs and times.

The Playhouse

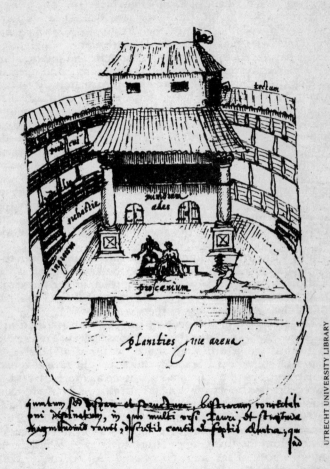

This early copy of a drawing by Johannes de Witt of the Swan Theatre in London (c. 1596), made by his friend Arend van Buchell, is the only surviving contemporary sketch of the interior of a public theater in the 1590s.

From other contemporary evidence, including the stage directions and dialogue of Elizabethan plays, we can surmise that the various public theaters where Shakespeare's plays were produced (the Theatre, the Curtain, the Globe) resembled the Swan in many important particulars, though there must have been some variations as well. The public playhouses were essentially round, or polygonal, and open to the sky, forming an acting arena approximately 70 feet in diameter; they did not have a large curtain with which to open and close a scene, such as we see today in opera and some traditional theater. A platform measuring approximately 43 feet across and 27 feet deep, referred to in the de Witt drawing as the *proscaenium*, projected into the yard, *planities sive arena*. The roof, *tectum*, above the stage and supported by two pillars, could contain machinery for ascents and descents, as were required in several of Shakespeare's late plays. Above this roof was a hut, shown in the drawing with a flag flying atop it and a trumpeter at its door announcing the performance of a play. The underside of the stage roof, called the heavens, was usually richly decorated with symbolic figures of the sun, the moon, and the constellations. The platform stage stood at a height of 5½ feet or so above the yard, providing room under the stage for underworldly effects. A trapdoor, which is not visible in this drawing, gave access to the space below.

The structure at the back of the platform (labeled *mimorum aedes*), known as the tiring-house because it was the actors' attiring (dressing) space, featured at least two doors, as shown here. Some theaters seem to have also had a discovery space, or curtained recessed alcove, perhaps between the two doors—in which Falstaff could have hidden from the sheriff (*1 Henry IV*, 2.4) or Polonius could have eavesdropped on Hamlet and his mother (*Hamlet*, 3.4). This discovery space probably gave the actors a means of access to and from the tiring-house. Curtains may also have been hung in front of the stage doors on occasion. The de Witt drawing shows a gallery above the doors that extends across the back and evidently contains spectators. On occasions when action "above" demanded the use of this space, as when Juliet appears at her "window" (*Romeo and Juliet*, 2.2 and 3.5), the gallery seems to have been used by the actors, but large scenes there were impractical.

The three-tiered auditorium is perhaps best described by Thomas Platter, a visitor to London in 1599 who saw on that occasion Shakespeare's *Julius Caesar* performed at the Globe:

> The playhouses are so constructed that they play on a raised platform, so that everyone has a good view. There are different galleries and places [*orchestra, sedilia, porticus*], however, where the seating is better and more comfortable and therefore more expensive. For whoever cares to stand below only pays one English penny, but if he wishes to sit, he enters by another door [*ingressus*] and pays another penny, while if he desires to sit in the most comfortable seats, which are cushioned, where he not only sees everything well but can also be seen, then he pays yet another English penny at another door. And during the performance food and drink are carried round the audience, so that for what one cares to pay one may also have refreshment.

Scenery was not used, though the theater building itself was handsome enough to invoke a feeling of order and hierarchy that lent itself to the splendor and pageantry onstage. Portable properties, such as thrones, stools, tables, and beds, could be carried or thrust on as needed. In the scene pictured here by de Witt, a lady on a bench, attended perhaps by her waiting-gentlewoman, receives the address of a male figure. If Shakespeare had written *Twelfth Night* by 1596 for performance at the Swan, we could imagine Malvolio appearing like this as he bows before the Countess Olivia and her gentlewoman, Maria.

HENRY IV,
PART TWO

The Actors' Names

RUMOR, *the Presenter*

KING HENRY THE FOURTH
PRINCE HENRY, *afterwards crowned* KING HENRY
   THE FIFTH
PRINCE JOHN OF LANCASTER, ⎫ *sons to*
HUMPHREY, [DUKE] OF GLOUCESTER, ⎬ *Henry IV*
THOMAS, [DUKE] OF CLARENCE, ⎭ *and brethren*
                    to Henry V

[EARL OF] NORTHUMBERLAND, ⎫
[SCROOP,] THE ARCHBISHOP
   OF YORK,
[LORD] MOWBRAY,
[LORD] HASTING, ⎬ *opposites against King*
LORD BARDOLPH,   *Henry IV*
TRAVERS,
MORTON,
[SIR JOHN] COLEVILLE, ⎭

[EARL OF] WARWICK, ⎫
[EARL OF] WESTMORLAND,
[EARL OF] SURREY,
GOWER, ⎬ *of the King's party*
HARCOURT,
[BLUNT],
LORD CHIEF JUSTICE,
[*His* SERVANT], ⎭

POINS, ⎫
[SIR JOHN] FALSTAFF,
BARDOLPH,
PISTOL, ⎬ *irregular humorists*
PETO,
[FALSTAFF'S] PAGE, ⎭

SHALLOW, ⎫ *both country justices*
SILENCE, ⎭
DAVY, *servant to Shallow*

FANG *and* SNARE, *two sergeants*
MOLDY, SHADOW, WART, FEEBLE, [*and*] BULLCALF, *country soldiers*
[FRANCIS, *a drawer*]

NORTHUMBERLAND'S WIFE
PERCY'S WIDOW [LADY PERCY]
HOSTESS QUICKLY
DOLL TEARSHEET

DRAWERS
BEADLES
GROOMS
[PORTER]

EPILOGUE

[*Lords, Attendants, Messengers, Pages, Musicians, Officers, etc.*]

[SCENE: *England*]

Induction

Enter Rumor, painted full of tongues.

RUMOR

Open your ears, for which of you will stop
The vent of hearing when loud Rumor speaks?
I, from the orient to the drooping west,
Making the wind my post-horse, still unfold   4
The acts commencèd on this ball of earth.
Upon my tongues continual slanders ride,
The which in every language I pronounce,
Stuffing the ears of men with false reports.
I speak of peace while covert enmity,
Under the smile of safety, wounds the world.
And who but Rumor, who but only I,
Make fearful musters and prepared defense,   12
Whiles the big year, swoll'n with some other grief,   13
Is thought with child by the stern tyrant War,
And no such matter? Rumor is a pipe   15
Blown by surmises, jealousies, conjectures,   16
And of so easy and so plain a stop   17
That the blunt monster with uncounted heads,   18
The still-discordant wavering multitude,
Can play upon it. But what need I thus   20
My well-known body to anatomize   21
Among my household? Why is Rumor here?   22
I run before King Harry's victory,

Induction. Location: Although the allegory of Rumor, based ultimately on Virgil's depiction of Fama as full of eyes, ears, and tongues, in the *Aeneid* (4.179–190), is timeless, Rumor is here represented as standing in front of Northumberland's castle, Warkworth. The play is supposed to open immediately after the battle of Shrewsbury, in which Henry Percy, or Hotspur, and the Scottish Earl of Douglas have been overthrown. We are concerned first of all with the news of the battle, with which *1 Henry IV* ended.
4 post-horse horse kept at an inn or post-house for the use of travelers.   **still** continually   **12 musters** assemblies of soldiers   **13 big** swollen, pregnant with disaster   **15 And no such matter** and yet there is no substance in such rumors.   **pipe** recorder (a wind instrument)   **16 jealousies** suspicions   **17 of . . . stop** i.e., whose stops or openings are so easily played on   **18 blunt** stupid, dull-witted   **20 what** why   **21 anatomize** lay open minutely, explain   **22 household** retinue, i.e., the audience

Who in a bloody field by Shrewsbury
Hath beaten down young Hotspur and his troops,
Quenching the flame of bold rebellion
Even with the rebels' blood. But what mean I
To speak so true at first? My office is
To noise abroad that Harry Monmouth fell   29
Under the wrath of noble Hotspur's sword,
And that the King before the Douglas' rage
Stooped his anointed head as low as death.
This have I rumored through the peasant towns   33
Between that royal field of Shrewsbury
And this worm-eaten hold of ragged stone,   35
Where Hotspur's father, old Northumberland,
Lies crafty-sick. The posts come tiring on,   37
And not a man of them brings other news
Than they have learned of me. From Rumor's tongues
They bring smooth comforts false, worse than true
     wrongs.   *Exit Rumor.* 40

---

29 Harry Monmouth Prince Hal (who was born at Monmouth in
Wales)   **33 peasant** rural, provincial   **35 hold** stronghold, fortress
37 crafty-sick feigning sickness.   **The . . . on** the messengers gallop hard,
exhausted by their effort   **40 worse . . . wrongs** i.e., false good news is
ultimately worse than hurtful truth

1.1   *Enter the Lord Bardolph at one door.*

LORD BARDOLPH
  Who keeps the gate here, ho?

    [*Enter the Porter.*]

                          Where is the Earl?   1
PORTER
  What shall I say you are?
LORD BARDOLPH   Tell thou the Earl
  That the Lord Bardolph doth attend him here.   3
PORTER
  His lordship is walked forth into the orchard.
  Please it your honor knock but at the gate,
  And he himself will answer.

    Enter the Earl [*of*] *Northumberland* [*in a*
    nightcap, supporting himself with a crutch].

LORD BARDOLPH   Here comes the Earl.
                        [*Exit Porter.*]

NORTHUMBERLAND
  What news, Lord Bardolph? Every minute now
  Should be the father of some stratagem.   8
  The times are wild. Contention, like a horse
  Full of high feeding, madly hath broke loose   10
  And bears down all before him.
LORD BARDOLPH   Noble Earl,
  I bring you certain news from Shrewsbury.   12
NORTHUMBERLAND
  Good, an God will!
LORD BARDOLPH   As good as heart can wish.   13
  The King is almost wounded to the death,
  And, in the fortune of my lord your son,   15
  Prince Harry slain outright; and both the Blunts
  Killed by the hand of Douglas. Young Prince John
  And Westmorland and Stafford fled the field,

1.1. Location: Warkworth. Before Northumberland's castle.
s.d. Lord Bardolph (An ally of the Percys; not to be confused with
Bardolph, Falstaff's red-faced companion.)   **1 keeps** guards   **3 attend**
await   **8 stratagem** violence   **10 high feeding** too-rich fodder
12 certain reliable   **13 an** if   **15 in the fortune of** by the good fortune
of, or, for what has befallen

And Harry Monmouth's brawn, the hulk Sir John,   19
Is prisoner to your son. O, such a day,
So fought, so followed, and so fairly won,   21
Came not till now to dignify the times
Since Caesar's fortunes!

NORTHUMBERLAND   How is this derived?   23
Saw you the field? Came you from Shrewsbury?

LORD BARDOLPH
I spake with one, my lord, that came from thence,
A gentleman well bred and of good name,
That freely rendered me these news for true.

Enter Travers.

NORTHUMBERLAND
Here comes my servant Travers, who I sent
On Tuesday last to listen after news.

LORD BARDOLPH
My lord, I overrode him on the way,   30
And he is furnished with no certainties
More than he haply may retail from me.   32

NORTHUMBERLAND
Now, Travers, what good tidings comes with you?

TRAVERS
My lord, Sir John Umfrevile turned me back   34
With joyful tidings and, being better horsed,
Outrode me. After him came spurring hard
A gentleman almost forspent with speed   37
That stopped by me to breathe his bloodied horse.   38
He asked the way to Chester, and of him
I did demand what news from Shrewsbury.
He told me that rebellion had ill luck
And that young Harry Percy's spur was cold.
With that, he gave his able horse the head,
And bending forward struck his armèd heels
Against the panting sides of his poor jade   45
Up to the rowel head, and starting so   46

---

19 brawn fat boar   **21 followed** carried through   **23 fortunes** successes.   **derived** learned, obtained   **30 overrode** outrode   **32 haply**
perhaps.   **retail** relate   **34 Sir John Umfrevile** (Perhaps the name of Lord
Bardolph in an earlier version of this scene.)   **37 forspent** exhausted
38 bloodied i.e., with spurring   **45 jade** nag   **46 rowel head** the end of
the spur, in which the barbed wheel turns.   **starting** springing forward

He seemed in running to devour the way,
Staying no longer question.

NORTHUMBERLAND　　　　　　　　Ha? Again. 　　　48
Said he young Harry Percy's spur was cold?
Of Hotspur, Coldspur? That rebellion
Had met ill luck?

LORD BARDOLPH　　　　My lord, I'll tell you what:
If my young lord your son have not the day, 　　　52
Upon mine honor, for a silken point 　　　53
I'll give my barony. Never talk of it.

NORTHUMBERLAND
Why should that gentleman that rode by Travers
Give then such instances of loss?

LORD BARDOLPH　　　　　　　　　Who, he?
He was some hilding fellow that had stol'n 　　　57
The horse he rode on and, upon my life,
Spoke at a venture. Look, here comes more news. 　　　59

　　　Enter Morton.

NORTHUMBERLAND
Yea, this man's brow, like to a title leaf, 　　　60
Foretells the nature of a tragic volume.
So looks the strand whereon the imperious flood 　　　62
Hath left a witnessed usurpation. 　　　63
Say, Morton, didst thou come from Shrewsbury?

MORTON
I ran from Shrewsbury, my noble lord,
Where hateful death put on his ugliest mask
To fright our party.

NORTHUMBERLAND　　　　How doth my son and brother?
Thou tremblest, and the whiteness in thy cheek
Is apter than thy tongue to tell thy errand.
Even such a man, so faint, so spiritless,
So dull, so dead in look, so woebegone,
Drew Priam's curtain in the dead of night 　　　72
And would have told him half his Troy was burnt;

48 Staying waiting for　**52 day** victory　**53 point** tag for fastening clothes (i.e., something of very small value)　**57 hilding** good-for-nothing　**59 at a venture** at random, recklessly　**60 title leaf** title page　**62 strand** shore　**63 witnessed usurpation** evidence of its (the sea's) invasion, encroachment. (Morton's brow is furrowed like wrinkled sand.)　**72 Priam** King of Troy.　**curtain** bedcurtain

But Priam found the fire ere he his tongue,
And I my Percy's death ere thou report'st it.
This thou wouldst say, "Your son did thus and thus;
Your brother thus; so fought the noble Douglas"—
Stopping my greedy ear with their bold deeds.   78
But in the end, to stop my ear indeed,   79
Thou hast a sigh to blow away this praise,
Ending with "Brother, son, and all are dead."

MORTON
Douglas is living, and your brother, yet;
But for my lord your son—

NORTHUMBERLAND   Why, he is dead.
See what a ready tongue suspicion hath!
He that but fears the thing he would not know
Hath by instinct knowledge from others' eyes
That what he feared is chancèd. Yet speak, Morton.   87
Tell thou an earl his divination lies,   88
And I will take it as a sweet disgrace
And make thee rich for doing me such wrong.

MORTON
You are too great to be by me gainsaid.   91
Your spirit is too true, your fears too certain.   92

NORTHUMBERLAND
Yet, for all this, say not that Percy's dead.   93
I see a strange confession in thine eye.
Thou shak'st thy head and hold'st it fear or sin
To speak a truth. If he be slain, say so.
The tongue offends not that reports his death;
And he doth sin that doth belie the dead,   98
Not he which says the dead is not alive.
Yet the first bringer of unwelcome news
Hath but a losing office, and his tongue   101
Sounds ever after as a sullen bell   102
Remembered tolling a departing friend.   103

LORD BARDOLPH
I cannot think, my lord, your son is dead.

---

78 Stopping filling   **79 stop . . . indeed** i.e., prevent my ever hearing
again   **87 is chancèd** has occurred   **88 divination** prophecy
91 gainsaid contradicted   **92 spirit** intuition, powers of perception
93 for in spite of   **98 belie** slander   **101 losing office** i.e., thankless
task   **102 sullen** mournful   **103 tolling** ringing the funeral bell for

MORTON
I am sorry I should force you to believe
That which I would to God I had not seen;
But these mine eyes saw him in bloody state,
Rend'ring faint quittance, wearied and outbreathed,   108
To Harry Monmouth, whose swift wrath beat down
The never-daunted Percy to the earth,
From whence with life he never more sprung up.
In few, his death, whose spirit lent a fire   112
Even to the dullest peasant in his camp,
Being bruited once, took fire and heat away   114
From the best-tempered courage in his troops;   115
For from his metal was his party steeled,   116
Which once in him abated, all the rest   117
Turned on themselves, like dull and heavy lead.   118
And as the thing that's heavy in itself
Upon enforcement flies with greatest speed,   120
So did our men, heavy in Hotspur's loss,
Lend to this weight such lightness with their fear
That arrows fled not swifter toward their aim
Than did our soldiers, aiming at their safety,
Fly from the field. Then was that noble Worcester
So soon ta'en prisoner; and that furious Scot,
The bloody Douglas, whose well-laboring sword
Had three times slain th' appearance of the King,   128
'Gan vail his stomach and did grace the shame   129
Of those that turned their backs, and in his flight,
Stumbling in fear, was took. The sum of all
Is that the King hath won and hath sent out
A speedy power to encounter you, my lord,   133
Under the conduct of young Lancaster   134
And Westmorland. This is the news at full.   135

---

108 quittance requital, i.e., resistance.   **outbreathed** out of breath
112 In few in few words   **114 bruited** rumored, reported   **115 best-
tempered** i.e., like the highest quality steel   **116 metal** (1) steel, continuing the metaphor of l. 115 (2) mettle, courage   **117 abated** (1) blunted
(2) slackened   **118 Turned on themselves** (1) bent backwards (2) turned
and ran   **120 Upon enforcement** when set forcibly in motion
128 appearance of the King i.e., warriors dressed like the King. (See
1 Henry IV, 5.3 and 5.4.25–38.)   **129 'Gan . . . stomach** began to abate or
lower his courage.   **grace** sanction (by his own running away)
133 power armed force   **134 conduct** command   **135 at** in

NORTHUMBERLAND
  For this I shall have time enough to mourn.
  In poison there is physic; and these news,   137
  Having been well, that would have made me sick,   138
  Being sick, have in some measure made me well.   139
  And as the wretch whose fever-weakened joints
  Like strengthless hinges buckle under life,   141
  Impatient of his fit, breaks like a fire   142
  Out of his keeper's arms, even so my limbs,   143
  Weakened with grief, being now enraged with grief,   144
  Are thrice themselves. Hence, therefore, thou nice
    crutch!   [*He throws away his crutch.*] 145
  A scaly gauntlet now with joints of steel   146
  Must glove this hand. And hence, thou sickly coif!   147
             [*He takes off his nightcap.*]
  Thou art a guard too wanton for the head   148
  Which princes, fleshed with conquest, aim to hit.   149
  Now bind my brows with iron, and approach
  The ragged'st hour that time and spite dare bring   151
  To frown upon th' enraged Northumberland!
  Let heaven kiss earth! Now let not Nature's hand
  Keep the wild flood confined! Let order die,   154
  And let this world no longer be a stage
  To feed contention in a lingering act;   156
  But let one spirit of the firstborn Cain   157
  Reign in all bosoms, that, each heart being set   158
  On bloody courses, the rude scene may end,
  And darkness be the burier of the dead!

LORD BARDOLPH
  This strainèd passion doth you wrong, my lord.   161

MORTON
  Sweet Earl, divorce not wisdom from your honor.

137 physic medicine   **138 Having . . . sick** that would have made me
sick if I had been well   **139 Being sick, have** I being sick, this same
news has   **141 buckle under life** bend under the weight of the living man
142 fit attack of illness   **143 keeper's** nurse's   **144 grief . . . grief** pain
and sickness . . . sorrow   **145 nice** delicate, effeminate   **146 scaly** i.e.,
mailed   **147 sickly coif** close-fitting cap worn by an invalid
148 wanton effeminate, luxurious   **149 fleshed** inflamed by foretaste of
blood and success   **151 ragged'st** roughest   **154 flood** river   **156 in . . .
act** in a drawn-out act (as of a play). (Northumberland wishes for an end
to the lingering dissolution of a world in conflict.)   **157 of . . . Cain** i.e.,
of murder   **158 that** so that   **161 strainèd** excessive

The lives of all your loving complices   163
Lean on your health, the which, if you give o'er
To stormy passion, must perforce decay.   165
You cast th' event of war, my noble lord,   166
And summed the account of chance, before you said
"Let us make head." It was your presurmise   168
That, in the dole of blows, your son might drop.   169
You knew he walked o'er perils, on an edge,
More likely to fall in than to get o'er;
You were advised his flesh was capable   172
Of wounds and scars, and that his forward spirit   173
Would lift him where most trade of danger ranged.   174
Yet did you say, "Go forth." And none of this,
Though strongly apprehended, could restrain
The stiff-borne action. What hath then befallen,   177
Or what hath this bold enterprise brought forth,
More than that being which was like to be?   179

LORD BARDOLPH
We all that are engagèd to this loss   180
Knew that we ventured on such dangerous seas
That if we wrought out life 'twas ten to one.   182
And yet we ventured, for the gain proposed
Choked the respect of likely peril feared;   184
And since we are o'erset, venture again.   185
Come, we will all put forth, body and goods.   186

MORTON
'Tis more than time. And, my most noble lord,
I hear for certain, and dare speak the truth,
The gentle Archbishop of York is up   189
With well-appointed powers. He is a man   190
Who with a double surety binds his followers.   191

---

163 complices allies   **165 perforce** necessarily   **166 cast th' event**
calculated the outcome   **168 make head** raise an army   **169 dole**
dealing out, distribution   **172 advised** aware   **173 Of** of receiving.
forward eager, ardent   **174 trade** trafficking   **177 stiff-borne** obsti-
nately carried out   **179 being** event; having occurred.   **like** likely
180 engaged to involved in   **182 if . . . one** if we came out alive we
survived ten-to-one odds   **184 Choked the respect** suppressed the
consideration   **185 o'erset** defeated, overthrown   **186 all put forth**
(1) all set out, as though putting out to sea (2) stake everything
189 gentle wellborn.   **Archbishop of York** i.e., Archbishop Scroop.
up in arms   **190 well-appointed powers** well-equipped armed forces
191 double surety i.e., a bond of allegiance in terms of body and soul

My lord your son had only but the corpse,   192
But shadows and the shows of men, to fight;   193
For that same word "rebellion" did divide
The action of their bodies from their souls,
And they did fight with queasiness, constrained,
As men drink potions, that their weapons only   197
Seemed on our side. But, for their spirits and souls,   198
This word "rebellion," it had froze them up
As fish are in a pond. But now the Bishop
Turns insurrection to religion.   201
Supposed sincere and holy in his thoughts,   202
He's followed both with body and with mind,
And doth enlarge his rising with the blood   204
Of fair King Richard, scraped from Pomfret stones;   205
Derives from heaven his quarrel and his cause;
Tells them he doth bestride a bleeding land,
Gasping for life under great Bolingbroke;   208
And more and less do flock to follow him.   209

NORTHUMBERLAND
I knew of this before, but to speak truth
This present grief had wiped it from my mind.
Go in with me, and counsel every man   212
The aptest way for safety and revenge.
Get posts and letters, and make friends with speed—   214
Never so few, and never yet more need.   *Exeunt.*

❖

1.2   *Enter Sir John [Falstaff] alone, with his Page*
bearing his sword and buckler.

FALSTAFF   Sirrah, you giant, what says the doctor to my   1
water?   2

---

192 only but only.   **corpse** i.e., corpses, living bodies without their
souls   **193 But** only.   **to fight** to use for fighting   **197 potions** medicine, poison   **198 for** as for   **201 to religion** into a sacred cause
202 Supposed i.e., rightly thought to be   **204 enlarge his rising** enhance
the merit of his insurrection   **205 Pomfret** i.e., Pontefract Castle in
Yorkshire, where Richard II was murdered   **208 Bolingbroke** i.e., King
Henry IV, here deprived of his title by the Archbishop   **209 more and
less** all classes   **212 counsel every man** let every man give advice as to
to   **214 posts** messengers.   **make** collect

1.2. Location: London. A street.
s.d. buckler shield   **1 Sirrah** (Form of address to a social inferior.)
1–2 to my water about my urine sample

PAGE He said, sir, the water itself was a good healthy
water, but for the party that owed it, he might have 4
more diseases than he knew for.   5

FALSTAFF Men of all sorts take a pride to gird at me. The 6
brain of this foolish-compounded clay, man, is not 7
able to invent anything that intends to laughter more 8
than I invent or is invented on me. I am not only witty
in myself, but the cause that wit is in other men. I do
here walk before thee like a sow that hath over-
whelmed all her litter but one. If the Prince put thee
into my service for any other reason than to set me off, 13
why then I have no judgment. Thou whoreson man- 14
drake, thou art fitter to be worn in my cap than to wait 15
at my heels. I was never manned with an agate till 16
now; but I will inset you neither in gold nor silver, but
in vile apparel, and send you back again to your master, for a jewel—the juvenal, the Prince your master, 19
whose chin is not yet fledge. I will sooner have a beard 20
grow in the palm of my hand than he shall get one of
his cheek, and yet he will not stick to say his face is a 22
face royal. God may finish it when he will, 'tis not a 23
hair amiss yet. He may keep it still at a face royal, for 24
a barber shall never earn sixpence out of it; and yet
he'll be crowing as if he had writ man ever since his 26
father was a bachelor. He may keep his own grace, but 27
he's almost out of mine, I can assure him. What said
Master Dommelton about the satin for my short cloak
and my slops?   30

---

4 owed owned   **5 knew for** was aware of   **6 gird** jeer   **7 foolish-
compounded** composed of folly   **8 intends** tends   **13 set me off** show
me to the best advantage   **14 whoreson** (A generalized term of abuse
meaning "vile" or "detestable.")   **14–15 mandrake** plant with a
forked, man-shaped root   **15 fitter . . . cap** i.e., as small and decorous
as a brooch worn in my hat   **15–16 wait at my heels** i.e., wait in
attendance on me, follow me about   **16 manned . . . agate** i.e., provided with a servant as small as the little figures cut in agate stone
for jewelry and seal rings   **19 juvenal** youth   **20 fledge** covered with
down   **22 stick** hesitate   **23 face royal** (punning on the *royal*, a coin
with the King's face stamped on it)   **23–24 a hair** (1) a single hair of
the beard (2) a jot   **24 at** at the value of   **26 writ man** attained
manhood   **27 grace** (1) title suited to his royal rank (2) favor
30 slops loose breeches

PAGE He said, sir, you should procure him better as- 31
surance than Bardolph. He would not take his bond 32
and yours; he liked not the security.

FALSTAFF Let him be damned like the glutton! Pray 34
God his tongue be hotter! A whoreson Achitophel! A 35
rascally yea-forsooth knave, to bear a gentleman in 36
hand and then stand upon security! The whoreson 37
smoothy-pates do now wear nothing but high shoes 38
and bunches of keys at their girdles; and if a man is 39
through with them in honest taking up, then they 40
must stand upon security. I had as lief they would put 41
ratsbane in my mouth as offer to stop it with security. 42
I looked 'a should have sent me two-and-twenty yards 43
of satin, as I am a true knight, and he sends me "secu-
rity"! Well he may sleep in security, for he hath the 45
horn of abundance, and the lightness of his wife 46
shines through it. And yet cannot he see, though he 47
have his own lantern to light him. Where's Bardolph? 48

PAGE He's gone into Smithfield to buy your worship a 49
horse.

FALSTAFF I bought him in Paul's, and he'll buy me a 51

31–32 **assurance** guarantee   32 **Bardolph** (One of Falstaff's followers, not the Lord Bardolph of scene 1.)   34 **the glutton** (A reference to the parable of Dives the rich man, Luke 16:19–31.)   35 **hotter** i.e., than Dives' tongue in hell.   **Achitophel** abettor of Absalom's treason against David. (2 Samuel 15–17.)   36 **yea-forsooth** i.e., yes-man
36–37 **bear . . . in hand** delude one with false hopes   37 **stand upon security** insist upon guarantee of payment (as also in l. 41)
38 **smoothy-pates** (Alludes to the short hair of tradesmen.)   38–39 **high shoes . . . keys** (Indications of their financial prosperity and pride.)
39–40 **is through . . . taking up** has agreed with them on an honest bargain   41 **lief** willingly   42 **ratsbane** rat poison   43 **looked 'a** expected that he   45 **security** i.e., a false and complacent sense of security   46 **horn of abundance** (1) cornucopia (2) cuckold's horn, a sign of his wife's infidelity.   **lightness** (1) wantonness (2) light showing through a lantern (which would have windows of *horn*, thereby giving the cuckold a lantern in his own forehead)   47 **cannot he see** i.e., he cannot see his own wife's infidelity   48 **lantern** (The old spelling "lanthorn" preserves Falstaff's continued joke about cuckold's horns.)   49 **Smithfield** district near Saint Paul's Cathedral, famous as a livestock market   51 **Paul's** i.e., Saint Paul's Cathedral nave, resort of servingmen seeking employment

horse in Smithfield. An I could get me but a wife in 52
the stews, I were manned, horsed, and wived.   53

    Enter [the] Lord Chief Justice [and Servant].

PAGE Sir, here comes the nobleman that committed the 54
  Prince for striking him about Bardolph.

FALSTAFF Wait close; I will not see him.   56
                                   [He tries to slip away.]

CHIEF JUSTICE What's he that goes there?

SERVANT Falstaff, an 't please your lordship.

CHIEF JUSTICE He that was in question for the robbery? 59

SERVANT He, my lord. But he hath since done good service at Shrewsbury, and, as I hear, is now going with
  some charge to the Lord John of Lancaster.   62

CHIEF JUSTICE What, to York? Call him back again.

SERVANT Sir John Falstaff!

FALSTAFF Boy, tell him I am deaf.

PAGE You must speak louder; my master is deaf.

CHIEF JUSTICE I am sure he is, to the hearing of anything good. Go pluck him by the elbow; I must speak
  with him.

SERVANT Sir John!

FALSTAFF What, a young knave, and begging? Is there
  not wars? Is there not employment? Doth not the King
  lack subjects? Do not the rebels need soldiers? Though
  it be a shame to be on any side but one, it is worse
  shame to beg than to be on the worst side, were it
  worse than the name of rebellion can tell how to
  make it.   77

SERVANT You mistake me, sir.

FALSTAFF Why, sir, did I say you were an honest man?
  Setting my knighthood and my soldiership aside, I
  had lied in my throat if I had said so.

SERVANT I pray you, sir, then set your knighthood and

---

52 An if **53 stews** brothels. **I . . . wived** (Proverbially, to be thus
manned, horsed, and wived at Saint Paul's, Smithfield, and the stews
respectively, was to be taken for a sucker.) **54 committed** i.e., to prison.
(According to an apocryphal story, Hal boxed the ears of the Lord Chief
Justice; see *1 Henry IV*, 3.2.32–33 and note, and *2 Henry IV*, 5.2.70–71
and notes.) **56 close** concealed **59 in question** under judicial examina-
tion **62 charge** command of soldiers **77 make** regard

your soldiership aside and give me leave to tell you 83
you lie in your throat if you say I am any other than 84
an honest man.

FALSTAFF I give thee leave to tell me so? I lay aside that
which grows to me? If thou gett'st any leave of me, 87
hang me; if thou tak'st leave, thou wert better be
hanged. You hunt counter. Hence! Avaunt! 89

SERVANT Sir, my lord would speak with you.

CHIEF JUSTICE Sir John Falstaff, a word with you.

FALSTAFF My good lord! God give your lordship good
time of day. I am glad to see your lordship abroad. I 93
heard say your lordship was sick. I hope your lordship
goes abroad by advice. Your lordship, though not 95
clean past your youth, have yet some smack of age
in you, some relish of the saltness of time in you, and
I most humbly beseech your lordship to have a reverent care of your health.

CHIEF JUSTICE Sir John, I sent for you before your expedition to Shrewsbury.

FALSTAFF An 't please your lordship, I hear His Majesty
is returned with some discomfort from Wales.

CHIEF JUSTICE I talk not of His Majesty. You would not
come when I sent for you.

FALSTAFF And I hear, moreover, His Highness is fallen
into this same whoreson apoplexy.

CHIEF JUSTICE Well, God mend him! I pray you, let me
speak with you.

FALSTAFF This apoplexy, as I take it, is a kind of leth-
argy, an 't please your lordship, a kind of sleeping in
the blood, a whoreson tingling.

CHIEF JUSTICE What tell you me of it? Be it as it is. 113

FALSTAFF It hath its original from much grief, from 114
study, and perturbation of the brain. I have read the
cause of his effects in Galen. It is a kind of deafness. 116

CHIEF JUSTICE I think you are fallen into the disease, for
you hear not what I say to you.

FALSTAFF Very well, my lord, very well. Rather, an 't

---

83 leave permission **84 in your throat** i.e., outrageously **87 grows to**
is an integral part of **89 hunt counter** i.e., run backward on the trail.
(A hunting term.) **93 abroad** out of doors **95 by advice** by medical
advice **113 What** why **114 its original** its origin **116 his** its. **Galen**
the famous Greek authority on medicine

please you, it is the disease of not listening, the malady
of not marking, that I am troubled withal.

CHIEF JUSTICE To punish you by the heels would   122
amend the attention of your ears, and I care not if I do
become your physician.

FALSTAFF I am as poor as Job, my lord, but not so patient. Your lordship may minister the potion of imprisonment to me in respect of poverty; but how I   127
should be your patient to follow your prescriptions,
the wise may make some dram of a scruple, or indeed   129
a scruple itself.

CHIEF JUSTICE I sent for you, when there were matters
against you for your life, to come speak with me.   132

FALSTAFF As I was then advised by my learned counsel
in the laws of this land service, I did not come.   134

CHIEF JUSTICE Well, the truth is, Sir John, you live in
great infamy.

FALSTAFF He that buckles himself in my belt cannot live
in less.

CHIEF JUSTICE Your means are very slender, and your   139
waste is great.

FALSTAFF I would it were otherwise; I would my means
were greater, and my waist slenderer.

CHIEF JUSTICE You have misled the youthful Prince.

FALSTAFF The young Prince hath misled me. I am the
fellow with the great belly, and he my dog.

CHIEF JUSTICE Well, I am loath to gall a new-healed
wound. Your day's service at Shrewsbury hath a little
gilded over your night's exploit on Gad's Hill. You may   148
thank th' unquiet time for your quiet o'erposting that   149
action.

FALSTAFF My lord?

CHIEF JUSTICE But since all is well, keep it so. Wake not
a sleeping wolf.

---

122 punish . . . heels i.e., by setting you in the stocks or fetters   127 in
. . . poverty i.e., by reason of my being too poor to pay a fine   129 make
. . . scruple entertain some small portion of doubt. (*Dram* and *scruple*
are small apothecaries' weights.)   132 for your life i.e., carrying the
death penalty   134 land service military service (with a pun on avoiding
the "service" of a legal summons)   139 means financial resources
148 exploit i.e., the famous robbery in *1 Henry IV*, 2.2   149 o'erposting
escaping the consequences of

FALSTAFF   To wake a wolf is as bad as smell a fox.   154

CHIEF JUSTICE   What, you are as a candle, the better part burnt out.

FALSTAFF   A wassail candle, my lord, all tallow. If I did   157
say of wax, my growth would approve the truth.   158

CHIEF JUSTICE   There is not a white hair on your face but should have his effect of gravity.   160

FALSTAFF   His effect of gravy, gravy, gravy.   161

CHIEF JUSTICE   You follow the young Prince up and down, like his ill angel.   163

FALSTAFF   Not so, my lord. Your ill angel is light, but I   164
hope he that looks upon me will take me without   165
weighing. And yet in some respects I grant I cannot   166
go. I cannot tell. Virtue is of so little regard in these   167
costermongers' times that true valor is turned bear-   168
ward; pregnancy is made a tapster, and his quick wit   169
wasted in giving reckonings. All the other gifts appur-   170
tenant to man, as the malice of this age shapes them,   171
are not worth a gooseberry. You that are old consider
not the capacities of us that are young; you do measure
the heat of our livers with the bitterness of your galls.   174
And we that are in the vaward of our youth, I must con-   175
fess, are wags too.

CHIEF JUSTICE   Do you set down your name in the scroll

---

154 smell a fox suspect something. (Cf. "smell a rat.")   **157 wassail candle** large candle lighted up at a feast.   **tallow** a mixture of animal fats (which Falstaff thinks is more appropriate for him than a candle made of bees' *wax*)   **158 wax** beeswax (with a pun on "growth"). **approve** prove   **160 his effect** its sign   **161 gravy** (Sweat was thought to be fat exuded from the flesh, like gravy from meat.)   **163 ill angel** evil attendant spirit. (But Falstaff quibbles on the meaning "a clipped angel," a coin worth 6 shillings 8 pence.)   **164 light** i.e., underweight (because the coin is "clipped"). (Refers also to Satan, "an angel of light," 2 Corinthians 11.14.)   **165 take me** accept me at face value **166 weighing** (1) putting me on the scales (2) considering further, interpreting   **167 go** (1) walk (2) pass current.   **cannot tell** (1) don't know what to think (2) don't count as good money   **168 costermongers'** i.e., commercial. (A costermonger is a hawker of fruits or vegetables.) **168–169 bearward** one who handles tame bears   **169 pregnancy** quickness (of wit), intellectual capacity   **170 reckonings** tavern bills **170–171 appurtenant** belonging   **174 heat . . . galls** (The liver was thought to be the source of passion and to be active in youth; the gall was thought the seat of melancholy and rancor, and to be prevalent in age.)   **175 vaward** vanguard, forefront

of youth, that are written down old with all the char- 178
acters of age? Have you not a moist eye, a dry hand, a 179
yellow cheek, a white beard, a decreasing leg, an increasing belly? Is not your voice broken, your wind
short, your chin double, your wit single, and every 182
part about you blasted with antiquity? And will you 183
yet call yourself young? Fie, fie, fie, Sir John!

FALSTAFF   My lord, I was born about three of the clock
in the afternoon, with a white head and something a 186
round belly. For my voice, I have lost it with halloing 187
and singing of anthems. To approve my youth further, 188
I will not. The truth is, I am only old in judgment and
understanding; and he that will caper with me for a 190
thousand marks, let him lend me the money, and have 191
at him! For the box of the ear that the Prince gave you, 192
he gave it like a rude prince, and you took it like a
sensible lord. I have checked him for it, and the young 194
lion repents—[Aside] marry, not in ashes and sack- 195
cloth, but in new silk and old sack. 196

CHIEF JUSTICE   Well, God send the Prince a better companion!

FALSTAFF   God send the companion a better prince! I
cannot rid my hands of him.

CHIEF JUSTICE   Well, the King hath severed you and
Prince Harry. I hear you are going with Lord John of
Lancaster against the Archbishop and the Earl of
Northumberland.

FALSTAFF   Yea, I thank your pretty sweet wit for it. But
look you pray, all you that kiss my lady Peace at home, 206
that our armies join not in a hot day; for, by the Lord,
I take but two shirts out with me, and I mean not to
sweat extraordinarily. If it be a hot day, and I brandish
anything but a bottle, I would I might never spit white 210

178–179 characters (1) characteristics (2) letters   **182 single** i.e., feeble
183 blasted withered, blighted   **186 something a** a somewhat
187 halloing shouting to hounds   **188 approve** prove   **190 caper with
me** compete with me in dancing   **191 marks** coins worth 13 shillings 4
pence   **192 For** as for.   **box of the ear** (See note to l. 54, above.)
194 sensible (1) intelligent (2) capable of receiving physical sensations.
checked rebuked   **195 marry** indeed. (Literally, "by the Virgin
Mary.")   **196 sack** a white Spanish wine   **206 look** be sure, take care
210 spit white i.e., from thirst

again. There is not a dangerous action can peep
out his head but I am thrust upon it. Well, I cannot last
ever. But it was alway yet the trick of our English na-   213
tion, if they have a good thing, to make it too common. If ye will needs say I am an old man, you should
give me rest. I would to God my name were not so
terrible to the enemy as it is. I were better to be eaten
to death with a rust than to be scoured to nothing with
perpetual motion.

CHIEF JUSTICE   Well, be honest, be honest; and God
bless your expedition!

FALSTAFF   Will your lordship lend me a thousand pound
to furnish me forth?   223

CHIEF JUSTICE   Not a penny, not a penny. You are too
impatient to bear crosses. Fare you well. Commend   225
me to my cousin Westmorland.

        [*Exeunt Chief Justice and Servant.*]

FALSTAFF   If I do, fillip me with a three-man beetle. A   227
man can no more separate age and covetousness than
'a can part young limbs and lechery; but the gout galls
the one, and the pox pinches the other, and so both   230
the degrees prevent my curses. Boy!   231

PAGE   Sir?

FALSTAFF   What money is in my purse?

PAGE   Seven groats and two pence.   234

FALSTAFF   I can get no remedy against this consumption
of the purse; borrowing only lingers and lingers it out,   236
but the disease is incurable. [*He gives letters.*] Go bear
this letter to my lord of Lancaster, this to the Prince,
this to the Earl of Westmorland, and this to old Mistress Ursula, whom I have weekly sworn to marry
since I perceived the first white hair of my chin. About
it. You know where to find me. [*Exit Page.*] A pox of
this gout! Or, a gout of this pox! For the one or the
other plays the rogue with my great toe. 'Tis no matter

---

213 alway yet always.   **trick** habit   **223 furnish** equip   **225 crosses**
(1) afflictions (2) silver coins stamped with the figure of the cross
227 fillip knock.   **three-man beetle** a huge pile-driving mallet requiring
three men to wield it   **230–231 both the degrees** i.e., age and youth, the
one afflicted with gout and the other with *pox* or syphilis   **231 prevent**
anticipate   **234 groats** coins worth 4 pence   **236 lingers** prolongs,
draws

if I do halt; I have the wars for my color, and my pen- 245
sion shall seem the more reasonable. A good wit will
make use of anything. I will turn diseases to com- 247
modity.   [*Exit.*] 248

✤

1.3   *Enter the Archbishop [of York], Thomas
          Mowbray (Earl Marshal), the Lord Hastings,
          and [Lord] Bardolph.*

ARCHBISHOP
  Thus have you heard our cause and known our means;
  And, my most noble friends, I pray you all,
  Speak plainly your opinions of our hopes.
  And first, Lord Marshal, what say you to it?
MOWBRAY
  I well allow the occasion of our arms,   5
  But gladly would be better satisfied
  How in our means we should advance ourselves   7
  To look with forehead bold and big enough   8
  Upon the power and puissance of the King.   9
HASTINGS
  Our present musters grow upon the file   10
  To five-and-twenty thousand men of choice;   11
  And our supplies live largely in the hope   12
  Of great Northumberland, whose bosom burns
  With an incensèd fire of injuries.
LORD BARDOLPH
  The question then, Lord Hastings, standeth thus:
  Whether our present five-and-twenty thousand
  May hold up head without Northumberland?   17
HASTINGS
  With him, we may.
LORD BARDOLPH   Yea, marry, there's the point.

---

245 halt limp. **color** excuse **247–248 commodity** profit

1.3. Location: York. The Archbishop's palace.
s.d. Thomas Mowbray son of Thomas Mowbray, Duke of Norfolk, who was
banished by Richard II **5 allow . . . arms** concede the justice of our arm-
ing **7 in** with **8 forehead** i.e., assurance, defiant gaze **9 puissance**
strength **10 file** roll **11 men of choice** choice men **12 supplies** reinforce-
ments. **largely** abundantly **17 hold up head** i.e., succeed, be confident

But if without him we be thought too feeble,
My judgment is we should not step too far
Till we had his assistance by the hand;
For in a theme so bloody-faced as this   22
Conjecture, expectation, and surmise
Of aids incertain should not be admitted.

ARCHBISHOP
'Tis very true, Lord Bardolph, for indeed
It was young Hotspur's case at Shrewsbury.

LORD BARDOLPH
It was, my lord; who lined himself with hope,   27
Eating the air on promise of supply,   28
Flattering himself in project of a power   29
Much smaller than the smallest of his thoughts,
And so, with great imagination
Proper to madmen, led his powers to death   32
And winking leapt into destruction.   33

HASTINGS
But, by your leave, it never yet did hurt
To lay down likelihoods and forms of hope.

LORD BARDOLPH
Yes, if this present quality of war—   36
Indeed the instant action, a cause on foot—   37
Lives so in hope, as in an early spring   38
We see th' appearing buds, which to prove fruit   39
Hope gives not so much warrant as despair   40
That frosts will bite them. When we mean to build,   41
We first survey the plot, then draw the model;   42
And when we see the figure of the house,   43
Then must we rate the cost of the erection,   44
Which if we find outweighs ability,   45

22 theme business   **27 lined** strengthened   **28 Eating . . . supply** i.e.,
living in false hopes of reinforcement   **29 project . . . power** anticipation of the arrival of an armed force   **32 powers** forces   **33 winking**
shutting his eyes   **36–41 Yes . . . them** i.e., Yes (replying to Lord .
Hastings), it can do hurt to be too hopeful about war; if, for example,
this present business of war—indeed, the very campaign we anticipate, the matter that is now afoot—depends merely on such desperate
hopes as we experience about buds appearing too early in the spring,
since in reality hope gives us not so much warrant to expect their
maturing into fruit as despair that frosts will bite them. (The text may
be corrupt here.)   **42 model** plan   **43 figure** design   **44 rate** estimate   **45 ability** i.e., ability to pay

What do we then but draw anew the model
In fewer offices, or at least desist   47
To build at all? Much more, in this great work,
Which is almost to pluck a kingdom down
And set another up, should we survey
The plot of situation and the model,
Consent upon a sure foundation,   52
Question surveyors, know our own estate,   53
How able such a work to undergo,
To weigh against his opposite; or else   55
We fortify in paper and in figures,   56
Using the names of men instead of men,
Like one that draws the model of an house
Beyond his power to build it, who, half through,
Gives o'er and leaves his part-created cost   60
A naked subject to the weeping clouds   61
And waste for churlish winter's tyranny.

HASTINGS
Grant that our hopes, yet likely of fair birth,   63
Should be stillborn, and that we now possessed
The utmost man of expectation,   65
I think we are a body strong enough,
Even as we are, to equal with the King.   67

LORD BARDOLPH
What, is the King but five-and-twenty thousand?

HASTINGS
To us no more, nay, not so much, Lord Bardolph.
For his divisions, as the times do brawl,   70
Are in three heads: one power against the French,   71
And one against Glendower; perforce a third   72
Must take up us. So is the unfirm King   73
In three divided, and his coffers sound   74
With hollow poverty and emptiness.

---

47 offices rooms.   **at least** at the worst   **52 Consent** agree
53 surveyors architects.   **estate** wealth   **55 his opposite** adverse conditions   **56 in paper** merely on paper   **60 part-created cost** partly finished splendor   **61 naked subject** exposed (i.e., helpless) victim   **63 yet**
still   **65 The . . . expectation** i.e., all the men that we might hope to
have   **67 equal** match   **70 as . . . brawl** in accordance with the discor-
dant necessity of the time   **71 heads** armies   **72 perforce** necessarily
73 take up encounter, oppose   **74 sound** resound, echo

ARCHBISHOP
  That he should draw his several strengths together   76
  And come against us in full puissance
  Need not to be dreaded.
HASTINGS   If he should do so,
  To French and Welsh he leaves his back unarmed,
  They baying him at the heels. Never fear that.   80
LORD BARDOLPH
  Who is it like should lead his forces hither?   81
HASTINGS
  The Duke of Lancaster and Westmorland;
  Against the Welsh, himself and Harry Monmouth.
  But who is substituted 'gainst the French   84
  I have no certain notice.
ARCHBISHOP   Let us on,
  And publish the occasion of our arms.   86
  The commonwealth is sick of their own choice;
  Their overgreedy love hath surfeited.
  An habitation giddy and unsure
  Hath he that buildeth on the vulgar heart.   90
  O thou fond many, with what loud applause   91
  Didst thou beat heaven with blessing Bolingbroke,   92
  Before he was what thou wouldst have him be!
  And being now trimmed in thine own desires,   94
  Thou, beastly feeder, art so full of him
  That thou provok'st thyself to cast him up.
  So, so, thou common dog, didst thou disgorge   97
  Thy glutton bosom of the royal Richard;
  And now thou wouldst eat thy dead vomit up,
  And howl'st to find it. What trust is in these times?
  They that, when Richard lived, would have him die,
  Are now become enamored on his grave.
  Thou, that threw'st dust upon his goodly head
  When through proud London he came sighing on
  After th' admirèd heels of Bolingbroke,
  Criest now "O earth, yield us that king again,

---

76 several strengths various armies   **80 baying** pursuing (like hunting
dogs)   **81 Who . . . should** who is likely to   **84 substituted** delegated
86 arms hostilities   **90 vulgar** common, plebeian   **91 fond many** foolish
multitude   **92 beat heaven** assail heaven with prayers   **94 trimmed in**
furnished with, dressed in   **97 disgorge** vomit

And take thou this!" O thoughts of men accurst!
Past and to come seems best; things present worst.

MOWBRAY

Shall we go draw our numbers and set on?   109

HASTINGS

We are time's subjects, and time bids begone.

Exeunt.

❖

---

109 draw our numbers assemble or muster our forces.   **set on** march

2.1 *Enter Hostess [Quickly] of the tavern and two officers: [Fang, followed by Snare].*

HOSTESS   Master Fang, have you entered the action?   1
FANG   It is entered.
HOSTESS   Where's your yeoman? Is 't a lusty yeoman?   3
Will 'a stand to 't?   4
FANG [*Looking around him*]   Sirrah—where's Snare?
HOSTESS   O Lord, ay, good Master Snare.
SNARE [*From behind them*]   Here, here.
FANG   Snare, we must arrest Sir John Falstaff.
HOSTESS   Yea, good Master Snare, I have entered him   9
and all.
SNARE   It may chance cost some of us our lives, for he   11
will stab.
HOSTESS   Alas the day, take heed of him! He stabbed me
in mine own house, most beastly, in good faith. 'A
cares not what mischief he does, if his weapon be out.
He will foin like any devil; he will spare neither man,   16
woman, nor child.
FANG   If I can close with him, I care not for his thrust.   18
HOSTESS   No, nor I neither. I'll be at your elbow.
FANG   An I but fist him once, and 'a come but within   20
my vice—   21
HOSTESS   I am undone by his going. I warrant you, he's   22
an infinitive thing upon my score. Good Master Fang,   23
hold him sure. Good Master Snare, let him not scape.
'A comes continuantly to Pie Corner—saving your   25
manhoods—to buy a saddle; and he is indited to din-   26

2.1. Location: London. A street.
1 entered the action begun the lawsuit   **3 yeoman** sheriff's man   **4 Will
. . . to 't** will he fight boldly   **9 entered** brought action against in
court   **11 chance** possibly   **16 foin** thrust in fencing; with unintended
sexual double meaning, as also in *stabbed, weapon, thrust, entered,
undone, saddle* (suggesting a prostitute), *case* (female pudendum), *openly
known to the world, brought in, long one, borne, fubbed off* (meaning
also to be put off with excuses), *do me, stand to me*, etc.   **18 close**
grapple   **20 fist** i.e., seize   **21 vice** vise, grip   **22 going** i.e., going
without paying   **23 infinitive** (Hostess Quickly's malapropism for
infinite, endless.)   **score** accounts   **25 continuantly** (Perhaps a mixup of
continually and *incontinently*, immediately.)   **Pie Corner** a corner in the
Smithfield district of London known for its cooks' shops   **25–26 saving
your manhoods** i.e., with apologies for mentioning anything so indeli-
cate   **26 indited** i.e., invited

ner to the Lubber's Head in Lumbert Street, to Master 27
Smooth's the silkman. I pray you, since my exion is 28
entered and my case so openly known to the world, let
him be brought in to his answer. A hundred mark is 30
a long one for a poor lone woman to bear; and I have 31
borne, and borne, and borne, and have been fubbed
off, and fubbed off, and fubbed off, from this day to
that day, that it is a shame to be thought on. There is
no honesty in such dealing, unless a woman should
be made an ass and a beast, to bear every knave's
wrong. Yonder he comes, and that arrant malmsey- 37
nose knave, Bardolph, with him. Do your offices, do 38
your offices. Master Fang and Master Snare, do me, do 39
me, do me your offices.

> *Enter Sir John [Falstaff], and Bardolph, and the*
> *Boy [Page].*

FALSTAFF How now, whose mare's dead? What's the 41
matter?

FANG Sir John, I arrest you at the suit of Mistress
Quickly.

FALSTAFF Away, varlets! Draw, Bardolph. Cut me off
the villain's head. Throw the quean in the channel.   46
> *[They draw.]*

HOSTESS Throw me in the channel? I'll throw thee in the
channel. Wilt thou? Wilt thou? Thou bastardly rogue!
Murder, murder! Ah, thou honeysuckle villain! Wilt 49
thou kill God's officers and the King's? Ah, thou hon- 50
eyseed rogue! Thou art a honeyseed, a man-queller, 51
and a woman-queller.   52

FALSTAFF Keep them off, Bardolph.

OFFICERS A rescue! A rescue!   54

---

27 Lubber's Head i.e., Libbard's Head, Leopard's Head Inn. **Lumbert**
i.e., Lombard **28 exion** action, lawsuit **30 mark** (Worth 13 shillings 4
pence.) **31 long one** huge reckoning (with unconscious sexual suggestion) **37–38 malmsey-nose** red-nosed (from drinking malmsey, a sweet
red wine) **39 do me** i.e., do your duty for me (with unintended sexual
suggestion) **41 whose mare's dead** i.e., what's all the fuss about
46 quean slut, hussy. **channel** street gutter **49 honeysuckle** (For
homicidal.) **50–51 honeyseed** (For *homicide*.) **51 man-queller** mur-
derer **52 woman-queller** destroyer of women (but with suggestion also
of "seducer") **54 A rescue** i.e., come help the officers in their rescue of
the hostess. (Said to anyone within earshot.)

HOSTESS Good people, bring a rescue or two. Thou
woo't, woo't thou? Thou woo't, woo't ta? Do, do, 56
thou rogue! Do, thou hempseed!   57
PAGE Away, you scullion, you rampallian, you fus- 58
tilarian! I'll tickle your catastrophe.   59

Enter [the] Lord Chief Justice and his men.

CHIEF JUSTICE
What is the matter? Keep the peace here, ho!
HOSTESS Good my lord, be good to me. I beseech you,
stand to me.   62
CHIEF JUSTICE
How now, Sir John? What are you brawling here?   63
Doth this become your place, your time, and business?
You should have been well on your way to York.
[*To an officer.*] Stand from him, fellow. Wherefore
   hang'st thou upon him?
HOSTESS O my most worshipful lord, an 't please Your
Grace, I am a poor widow of Eastcheap, and he is ar-
rested at my suit.
CHIEF JUSTICE For what sum?
HOSTESS It is more than for some, my lord, it is for all,
all I have. He hath eaten me out of house and home; he
hath put all my substance into that fat belly of his. But
I will have some of it out again, [*To Falstaff*] or I will ride
thee o' nights like the mare.   75
FALSTAFF I think I am as like to ride the mare, if I have
any vantage of ground to get up.   77
CHIEF JUSTICE How comes this, Sir John? What man of
good temper would endure this tempest of exclama- 79
tion? Are you not ashamed to enforce a poor widow to
so rough a course to come by her own?   81
FALSTAFF What is the gross sum that I owe thee?   82
HOSTESS Marry, if thou wert an honest man, thyself and

---

56 woo't thou wilt thou. **ta** thou **57 hempseed** (Alludes to the hang-
man's rope; Mistress Quickly probably means *homicide*.) **58 scullion**
kitchen wench. **rampallian** scoundrel, ruffian **58–59 fustilarian** fat,
frowsy woman **59 catastrophe** backside **62 stand to** help (with bawdy
suggestion) **63 What** why **75 o' nights** by night. **mare** nightmare
77 vantage of ground superior position. **get up** mount (with intended
sexual suggestion, continued from *ride the mare* in l. 76) **79 temper**
disposition **81 come by her own** get what is hers **82 gross** whole

the money too. Thou didst swear to me upon a parcel- 84
gilt goblet, sitting in my Dolphin chamber, at the 85
round table, by a seacoal fire, upon Wednesday in 86
Wheeson week, when the Prince broke thy head for 87
liking his father to a singing-man of Windsor, thou 88
didst swear to me then, as I was washing thy wound,
to marry me and make me my lady thy wife. Canst
thou deny it? Did not goodwife Keech, the butcher's 91
wife, come in then and call me gossip Quickly? Com- 92
ing in to borrow a mess of vinegar, telling us she had 93
a good dish of prawns, whereby thou didst desire to 94
eat some, whereby I told thee they were ill for a green 95
wound? And didst thou not, when she was gone
downstairs, desire me to be no more so familiarity 97
with such poor people, saying that ere long they
should call me madam? And didst thou not kiss me
and bid me fetch thee thirty shillings? I put thee now
to thy book oath. Deny it if thou canst.   101

FALSTAFF My lord, this is a poor mad soul, and she says
up and down the town that her eldest son is like you.
She hath been in good case, and the truth is, poverty 104
hath distracted her. But for these foolish officers, I be- 105
seech you I may have redress against them.

CHIEF JUSTICE Sir John, Sir John, I am well acquainted
with your manner of wrenching the true cause the
false way. It is not a confident brow, nor the throng of
words that come with such more than impudent
sauciness from you, can thrust me from a level consid- 111
eration. You have, as it appears to me, practiced upon
the easy-yielding spirit of this woman and made her
serve your uses both in purse and in person.   114

HOSTESS Yea, in truth, my lord.

84–85 parcel-gilt partly gilded   85 Dolphin chamber (The name of a room in
her inn; *Dolphin* means "Dauphin.")   86 seacoal bituminous coal, brought
in by sea   87 Wheeson Whitsun (Pentecost).   broke hit, made a cut on
88 liking comparing.   singing-man chorister   91 goodwife (Title of a married woman.)   Keech (Literally, "a lump of tallow.")   92 gossip (Literally, a
fellow godparent; hence, a female friend.)   93 mess small quantity
94 prawns shrimps.   whereby whereupon   95 green raw   97 familiarity
(The hostess's word for "familiar.")   101 book oath oath on a Bible   104 in
good case well to do (perhaps with bawdy suggestion)   105 distracted her
driven her mad   111 level fair-minded, evenhanded   114 serve your uses
(with erotic suggestion)

CHIEF JUSTICE Pray thee, peace.—Pay her the debt you
owe her, and unpay the villainy you have done her.
The one you may do with sterling money, and the
other with current repentance.   119

FALSTAFF My lord, I will not undergo this sneap with-   120
out reply. You call honorable boldness impudent
sauciness. If a man will make curtsy and say nothing,   122
he is virtuous. No, my lord, my humble duty re-   123
membered, I will not be your suitor. I say to you, I do   124
desire deliverance from these officers, being upon
hasty employment in the King's affairs.

CHIEF JUSTICE You speak as having power to do wrong.
But answer in th' effect of your reputation, and satisfy   128
the poor woman.

FALSTAFF Come hither, hostess. [*He takes her aside.*]

        Enter a messenger [*Gower*].

CHIEF JUSTICE Now, Master Gower, what news?

GOWER
The King, my lord, and Harry Prince of Wales
Are near at hand. The rest the paper tells.
        [*He gives a letter. The Chief Justice reads.*]

FALSTAFF [*To Mistress Quickly*] As I am a gentleman.

HOSTESS Faith, you said so before.

FALSTAFF As I am a gentleman. Come, no more words
of it.

HOSTESS By this heavenly ground I tread on, I must be
fain to pawn both my plate and the tapestry of my   139
dining chambers.

FALSTAFF Glasses, glasses, is the only drinking. And for   141
thy walls, a pretty slight drollery, or the story of the   142
Prodigal, or the German hunting in water work, is   143

---

119 current genuine (with an allusion to current, or lawful, coin, the
sterling of l. 118)   **120 sneap** reproof   **122 curtsy** bow   **123–124 my . . .
remembered** i.e., with all due consideration of the respect I owe to your
position   **128 in . . . reputation** i.e., in a manner becoming a man of
your reputation   **139 fain** obliged, content   **141 Glasses . . . drinking**
i.e., glasses are all the fashion now for drinking, instead of metal tan-
kards   **142 drollery** comic picture   **142–143 the Prodigal** the Prodigal
Son. (See Luke 15.11–32.)   **143 German hunting** hunting scene painted
by a German or Dutch artist.   **water work** watercolor

worth a thousand of these bed-hangers and these fly- 144
bitten tapestries. Let it be ten pound, if thou canst.
Come, an 'twere not for thy humors, there's not a 146
better wench in England. Go wash thy face, and draw 147
the action. Come, thou must not be in this humor
with me. Dost not know me? Come, come, I know
thou wast set on to this.

HOSTESS   Pray thee, Sir John, let it be but twenty nobles. 151
I' faith, I am loath to pawn my plate, so God save 152
me, la!

FALSTAFF   Let it alone; I'll make other shift. You'll be a 154
fool still.

HOSTESS   Well, you shall have it, though I pawn my
gown. I hope you'll come to supper. You'll pay me all
together?

FALSTAFF   Will I live? [*To Bardolph.*] Go, with her, with 159
her; hook on, hook on. 160

HOSTESS   Will you have Doll Tearsheet meet you at
supper?

FALSTAFF   No more words. Let's have her.
                    Exeunt Hostess and Sergeant [Fang,
                              Bardolph, and others].

CHIEF JUSTICE   I have heard better news.

FALSTAFF   What's the news, my lord?

CHIEF JUSTICE   Where lay the King tonight? 166

GOWER   At Basingstoke, my lord. 167

FALSTAFF   I hope, my lord, all's well. What is the news,
my lord?

CHIEF JUSTICE   Come all his forces back?

GOWER
No, fifteen hundred foot, five hundred horse 171
Are marched up to my lord of Lancaster, 172
Against Northumberland and the Archbishop.

FALSTAFF   Comes the King back from Wales, my noble
lord?

---

144 bed-hangers curtains around a four-poster bed   **146 an 'twere** if it
were.   **humors** whims, vagaries   **147 draw** withdraw   **151 nobles** coins
current at 6 shillings 8 pence   **152 loath** reluctant   **154 shift** expedient   **159 Will I live** i.e., as sure as I live   **160 hook on** i.e., follow her
166 tonight this past night   **167 Basingstoke** a town in Hampshire
171 foot foot soldiers.   **horse** cavalry troops   **172 to** i.e., led by

CHIEF JUSTICE
  You shall have letters of me presently.   176
  Come, go along with me, good Master Gower.

[He starts to go.]

FALSTAFF My lord!

CHIEF JUSTICE What's the matter?

FALSTAFF Master Gower, shall I entreat you with me to
dinner?

GOWER I must wait upon my good lord here, I thank   182
you, good Sir John.

CHIEF JUSTICE Sir John, you loiter here too long, being   184
you are to take soldiers up in counties as you go.   185

FALSTAFF Will you sup with me, Master Gower?

CHIEF JUSTICE What foolish master taught you these
manners, Sir John?

FALSTAFF Master Gower, if they become me not, he was
a fool that taught them me. This is the right fencing
grace, my lord—tap for tap, and so part fair.   191

CHIEF JUSTICE Now the Lord lighten thee! Thou art a   192
great fool.   *[Exeunt separately.]*

✤

2.2   *Enter the Prince [Henry], Poins, with others.*

PRINCE Before God, I am exceeding weary.

POINS Is 't come to that? I had thought weariness durst
not have attached one of so high blood.   3

PRINCE Faith, it does me, though it discolors the com-   4
plexion of my greatness to acknowledge it. Doth it not   5
show vilely in me to desire small beer?   6

POINS Why, a prince should not be so loosely studied   7

---

176 presently immediately   **182 wait upon** accompany   **184–185 being
. . . up** seeing that you are to levy soldiers   **191 grace** form, style.
(Falstaff is saying that by refusing to answer the Chief Justice's questions in ll. 180 ff., Falstaff is only paying him back tit for tat for ignoring Falstaff's questions, ll. 165–177.) **fair** on good terms **192 lighten**
(1) enlighten (2) reduce in weight

2.2. Location: London. Prince Henry's dwelling.
3 attached seized **4–5 discolors . . . greatness** i.e., makes me blush or
look pale with weariness, and casts a shadow over my princely greatness **6 show** appear. **small beer** weak kind of beer, hence inferior
7 studied versed, inclined

as to remember so weak a composition.   8

PRINCE   Belike then my appetite was not princely got,   9
for, by my troth, I do now remember the poor crea-
ture, small beer. But indeed these humble considera-
tions make me out of love with my greatness. What a
disgrace is it to me to remember thy name! Or to know
thy face tomorrow! Or to take note how many pair of
silk stockings thou hast, viz., these, and those that   15
were thy peach-colored ones! Or to bear the inventory   16
of thy shirts, as, one for superfluity, and another for   17
use! But that the tennis-court keeper knows better   18
than I; for it is a low ebb of linen with thee when thou 19
keepest not racket there, as thou hast not done a great   20
while, because the rest of the low countries have made   21
a shift to eat up thy holland. And God knows whether   22
those that bawl out the ruins of thy linen shall inherit 23
His kingdom. But the midwives say the children are   24
not in the fault, whereupon the world increases and   25
kindreds are mightily strengthened.   26

POINS   How ill it follows, after you have labored so hard,
you should talk so idly! Tell me, how many good
young princes would do so, their fathers being so sick
as yours at this time is?

PRINCE   Shall I tell thee one thing, Poins?

POINS   Yes, faith, and let it be an excellent good thing.

PRINCE   It shall serve among wits of no higher breeding
than thine.

---

8 so . . . composition i.e., weak beer, trifles   **9 Belike** probably.   **got**
begotten   **15 viz.** namely. (An abbreviation of the Latin *videlicet*.)
16 bear bear in mind   **17 for superfluity** as a clean change (of shirt)
18–21 But . . . while i.e., the keeper of the tennis court knows that
Poins's inventory of shirts is at a low ebb, that he does not have a spare
clean shirt to shift into, because he has not been seen at the tennis
court lately   **21 the low countries** i.e., the brothels where Poins spends
his money (with a pun on "the Netherlands")   **21–22 made a shift**
contrived (with a pun on *shift*, shirt)   **22 eat . . . holland** i.e., used up all
the money you would spend on a linen shirt (with a pun on *Holland* as
one of the Low Countries)   **23 those . . . linen** i.e., your bastards, who
wear your cast-off shirts made into swaddling clothes.   **bawl out** cry
out from   **23–24 inherit His kingdom** i.e., go to heaven. (See Matthew
5.10, 25.34, or 19.14: "Suffer the little children . . . to come to me, for
of such is the kingdom of heaven.")   **25 in the fault** to be blamed (for
being illegitimate)   **26 kindreds** families. (The Prince's point is that
this is how families are increased in size.)

POINS   Go to. I stand the push of your one thing that 35
    you will tell.

PRINCE   Marry, I tell thee it is not meet that I should be 37
    sad, now my father is sick. Albeit I could tell to thee,
    as to one it pleases me, for fault of a better, to call my
    friend, I could be sad, and sad indeed too.

POINS   Very hardly upon such a subject.   41

PRINCE   By this hand, thou thinkest me as far in the
    devil's book as thou and Falstaff for obduracy and per-
    sistency. Let the end try the man. But I tell thee, my
    heart bleeds inwardly that my father is so sick. And
    keeping such vile company as thou art hath in reason
    taken from me all ostentation of sorrow.   47

POINS   The reason?

PRINCE   What wouldst thou think of me if I should
    weep?

POINS   I would think thee a most princely hypocrite.

PRINCE   It would be every man's thought, and thou art
    a blessed fellow to think as every man thinks. Never a
    man's thought in the world keeps the roadway better 54
    than thine. Every man would think me an hypocrite
    indeed. And what accites your most worshipful 56
    thought to think so?

POINS   Why, because you have been so lewd and so 58
    much engraffed to Falstaff.   59

PRINCE   And to thee.

POINS   By this light, I am well spoke on; I can hear it
    with mine own ears. The worst that they can say of
    me is that I am a second brother and that I am a proper 63
    fellow of my hands, and those two things I confess I 64
    cannot help. By the Mass, here comes Bardolph.

    Enter Bardolph and Boy [Page].

PRINCE   And the boy that I gave Falstaff. 'A had him

---

35 push attack, thrust   **37 meet** fitting, appropriate   **41 Very hardly**
scarcely, with difficulty   **47 ostentation** outward indication   **54 keeps
the roadway** i.e., follows the common way of thinking   **56 accites**
induces (with a quibble on "summons")   **58 lewd** base   **59 engraffed**
closely attached   **63 second brother** i.e., a younger son, without inheri-
tance   **63–64 proper . . . hands** i.e., good fighter

from me Christian, and look if the fat villain have not 67
transformed him ape.   68

BARDOLPH   God save Your Grace!

PRINCE   And yours, most noble Bardolph!

POINS [*To Bardolph*]   Come, you virtuous ass, you bash-
ful fool, must you be blushing? Wherefore blush you 72
now? What a maidenly man-at-arms are you become!
Is 't such a matter to get a pottle pot's maidenhead? 74

PAGE   'A calls me e'en now, my lord, through a red lat- 75
tice, and I could discern no part of his face from the 76
window. At last I spied his eyes, and methought he
had made two holes in the alewife's petticoat and
so peeped through.

PRINCE   Has not the boy profited?

BARDOLPH   Away, you whoreson upright rabbit, away!

PAGE   Away, you rascally Althaea's dream, away!   82

PRINCE   Instruct us, boy. What dream, boy?

PAGE   Marry, my lord, Althaea dreamt she was delivered
of a firebrand, and therefore I call him her dream.

PRINCE   A crown's worth of good interpretation. There 86
'tis, boy.   [*He gives money.*]

POINS   O, that this blossom could be kept from cankers! 88
Well, there is sixpence to preserve thee.   89
                                              [*He gives money.*]

BARDOLPH   An you do not make him be hanged among 90
you, the gallows shall have wrong.

PRINCE   And how doth thy master, Bardolph?

BARDOLPH   Well, my lord. He heard of Your Grace's
coming to town. There's a letter for you.
                                              [*He gives a letter.*]

67–68 have . . . ape i.e., has not dressed him fantastically   **72 blushing**
i.e., red-faced (from drink).   **Wherefore** why   **74 get . . . maidenhead**
i.e., knock off a two-quart tankard of ale   **75 e'en now** just now, a
moment ago   **75–76 red lattice** (Red lattices identified taverns.)
76 discern distinguish   **82 Althaea's dream** (Althaea dreamed that her
newborn son would live only so long as a brand on the fire lasted. The
Page mistakenly relates Hecuba's dream: when pregnant with Paris,
Hecuba dreamed she would be delivered of a firebrand that would
destroy Troy.)   **86 crown** i.e., 5 shillings   **88 cankers** cankerworms,
worms that destroy buds and leaves   **89 to preserve thee** (Allusion to
the cross on the sixpence.)   **90 An** if

POINS   Delivered with good respect. And how doth the 95
martlemas, your master? 96

BARDOLPH   In bodily health, sir.

POINS   Marry, the immortal part needs a physician, but
that moves not him. Though that be sick, it dies not.

PRINCE   I do allow this wen to be as familiar with me as 100
my dog, and he holds his place, for look you how he
writes.   [*He shows a letter to Poins.*]

POINS   [*Reading the superscription*]   "John Falstaff,
knight."—Every man must know that as oft as he has 104
occasion to name himself, even like those that are kin
to the King, for they never prick their finger but they
say, "There's some of the King's blood spilt." "How
comes that?" says he that takes upon him not to con- 108
ceive. The answer is as ready as a borrower's cap: "I 109
am the King's poor cousin, sir."

PRINCE   Nay, they will be kin to us, or they will fetch it 111
from Japheth. But the letter. [*He reads.*] "Sir John 112
Falstaff, knight, to the son of the King nearest his father,
Harry Prince of Wales, greeting."

POINS   Why, this is a certificate. 115

PRINCE   Peace! [*He reads.*] "I will imitate the honorable
Romans in brevity."

POINS   He sure means brevity in breath, short-winded.

PRINCE [*Reads*]   "I commend me to thee, I commend thee,
and I leave thee. Be not too familiar with Poins, for he
misuses thy favors so much that he swears thou art to
marry his sister Nell. Repent at idle times as thou
mayst, and so farewell.

"Thine, by yea and no, which is as much as to say, 124
as thou usest him, Jack Falstaff with my familiars, 125
John with my brothers and sisters, and Sir John
with all Europe."

---

95 good respect proper ceremony. (Said ironically.)   **96 martlemas** i.e.,
Martinmas beef, beef slaughtered on November 11 (and fattened before-
hand)   **100 wen** swelling, tumor   **104 Every . . . that** i.e., Falstaff wants
to make sure that everyone is aware of his knightly rank   **108–109 takes
. . . conceive** pretends not to understand   **109 as ready . . . cap** i.e., as
quick in coming forth as a cap is doffed by one seeking aid   **111–112 fetch
. . . Japheth** i.e., trace their ancestry back to Japheth, one of the sons of
Noah. (Genesis 10.2–5.)   **115 certificate** legal document   **124 by yea and
no** (A Puritan oath.)   **125 familiars** intimate friends

POINS   My lord, I'll steep this letter in sack and make   128
  him eat it.
PRINCE   That's to make him eat twenty of his words. But   130
  do you use me thus, Ned? Must I marry your sister?
POINS   God send the wench no worse fortune! But I
  never said so.
PRINCE   Well, thus we play the fools with the time, and
  the spirits of the wise sit in the clouds and mock us.—Is
  your master here in London?
BARDOLPH   Yea, my lord.
PRINCE   Where sups he? Doth the old boar feed in the
  old frank?   139
BARDOLPH   At the old place, my lord, in Eastcheap.
PRINCE   What company?
PAGE   Ephesians, my lord, of the old church.   142
PRINCE   Sup any women with him?
PAGE   None, my lord, but old Mistress Quickly and
  Mistress Doll Tearsheet.
PRINCE   What pagan may that be?   146
PAGE   A proper gentlewoman, sir, and a kinswoman of
  my master's.
PRINCE   Even such kin as the parish heifers are to the
  town bull. Shall we steal upon them, Ned, at supper?   150
POINS   I am your shadow, my lord; I'll follow you.
PRINCE   Sirrah, you boy, and Bardolph, no word to your
  master that I am yet come to town. There's for your
  silence.   [*He gives money.*]
BARDOLPH   I have no tongue, sir.
PAGE   And for mine, sir, I will govern it.
PRINCE   Fare you well; go. [*Exeunt Bardolph and Page.*]
  This Doll Tearsheet should be some road.   158
POINS   I warrant you, as common as the way between
  Saint Albans and London.
PRINCE   How might we see Falstaff bestow himself to-   161
  night in his true colors, and not ourselves be seen?

---

128 steep soak   **130 twenty** i.e., a considerable number   **139 frank** sty,
pen. (Often thought to refer to the Boar's Head Tavern.)   **142 Ephesians
. . . church** i.e., good fellows of the usual, disreputable fellowship
146 pagan i.e., harlot   **150 town bull** a communally owned bull that
local farmers could mate with their heifers   **158 should** must.   **road**
i.e., common whore   **161 bestow** behave

POINS   Put on two leathern jerkins and aprons, and wait 163
upon him at his table as drawers.   164
PRINCE   From a god to a bull? A heavy descension! It 165
was Jove's case. From a prince to a prentice? A low 166
transformation! That shall be mine, for in everything
the purpose must weigh with the folly. Follow me, 168
Ned.   *Exeunt.*

❖

2.3   *Enter Northumberland, his wife [Lady*
Northumberland], and the wife to Harry Percy
[Lady Percy].

NORTHUMBERLAND
I pray thee, loving wife and gentle daughter,   1
Give even way unto my rough affairs.   2
Put not you on the visage of the times   3
And be like them to Percy troublesome.
LADY NORTHUMBERLAND
I have given over; I will speak no more.
Do what you will; your wisdom be your guide.
NORTHUMBERLAND
Alas, sweet wife, my honor is at pawn,
And, but my going, nothing can redeem it.   8
LADY PERCY
O, yet for God's sake, go not to these wars!
The time was, Father, that you broke your word,
When you were more endeared to it than now,   11
When your own Percy, when my heart's dear Harry,
Threw many a northward look to see his father
Bring up his powers; but he did long in vain.   14
Who then persuaded you to stay at home?
There were two honors lost, yours and your son's.

---

163 jerkins jackets   **164 drawers** tapsters, tavern waiters   **165 heavy**
descension grievous descent   **166 Jove's case** (Jupiter, for the love of
Europa, transformed himself into a bull.)   **168 weigh with** match,
balance

2.3. Location: Warkworth. Before Northumberland's castle.
1 daughter i.e., daughter-in-law   **2 even way** free scope   **3 Put . . . times**
i.e., don't look as bleak or troubled as are the times   **8 but** except for
11 endeared pledged, bound by affection   **14 powers** armed forces

For yours, the God of heaven brighten it!   17
For his, it stuck upon him as the sun
In the gray vault of heaven, and by his light   19
Did all the chivalry of England move   20
To do brave acts. He was indeed the glass   21
Wherein the noble youth did dress themselves.
He had no legs that practiced not his gait;   23
And speaking thick, which nature made his blemish,   24
Became the accents of the valiant,
For those that could speak low and tardily
Would turn their own perfection to abuse   27
To seem like him. So that in speech, in gait,
In diet, in affections of delight,   29
In military rules, humors of blood,   30
He was the mark and glass, copy and book,   31
That fashioned others. And him, O, wondrous him!
O, miracle of men! Him did you leave,
Second to none, unseconded by you,   34
To look upon the hideous god of war
In disadvantage, to abide a field   36
Where nothing but the sound of Hotspur's name
Did seem defensible. So you left him.   38
Never, O, never do his ghost the wrong
To hold your honor more precise and nice   40
With others than with him! Let them alone.
The Marshal and the Archbishop are strong.
Had my sweet Harry had but half their numbers,
Today might I, hanging on Hotspur's neck,
Have talked of Monmouth's grave.
NORTHUMBERLAND   Beshrew your heart, 45
Fair daughter, you do draw my spirits from me
With new lamenting ancient oversights.   47

---

17 For as for **19 gray** sky-blue **20 chivalry** men-at-arms **21 glass** mirror **23 He . . . gait** i.e., there was no man alive and able to walk who did not imitate Hotspur's stride **24 thick** impulsively, impetuously **27 turn . . . abuse** i.e., debase their own manner of speech and adopt his **29 affections of delight** choice of pleasurable occupations **30 humors of blood** temperament **31 mark** pattern, guiding object **34 unseconded** unsupported **36 In disadvantage** i.e., outnumbered. **abide a field** face a battle **38 defensible** able to make defense **40 nice** punctilious **45 Monmouth's** i.e., Prince Hal's (since he was born at Monmouth). **Beshrew your heart** (A reproachful oath.) **47 new lamenting** lamenting anew

But I must go and meet with danger there,
Or it will seek me in another place
And find me worse provided.

LADY NORTHUMBERLAND   O, fly to Scotland,   50
Till that the nobles and the armèd commons
Have of their puissance made a little taste.   52

LADY PERCY
If they get ground and vantage of the King,   53
Then join you with them like a rib of steel,
To make strength stronger; but, for all our loves,
First let them try themselves. So did your son;   56
He was so suffered. So came I a widow,   57
And never shall have length of life enough
To rain upon remembrance with mine eyes,   59
That it may grow and sprout as high as heaven
For recordation to my noble husband.   61

NORTHUMBERLAND
Come, come, go in with me. 'Tis with my mind
As with the tide swelled up unto his height,
That makes a still-stand, running neither way.   64
Fain would I go to meet the Archbishop,   65
But many thousand reasons hold me back.
I will resolve for Scotland. There am I,   67
Till time and vantage crave my company.   *Exeunt.* 68

❖

2.4   *Enter a Drawer, [Francis, and another].*

FRANCIS What the devil hast thou brought there?
Applejohns? Thou knowest Sir John cannot endure   2
an applejohn.

---

50 provided prepared   **52 taste** trial   **53 get . . . of** achieve a military
advantage over   **56 try** test   **57 suffered** allowed to proceed.   **came**
became   **59 rain . . . eyes** water remembrance with my tears, as though
it were a plant like rosemary   **61 recordation** remembrance, memo-
rial   **64 still-stand** point of balance, standstill   **65 Fain** gladly
67 resolve for decide to go to   **68 vantage** opportunity

**2.4. Location: London. A tavern in Eastcheap, usually identified as the
Boar's Head. Some tavern furniture is provided.**
2 Applejohns a kind of apple eaten when shriveled and withered

SECOND DRAWER   Mass, thou sayst true. The Prince 4
  once set a dish of applejohns before him, and told
  him there were five more Sir Johns, and, putting off
  his hat, said, "I will now take my leave of these six dry,
  round, old, withered knights." It angered him to the
  heart. But he hath forgot that.

FRANCIS   Why, then, cover, and set them down. And 10
  see if thou canst find out Sneak's noise; Mistress Tear- 11
  sheet would fain hear some music.

  Enter Will [a third Drawer].

THIRD DRAWER   Dispatch! The room where they supped 13
  is too hot; they'll come in straight.   14

FRANCIS   Sirrah, here will be the Prince and Master
  Poins anon, and they will put on two of our jerkins
  and aprons, and Sir John must not know of it. Bardolph hath brought word.

THIRD DRAWER   By the Mass, here will be old utas. It 19
  will be an excellent stratagem.

SECOND DRAWER   I'll see if I can find out Sneak.   *Exit.*

  *Enter Mistress Quickly [the hostess] and Doll
  Tearsheet.*

HOSTESS   I' faith, sweetheart, methinks now you are in
  an excellent good temperality. Your pulsidge beats as 23
  extraordinarily as heart would desire, and your color, 24
  I warrant you, is as red as any rose, in good truth, la!
  But, i' faith, you have drunk too much canaries, and 26
  that's a marvelous searching wine, and it perfumes 27
  the blood ere one can say, "What's this?" How do
  you now?

DOLL   Better than I was. Hem!

HOSTESS   Why, that's well said. A good heart's worth
  gold. Lo, here comes Sir John.

  Enter Sir John [Falstaff].

---

4 Mass i.e., by the Mass   **10 cover** spread the cloth, set the table
11 noise band of musicians   **13 Dispatch** hurry up   **14 straight** very
soon   **19 old utas** i.e., rare fun   **23 temperality** i.e., temper.   **pulsidge**
i.e., pulse   **24 extraordinarily** i.e., ordinarily   **26 canaries** (A light,
sweet wine from the Canary Islands.)   **27 searching** potent

FALSTAFF [*Singing*] "When Arthur first in court"— 33
Empty the jordan. [*Exit a Drawer.*]—[*Singing.*] "And 34
was a worthy king." How now, Mistress Doll?

HOSTESS   Sick of a calm, yea, good faith.   36

FALSTAFF   So is all her sect. An they be once in a calm, 37
they are sick.

DOLL   A pox damn you, you muddy rascal, is that all
the comfort you give me?

FALSTAFF   You make fat rascals, Mistress Doll.   41

DOLL   I make them? Gluttony and diseases make them;
I make them not.

FALSTAFF   If the cook help to make the gluttony, you
help to make the diseases, Doll. We catch of you, Doll,
we catch of you. Grant that, my poor virtue, grant that.

DOLL   Yea, joy, our chains and our jewels.   47

FALSTAFF   "Your brooches, pearls, and ouches." For to 48
serve bravely is to come halting off, you know; to
come off the breach with his pike bent bravely, and to
surgery bravely; to venture upon the charged cham- 51
bers bravely—   52

DOLL   Hang yourself, you muddy conger, hang yourself!

HOSTESS   By my troth, this is the old fashion. You two
never meet but you fall to some discord. You are both,
i' good truth, as rheumatic as two dry toasts; you can- 57
not one bear with another's confirmities. What the 58
goodyear! One must bear, and that [*To Doll*] must be 59
you. You are the weaker vessel, as they say,
the emptier vessel.

DOLL   Can a weak empty vessel bear such a huge full

---

33 When . . . court (A fragment from the ballad "Sir Launcelot du
Lake.")   **34 jordan** chamber pot   **36 calm** i.e., qualm   **37 sect** sex
41 rascals (1) lean deer (2) good-for-nothings   **47 Yea . . . jewels** i.e., yes,
indeed, you *catch* or steal our valuables   **48 ouches** jewels. (The line is
from a ballad.)   **51–52 charged chambers** small cannon; with bawdy
double meaning, as also in *breach, pike, surgery* (venereal treatment),
conger (eel, with sexual connotation), *bear*   **57 rheumatic** (Blunder for
choleric or *splenetic*?)   **58 confirmities** (For *infirmities*.)   **58–59 What
the goodyear** (An expletive, meaning something like "what the devil.")
59 bear (1) put up with another's infirmities (2) bear the weight of a
lover (3) bear children

hogshead? There's a whole merchant's venture of Bor- 63
deaux stuff in him; you have not seen a hulk better 64
stuffed in the hold.—Come, I'll be friends with thee,
Jack. Thou art going to the wars, and whether I shall
ever see thee again or no there is nobody cares.

   Enter Drawer.

DRAWER   Sir, Ancient Pistol's below, and would speak 68
with you.
DOLL   Hang him, swaggering rascal! Let him not come
hither. It is the foul-mouthed'st rogue in England.
HOSTESS   If he swagger, let him not come here. No, by
my faith, I must live among my neighbors. I'll no 73
swaggerers. I am in good name and fame with the
very best. Shut the door; there comes no swaggerers
here. I have not lived all this while to have swaggering
now. Shut the door, I pray you.
FALSTAFF   Dost thou hear, Hostess?
HOSTESS   Pray ye, pacify yourself, Sir John. There comes
no swaggerers here.
FALSTAFF   Dost thou hear? It is mine ancient.
HOSTESS   Tilly-fally, Sir John, ne'er tell me. An your an- 82
cient swagger, 'a comes not in my doors. I was before 83
Master Tisick, the debuty, t'other day, and, as he said 84
to me, 'twas no longer ago than Wednesday last, i' good
faith, "Neighbor Quickly," says he—Master Dumbe,
our minister, was by then—"Neighbor Quickly," says
he, "receive those that are civil, for," said he, "you are 88
in an ill name." Now 'a said so, I can tell where- 89
upon. "For," says he, "you are an honest woman, and 90
well thought on; therefore take heed what guests you
receive. Receive," says he, "no swaggering compan- 92
ions." There comes none here. You would bless you 93
to hear what he said. No, I'll no swaggerers.

---

63 hogshead large cask.   **venture** cargo   **63–64 Bordeaux stuff** i.e.,
wine   **64 hulk** large, unwieldy cargo ship   **68 Ancient** ensign, standard-
bearer   **73 I'll no** I'll have no   **82 Tilly-fally** i.e., fiddlesticks   **82–83 An
your ancient swagger, 'a** if your ensign is going to swagger, he   **84 Tisick**
(Literally, phthisic, a cough or consumption.)   **debuty** deputy, deputy
alderman   **88–89 are . . . name** have a bad reputation   **89–90 whereupon** upon what grounds   **92–93 companions** ruffians   **93 bless you**
i.e., feel yourself fortunate

FALSTAFF   He's no swaggerer, hostess; a tame cheater, i' 95
faith; you may stroke him as gently as a puppy grey-
hound. He'll not swagger with a Barbary hen, if her 97
feathers turn back in any show of resistance. Call him
up, drawer.   [*Exit Drawer.*]
HOSTESS   Cheater, call you him? I will bar no honest 100
man my house, nor no cheater, but I do not love swaggering, by my troth. I am the worse when one says
"swagger." Feel, masters, how I shake; look you, I warrant you.
DOLL   So you do, Hostess.
HOSTESS   Do I? Yea, in very truth, do I, an 'twere an 106
aspen leaf. I cannot abide swaggerers.

Enter Ancient Pistol, [Bardolph,] and Boy [Page].

PISTOL   God save you, Sir John!
FALSTAFF   Welcome, Ancient Pistol. Here, Pistol, I
charge you with a cup of sack. Do you discharge upon 110
mine hostess.
PISTOL   I will discharge upon her, Sir John, with two
bullets.
FALSTAFF   She is pistol-proof, sir; you shall not hardly 114
offend her.   115
HOSTESS   Come, I'll drink no proofs nor no bullets. I'll
drink no more than will do me good, for no man's
pleasure, I.
PISTOL   Then to you, Mistress Dorothy; I will charge
you.
DOLL   Charge me? I scorn you, scurvy companion.
What, you poor, base, rascally, cheating, lack-linen 122
mate? Away, you moldy rogue, away! I am meat for 123
your master.
PISTOL   I know you, Mistress Dorothy.

---

95 cheater decoy in a team of confidence men   **97 Barbary hen** guinea
hen. (Slang term for a prostitute.)   **100 Cheater** (Mistress Quickly may
understand the word as *escheator*, an officer of the King's exchequer.)
106 an 'twere i.e., as if I were   **110 charge** pledge, drink to.   **discharge
upon** toast; with bawdy double meaning; see also *charge, Pistol, bullets*
(testicles), *meat* (slang for "whore"), etc.   **114 shall not** i.e., shall. (A
colloquial expression.)   **115 offend** wound   **122 lack-linen** i.e., without
a shirt to your name   **123 mate** low fellow.   **meat** (with a pun on *mate*;
pronounced alike)

DOLL Away, you cutpurse rascal! You filthy bung, 126
away! By this wine, I'll thrust my knife in your moldy
chops, an you play the saucy cuttle with me. Away, 128
you bottle-ale rascal! You basket-hilt stale juggler, you! 129
Since when, I pray you, sir? God's light, with two 130
points on your shoulders? Much! 131

PISTOL God let me not live, but I will murder your ruff 132
for this.

FALSTAFF No more, Pistol, I would not have you go off
here. Discharge yourself of our company, Pistol.

HOSTESS No, good Captain Pistol, not here, sweet Captain.

DOLL Captain? Thou abominable damned cheater, art
thou not ashamed to be called captain? An captains
were of my mind, they would truncheon you out for 140
taking their names upon you before you have earned
them. You a captain? You slave, for what? For tearing
a poor whore's ruff in a bawdy house? He a captain?
Hang him, rogue! He lives upon moldy stewed prunes 144
and dried cakes. A captain? God's light, these villains
will make the word as odious as the word "occupy," 146
which was an excellent good word before it was ill 147
sorted. Therefore captains had need look to 't. 148

BARDOLPH Pray thee, go down, good Ancient. 149

FALSTAFF Hark thee hither, Mistress Doll.

PISTOL Not I. I tell thee what, Corporal Bardolph, I
could tear her. I'll be revenged of her.

PAGE Pray thee, go down.

PISTOL I'll see her damned first, to Pluto's damned lake, 154
by this hand, to th' infernal deep,
With Erebus and tortures vile also. 156

126 bung (1) pickpocket (2) something that fills a hole 128 chops
cheeks. cuttle cutthroat or cutpurse 129 basket-hilt basketlike hilt or
handguard for a practice weapon only; see 3.2.65, note. (Doll scornfully
accuses Pistol of avoiding danger by not using a real sword.) juggler
imposter 130 Since when i.e., since when do you claim to be so brave
and military? 131 points lace tags (for securing armor to the shoulders). Much (An exclamation of scornful incredulity.) 132 murder i.e.,
tear. ruff pleated, starched collar 140 truncheon cudgel 144 stewed
prunes (Associated with brothels.) 146 occupy fornicate 147–148 ill
sorted corrupted, put in such bad company 148 had need would do
well to 149 go down calm down, or, go downstairs and leave
154 Pluto's damned lake the river of the underworld 156 Erebus the
underworld

Hold hook and line, say I.
Down, down, dogs! Down, faitors!   158
Have we not Hiren here?   159

HOSTESS   Good Captain Peesel, be quiet; 'tis very late, i'
faith. I beseek you now, aggravate your choler.   161

PISTOL

These be good humors, indeed! Shall packhorses   162
And hollow pampered jades of Asia,
Which cannot go but thirty mile a day,
Compare with Caesars, and with Cannibals,   165
And Troiant Greeks? Nay, rather damn them with   166
King Cerberus, and let the welkin roar.   167
Shall we fall foul for toys?   168

HOSTESS   By my troth, Captain, these are very bitter
words.

BARDOLPH   Begone, good Ancient. This will grow to a
brawl anon.

PISTOL

Die men like dogs! Give crowns like pins! Have we not
Hiren here?   173

HOSTESS   O' my word, Captain, there's none such here.   174
What the goodyear, do you think I would deny her?   175
For God's sake, be quiet.

PISTOL

Then feed, and be fat, my fair Calipolis.   177
Come, give 's some sack.

---

158 faitors imposters, cheats   **159 Hiren** i.e., Pistol's fanciful name for
his sword, with a seeming allusion to a lost play by Peele, *The Turkish
Mahomet and Hiren the Fair Greek. Hiren* means Irene. (Throughout,
Pistol's colorful speech is full of echoes from the contemporary the-
ater.)   **161 beseek** beseech.   **aggravate** (For *moderate.*)   **162 humors**
whimsies of conduct   **162–166 Shall . . . Greeks** (Misquotation from
Marlowe's *Second Part of Tamburlaine,* 4.4.1–2.)   **165 Cannibals** (The
association here with Caesar would seem to suggest *Hannibals,* but
Cannibals appears in the apparent source for this passage, John Eliot's
Ortho-epia Gallica, 1593. Pistol is ready to take on Cannibals, Trojan
Greeks, or anybody.)   **166 Troiant** Trojan   **167 Cerberus** three-headed
dog guarding the entrance to Hades.   **welkin** heavens   **168 fall . . . toys**
fall out over trifles   **173 Give crowns like pins** pass out kingdoms as if
they were of the value of a pin (as Tamburlaine does to his followers)
174 there's none such here (The hostess seems to think that Pistol is
asking after Hiren or Irene as though she were a boarder or habitué of
the tavern.)   **175 deny her** deny that she was here, if she were
177 Then . . . Calipolis (Garbled version of a line in Peele's *The Battle of
Alcazar,* 2.3.70.)

Si fortune me tormente, sperato me contento.   179
Fear we broadsides? No, let the fiend give fire.   180
Give me some sack, and, sweetheart, lie thou there.
                              [*He lays down his sword.*]
Come we to full points here, and are etceteras nothings? 182
FALSTAFF   Pistol, I would be quiet.

PISTOL
Sweet knight, I kiss thy neaf.   184
What, we have seen the seven stars.   185
DOLL   For God's sake, thrust him downstairs. I cannot
endure such a fustian rascal.   187

PISTOL
Thrust him downstairs? Know we not Galloway nags?   188
FALSTAFF   Quoit him down, Bardolph, like a shove-   189
groat shilling. Nay, an 'a do nothing but speak noth-   190
ing, 'a shall be nothing here.   191
BARDOLPH   Come, get you downstairs.

PISTOL [*Snatching up his sword*]
What, shall we have incision? Shall we imbrue?   193
Then death rock me asleep, abridge my doleful days!   194
Why then, let grievous, ghastly, gaping wounds
Untwine the Sisters Three! Come, Atropos, I say!   196
HOSTESS   Here's goodly stuff toward!   197
FALSTAFF   Give me my rapier, boy.
DOLL   I pray thee, Jack, I pray thee, do not draw.
FALSTAFF   Get you downstairs.   [*They fight.*]
HOSTESS   Here's a goodly tumult! I'll forswear keeping
house afore I'll be in these tirrits and frights. So, mur- 202

---

179 Si . . . contento if fortune torments me, hope contents me. (An
ignorant medley of Spanish and Italian.)   **180 broadsides** volleys fired
from one side of a ship.   **give fire** shoot   **182 full points** full stops,
periods; also, swords' points.   **etceteras** (Probably with bawdy suggestion.)   **184 neaf** fist   **185 the seven stars** the Pleiades. (Pistol means
they have enjoyed themselves at night.)   **187 fustian** bombast, worth-
less   **188 Galloway nags** a Scottish breed of small but swift horses (here
used abusively to mean "harlots")   **189 Quoit** throw   **189–190 shove-
groat shilling** an Edward VI shilling used in shove-groat, a game in
which the coins were shoved toward a mark   **190 an 'a** if he
190–191 speak nothing speak nonsense   **191 nothing here** gone from
here   **193 incision** bloodshed.   **imbrue** shed blood   **194 death . . .
asleep** (Quotation from a current poem about Anne Boleyn and her
brother as they awaited execution.)   **196 Sisters Three** i.e., the three
Fates, Clotho, Lachesis, and Atropos. Atropos severed the thread of
life.   **197 toward** forthcoming   **202 tirrits** fits of temper

der, I warrant now. Alas, alas, put up your naked
weapons, put up your naked weapons.

[*Exit Bardolph, driving Pistol out.*]

DOLL   I pray thee, Jack, be quiet; the rascal's gone. Ah,
you whoreson little valiant villain, you!

HOSTESS   Are you not hurt i' the groin? Methought 'a
made a shrewd thrust at your belly.   208

[*Enter Bardolph.*]

FALSTAFF   Have you turned him out o' doors?

BARDOLPH   Yea, sir. The rascal's drunk. You have hurt
him, sir, i' the shoulder.

FALSTAFF   A rascal! To brave me?

DOLL   Ah, you sweet little rogue, you! Alas, poor ape,
how thou sweat'st! Come, let me wipe thy face. Come
on, you whoreson chops. Ah, rogue, i' faith, I love   215
thee. Thou art as valorous as Hector of Troy, worth   216
five of Agamemnon, and ten times better than the   217
Nine Worthies. Ah, villain!   218

FALSTAFF   A rascally slave! I will toss the rogue in a
blanket.

DOLL   Do, an thou dar'st for thy heart. An thou dost, I'll   221
canvass thee between a pair of sheets.   222

Enter Music.

PAGE   The music is come, sir.

FALSTAFF   Let them play. Play, sirs. Sit on my knee,
Doll. A rascal bragging slave! The rogue fled from me
like quicksilver.

DOLL [*Sitting on his knee*]   I' faith, and thou followedst
him like a church. Thou whoreson little tidy Bartholo-   228
mew boar-pig, when wilt thou leave fighting o' days   229

---

208 shrewd vicious   **215 chops** fat jaws   **216 Hector of Troy** leader of
the Trojans; the type of valor   **217 Agamemnon** leader of the Greeks at
Troy   **218 Nine Worthies** Arthur, Charlemagne, Godfrey of Boulogne;
Hector, Alexander, Julius Caesar; Joshua, David, Judas Maccabaeus
221 for thy heart to save your life   **222 canvass** toss. (Doll gives a sexual
interpretation to Falstaff's phrase, *toss . . . in a blanket*, which means to
subject a coward to ignominious treatment.)   **s.d. Music** musicians
228 a church i.e., a ponderous structure (?)   **tidy** plump, tender
228–229 Bartholomew boar-pig (Allusion to the serving of roast pig at
Bartholomew Fair, August 24, in Smithfield.)

and foining o' nights, and begin to patch up thine old   230
body for heaven?

    Enter [behind] Prince and Poins [disguised as drawers].

FALSTAFF Peace, good Doll, do not speak like a death's-   232
head; do not bid me remember mine end.   233
DOLL Sirrah, what humor's the Prince of?   234
FALSTAFF A good shallow young fellow. 'A would have
made a good pantler, 'a would ha' chipped bread well.   236
DOLL They say Poins has a good wit.
FALSTAFF He a good wit? Hang him, baboon! His wit's
as thick as Tewkesbury mustard. There's no more con-   239
ceit in him than is in a mallet.   240
DOLL Why does the Prince love him so, then?
FALSTAFF Because their legs are both of a bigness, and   242
'a plays at quoits well, and eats conger and fennel, and   243
drinks off candles' ends for flapdragons, and rides the   244
wild mare with the boys, and jumps upon joint   245
stools, and swears with a good grace, and wears his   246
boots very smooth like unto the sign of the Leg, and   247
breeds no bate with telling of discreet stories; and such   248
other gambol faculties 'a has that show a weak mind   249
and an able body, for the which the Prince admits
him. For the Prince himself is such another; the
weight of a hair will turn the scales between their
avoirdupois.   253

---

230 foining thrusting, fornicating   **232–233 death's-head** skull, used
emblematically as a reminder of the inevitability of death   **234 what
. . . of** what is the Prince's disposition, temperament, mood
236 pantler pantry worker.   **chipped bread** cut off the hard bread
crusts   **239 Tewkesbury mustard** (Tewkesbury in Gloucestershire was
famous for mustard balls.)   **239–240 conceit** wit   **240 mallet** wooden
hammer, heavy and not at all sharp   **242 of a bigness** of equal size
243 conger and fennel conger eel seasoned with a yellow-flowered herb.
(Rich fare, likely to dull the wits.)   **244 drinks . . . flapdragons** i.e.,
drinks liquor with a lighted candle floating in it. (An act of bravado.)
245 wild mare seesaw, or a game in which boys pile on top of one
another until the *mare* collapses   **245–246 joint stools** stools made by a
joiner or craftsman in furniture, etc.   **247 smooth** i.e., well-fitting. **sign
. . . Leg** sign over a bootmaker's shop   **248 breeds no bate** causes no
strife. (Falstaff may be saying sardonically that Poins is not one to make
his listeners impatient by limiting himself to discreet stories.)
249 gambol sportive   **253 avoirdupois** weight

PRINCE [*To Poins*] Would not this nave of a wheel have   254
his ears cut off?   255

POINS Let's beat him before his whore.   256

PRINCE Look whe'er the withered elder hath not his poll   257
clawed like a parrot.   258

POINS Is it not strange that desire should so many years
outlive performance?

FALSTAFF Kiss me, Doll.

PRINCE [*To Poins*] Saturn and Venus this year in con-   262
junction? What says th' almanac to that?   263

POINS And look whether the fiery Trigon, his man, be   264
not lisping to his master's old tables, his notebook,   265
his counsel keeper.

FALSTAFF Thou dost give me flattering busses.   267

DOLL By my troth, I kiss thee with a most constant
heart.

FALSTAFF I am old, I am old.

DOLL I love thee better than I love e'er a scurvy young
boy of them all.

FALSTAFF What stuff wilt have a kirtle of? I shall receive   273
money o' Thursday; shalt have a cap tomorrow. A
merry song, come. It grows late; we'll to bed. Thou'lt
forget me when I am gone.

DOLL By my troth, thou'lt set me a-weeping an thou   277
sayst so. Prove that ever I dress myself handsome till
thy return—well, hearken a' th' end.   279

FALSTAFF Some sack, Francis.

---

254 nave hub. (Refers to Falstaff's rotundity; with a pun on *knave*.)
254–255 have . . . off i.e., as the punishment for slandering royalty
256 before in front of   **257 elder** (1) elder tree (2) old man   **257–258 poll
. . . parrot** (Doll is probably rumpling the hair on Falstaff's head, his
poll.)   **262–263 Saturn . . . conjunction** i.e., will the planets that govern old
age and love be near one another in the heavens   **264 fiery Trigon** (The
twelve signs of the zodiac were divided into four *trigons* or triangles,
one of which, consisting of Aries, Leo, and Sagittarius, was characterized as fiery. These three form a triangle because they are not contigu-
ous on the circle of the zodiac but occur at points equivalent roughly to
April, August, and December, at 120-degree intervals. The other three
trigons were characterized as watery, airy, and earthy. The joke here is
directed against Bardolph's fiery face.)   **265 lisping . . . notebook**
whispering lovingly to Falstaff's old confidante, i.e., Mistress Quickly.
tables notebook (for assignations)   **267 busses** kisses   **273 stuff** material.   **kirtle** skirt   **277 an** if   **279 hearken a' th' end** i.e., wait to see
how it turns out

PRINCE, POINS [*Coming forward*] Anon, anon, sir. 281

FALSTAFF Ha? A bastard son of the King's? And art not thou Poins his brother?

PRINCE Why, thou globe of sinful continents, what a 284 life dost thou lead!

FALSTAFF A better than thou. I am a gentleman; thou art a drawer.

PRINCE Very true, sir, and I come to draw you out by 288 the ears. 289

HOSTESS O, the Lord preserve Thy Grace! By my troth, welcome to London. Now, the Lord bless that sweet face of thine! O Jesu, are you come from Wales?

FALSTAFF Thou whoreson mad compound of majesty, 293 by this light flesh and corrupt blood, thou art wel- 294 come.

DOLL How, you fat fool! I scorn you.

POINS My lord, he will drive you out of your revenge and turn all to a merriment, if you take not the heat. 298

PRINCE You whoreson candle-mine you, how vilely 299 did you speak of me even now before this honest, vir- 300 tuous, civil gentlewoman!

HOSTESS God's blessing of your good heart! And so she is, by my troth.

FALSTAFF Didst thou hear me?

PRINCE Yea, and you knew me, as you did when you 305 ran away by Gad's Hill. You knew I was at your back, 306 and spoke it on purpose to try my patience.

FALSTAFF No, no, no, not so, I did not think thou wast within hearing.

PRINCE I shall drive you then to confess the willful abuse, and then I know how to handle you.

FALSTAFF No abuse, Hal, o' mine honor, no abuse.

PRINCE Not? To dispraise me, and call me pantler and 313 bread-chipper and I know not what?

---

281 Anon, anon (The cry of the drawer, or tapster, in answering his customers' demands for service, as in *1 Henry IV*, 2.4.21 ff.) **284 globe** (1) terrestrial globe (2) sphere. **continents** (1) the continents of the earth (2) contents (3) containers (of sin) **288–289 draw . . . ears** (as one might grab by the ears a naughty child caught in some mischief) **293 compound** lump, mass **294 light . . . blood** i.e., Doll **298 if . . . heat** if you don't strike while the iron is hot **299 candle-mine** magazine or storehouse of tallow **300 honest** chaste **305–306 Yea . . . Gad's Hill** (See *1 Henry IV*, 2.4.) **313 Not** i.e., you mean it's not abuse?

FALSTAFF No abuse, Hal.

POINS No abuse?

FALSTAFF No abuse, Ned, i' the world, honest Ned, none. I dispraised him before the wicked, that the wicked might not fall in love with thee [*To Hal*]; in which doing, I have done the part of a careful friend and a true subject, and thy father is to give me thanks for it. No abuse, Hal. None, Ned, none. No, faith, boys, none.

PRINCE See now whether pure fear and entire coward- 324
ice doth not make thee wrong this virtuous gentlewoman to close with us. Is she of the wicked? Is thine 326
hostess here of the wicked? Or is thy boy of the
wicked? Or honest Bardolph, whose zeal burns in his
nose, of the wicked?

POINS Answer, thou dead elm, answer.

FALSTAFF The fiend hath pricked down Bardolph irre- 331
coverable, and his face is Lucifer's privy kitchen, 332
where he doth nothing but roast maltworms. For the 333
boy, there is a good angel about him, but the devil
blinds him too.   335

PRINCE For the women?

FALSTAFF For one of them, she's in hell already and
burns poor souls. For th' other, I owe her money, and 338
whether she be damned for that I know not.   339

HOSTESS No, I warrant you.

FALSTAFF No, I think thou art not; I think thou art quit 341
for that. Marry, there is another indictment upon thee, 342
for suffering flesh to be eaten in thy house, contrary to 343
the law, for the which I think thou wilt howl.   344

HOSTESS All victuallers do so. What's a joint of mutton or 345
two in a whole Lent?

PRINCE You, gentlewoman—

---

324 entire sheer **326 close** come to terms, agree **331 pricked down** marked, or designated **332 privy** private **333 maltworms** topers, drunkards. **For** as for **335 blinds** (A textual crux. The Folio reads *outbids;* sometimes emended to *attends* or *binds*.) **338 burns** i.e., infects with venereal disease **339 damned** (since usury was condemned by the church as well as the state) **341–342 quit for that** (1) acquitted of that charge (2) repaid (as much as you are ever likely to be)
343 flesh to be eaten (Allusion to enactments to prevent the sale of meat in Lent; with sexual double entendre on *mutton,* whore.) **344 howl** (like damned souls in hell) **345 victuallers** i.e., innkeepers

DOLL What says Your Grace?

FALSTAFF His Grace says that which his flesh rebels 349
against.   *Peto knocks at door.*

HOSTESS Who knocks so loud at door? Look to the door
there, Francis.

[*Francis goes to the door. Enter Peto.*]

PRINCE Peto, how now, what news?

PETO
The King your father is at Westminster,
And there are twenty weak and wearied posts 355
Come from the north. And as I came along
I met and overtook a dozen captains,
Bareheaded, sweating, knocking at the taverns,
And asking everyone for Sir John Falstaff.

PRINCE
By heaven, Poins, I feel me much to blame,
So idly to profane the precious time,
When tempest of commotion, like the south 362
Borne with black vapor, doth begin to melt 363
And drop upon our bare unarmèd heads.—
Give me my sword and cloak.—Falstaff, good night.
                    Exeunt Prince and Poins, [and Peto].

FALSTAFF Now comes in the sweetest morsel of the
night, and we must hence and leave it unpicked.
[*Knocking within. Bardolph goes to the door.*] More
knocking at the door!

[*Bardolph returns.*]

How now, what's the matter?

BARDOLPH
You must away to court, sir, presently. 371
A dozen captains stay at door for you. 372

FALSTAFF [*To the Page*] Pay the musicians, sirrah. Farewell, hostess; farewell, Doll. You see, my good
wenches, how men of merit are sought after. The un-

---

349 Grace (1) royal grace (2) inclination toward spiritual grace. (The
Prince may call Doll "gentlewoman," says Falstaff, but the flesh is ever
rebellious; the Prince as a man knows Doll to be something very different.) **355 posts** messengers **362 commotion** insurrection. **south**
south wind (regarded as a breeder of tempests) **363 Borne** laden
371 presently immediately **372 stay** wait

deserver may sleep, when the man of action is called
on. Farewell, good wenches. If I be not sent away post, 377
I will see you again ere I go.

DOLL I cannot speak. If my heart be not ready to
burst—well, sweet Jack, have a care of thyself.

FALSTAFF Farewell, farewell.

       Exit [with Bardolph and Page].

HOSTESS Well, fare thee well. I have known thee these
twenty-nine years, come peascod time, but an honest- 383
er and truer-hearted man—well, fare thee well.

BARDOLPH *[At the door]* Mistress Tearsheet!

HOSTESS What's the matter?

BARDOLPH Bid Mistress Tearsheet come to my master.

HOSTESS O, run, Doll, run; run, good Doll. Come.—
She comes blubbered.—Yea, will you come, Doll? 389

          Exeunt.

❖

---

377 post immediately **383 peascod time** i.e., early summer, when peas
are still unripe **389 blubbered** disfigured with weeping

3.1   *Enter the King in his nightgown, alone [with a Page].*

KING
  Go call the Earls of Surrey and of Warwick;
  But ere they come, bid them o'erread these letters   2
  And well consider of them. Make good speed.
                  [He gives letters. Exit Page.]
  How many thousand of my poorest subjects
  Are at this hour asleep! O sleep, O gentle sleep,
  Nature's soft nurse, how have I frighted thee,
  That thou no more wilt weigh my eyelids down
  And steep my senses in forgetfulness?
  Why rather, sleep, liest thou in smoky cribs,   9
  Upon uneasy pallets stretching thee,   10
  And hushed with buzzing night-flies to thy slumber,
  Than in the perfumed chambers of the great,
  Under the canopies of costly state,   13
  And lulled with sound of sweetest melody?
  O thou dull god, why liest thou with the vile   15
  In loathsome beds, and leavest the kingly couch
  A watch-case or a common 'larum bell?   17
  Wilt thou upon the high and giddy mast
  Seal up the shipboy's eyes, and rock his brains
  In cradle of the rude imperious surge   20
  And in the visitation of the winds,   21
  Who take the ruffian billows by the top,   22
  Curling their monstrous heads and hanging them
  With deafing clamor in the slippery clouds,   24
  That, with the hurly, death itself awakes?   25
  Canst thou, O partial sleep, give thy repose
  To the wet sea-boy in an hour so rude,
  And, in the calmest and most stillest night,
  With all appliances and means to boot,   29

3.1. Location: Westminster. The royal court.
s.d. nightgown dressing gown   **2 o'erread** read over . **9 cribs** hovels
10 uneasy uncomfortable.   **thee** thyself   **13 state** magnificence   **15 dull**
drowsy.   **vile** low in rank   **17 watch-case** sentry box, or a space in
which the occupant is restlessly aware of the passage of time   **20 rude**
turbulent   **21 visitation** violent onset   **22 Who** which, i.e., the winds
24 deafing deafening.   **slippery** quickly slipping by   **25 That** so that.
hurly tumult   **29 appliances** devices.   **to boot** as well, besides

Deny it to a king? Then happy low, lie down!   30
Uneasy lies the head that wears a crown.   31

Enter Warwick, Surrey, and Sir John Blunt.

WARWICK
  Many good morrows to Your Majesty!
KING   Is it good morrow, lords?
WARWICK   'Tis one o'clock, and past.
KING
  Why, then, good morrow to you all, my lords.
  Have you read o'er the letters that I sent you?
WARWICK   We have, my liege.
KING
  Then you perceive the body of our kingdom
  How foul it is, what rank diseases grow,   39
  And with what danger, near the heart of it.
WARWICK
  It is but as a body yet distempered,   41
  Which to his former strength may be restored   42
  With good advice and little medicine.   43
  My Lord Northumberland will soon be cooled.
KING
  O God, that one might read the book of fate,
  And see the revolution of the times   46
  Make mountains level, and the continent,   47
  Weary of solid firmness, melt itself
  Into the sea, and other times to see
  The beachy girdle of the ocean
  Too wide for Neptune's hips, how chance's mocks   51
  And changes fill the cup of alteration
  With divers liquors! O, if this were seen,
  The happiest youth, viewing his progress through,   54
  What perils past, what crosses to ensue,   55
  Would shut the book, and sit him down and die.

30 low humble persons   **31 s.d. Sir John Blunt** (Since he says nothing
and is omitted from the Folio, his presence may be unnecessary, but see
l. 35, "to you all.")   **39 rank** festering   **41 distempered** sick   **42 his**
its   **43 little** a little   **46 revolution of** changes brought by   **47 continent**
dry land   **51 Too wide** i.e., vast in expanse, when the ocean recedes.
chance's mocks (A textual crux. The quarto and Folio read *chances
mocks;* sometimes emended to *chances mock*.)   **54 progress through**
life's progress from beginning to end   **55 crosses** afflictions

'Tis not ten years gone
Since Richard and Northumberland, great friends,
Did feast together, and in two years after
Were they at wars. It is but eight years since
This Percy was the man nearest my soul,   61
Who like a brother toiled in my affairs
And laid his love and life under my foot,   63
Yea, for my sake, even to the eyes of Richard   64
Gave him defiance. But which of you was by—
[*To Warwick*] You, cousin Nevil, as I may remember—   66
When Richard, with his eye brimful of tears,
Then checked and rated by Northumberland,   68
Did speak these words, now proved a prophecy?
"Northumberland, thou ladder by the which   70
My cousin Bolingbroke ascends my throne"—
Though then, God knows, I had no such intent,
But that necessity so bowed the state
That I and greatness were compelled to kiss—
"The time shall come," thus did he follow it,
"The time will come, that foul sin, gathering head,
Shall break into corruption"—so went on,   77
Foretelling this same time's condition   78
And the division of our amity.

WARWICK
There is a history in all men's lives,
Figuring the nature of the times deceased,   81
The which observed, a man may prophesy,
With a near aim, of the main chance of things   83
As yet not come to life, who in their seeds   84
And weak beginnings lie intreasurèd.   85
Such things become the hatch and brood of time,   86
And by the necessary form of this   87
King Richard might create a perfect guess
That great Northumberland, then false to him,
Would of that seed grow to a greater falseness,

61 This Percy i.e., Northumberland **63 under my foot** i.e., under my
control **64 to the eyes** i.e., face to face **66 Nevil** (An error; this Earl of
Warwick's surname is Beauchamp.) **68 checked and rated** rebuked
70–77 Northumberland . . . corruption (See *Richard II*, 5.1.55 ff.)
78 same present **81 Figuring** depicting. **deceased** past **83 main
chance** general probability **84 who** which **85 intreasurèd** stored up
86 hatch and brood offspring **87 necessary . . . this** logical consequence of this principle

Which should not find a ground to root upon
Unless on you.

KING   Are these things then necessities?
Then let us meet them like necessities;
And that same word even now cries out on us.   94
They say the Bishop and Northumberland
Are fifty thousand strong.

WARWICK   It cannot be, my lord.
Rumor doth double, like the voice and echo,
The numbers of the feared. Please it Your Grace
To go to bed. Upon my soul, my lord,
The powers that you already have sent forth
Shall bring this prize in very easily.
To comfort you the more, I have received
A certain instance that Glendower is dead.   103
Your Majesty hath been this fortnight ill,
And these unseasoned hours perforce must add   105
Unto your sickness.

KING   I will take your counsel.
And were these inward wars once out of hand,   107
We would, dear lords, unto the Holy Land.   *Exeunt.*

❖

3.2   *Enter Justice Shallow and Justice Silence.*

SHALLOW   Come on, come on, come on, give me your
hand, sir, give me your hand, sir. An early stirrer, by
the rood! And how doth my good cousin Silence?   3

SILENCE   Good morrow, good cousin Shallow.

SHALLOW   And how doth my cousin your bedfellow?
And your fairest daughter and mine, my goddaughter
Ellen?

SILENCE   Alas, a black ouzel, cousin Shallow!   8

SHALLOW   By yea and no, sir. I dare say my cousin Wil-

---

94 cries out on denounces   **103 certain instance** unquestionable proof
105 unseasoned unseasonable, late   **107 inward** civil.   **out of hand**
done with
**3.2. Location: Gloucestershire. Before Justice Shallow's house. A table
and chairs must be provided onstage.**
3 rood cross.   **cousin** kinsman (as also in ll. 4, 5, and 9)   **8 ouzel** black-
bird. (Ellen is *black* or dark-complexioned, not fair.)

liam is become a good scholar. He is at Oxford still, is
he not?

SILENCE   Indeed, sir, to my cost.

SHALLOW   'A must then to the Inns o' Court shortly. I   13
was once of Clement's Inn, where I think they will talk   14
of mad Shallow yet.

SILENCE   You were called "lusty Shallow" then, cousin.   16

SHALLOW   By the Mass, I was called anything, and I
would have done anything indeed too, and roundly   18
too. There was I, and Little John Doit of Staffordshire,
and black George Barnes, and Francis Pickbone, and
Will Squele, a Cotswold man. You had not four such   21
swinge-bucklers in all the Inns o' Court again. And I   22
may say to you, we knew where the bona-robas were   23
and had the best of them all at commandment. Then   24
was Jack Falstaff, now Sir John, a boy, and page to   25
Thomas Mowbray, Duke of Norfolk.   26

SILENCE   This Sir John, cousin, that comes hither anon
about soldiers?

SHALLOW   The same Sir John, the very same. I see him   29
break Scoggin's head at the court gate, when 'a was a   30
crack not thus high. And the very same day did I fight   31
with one Samson Stockfish, a fruiterer, behind
Gray's Inn. Jesu, Jesu, the mad days that I have spent!   33
And to see how many of my old acquaintance are
dead!

SILENCE   We shall all follow, cousin.

SHALLOW   Certain, 'tis certain, very sure, very sure.
Death, as the Psalmist saith, is certain to all, all shall   38
die. How a good yoke of bullocks at Stamford fair?   39

---

13 Inns o' Court legal societies of London   **14 Clement's Inn** one of the
Inns of Chancery; in Shallow's time, these institutions prepared one for
the Inns of Court   **16 lusty** merry, lascivious   **18 roundly** thoroughly,
without ceremony   **21 Cotswold** from the Cotswold Hills in Gloucestershire   **22 swinge-bucklers** swashbucklers, roisterers   **23 bona-robas**
good-looking wenches, smart prostitutes   **24 at commandment** at our
beck and call   **25–26 page to Thomas Mowbray** (Both Sir John Oldcastle, Falstaff's original, and Sir John Fastolfe, for whom Falstaff was
renamed, were pages to the Duke of Norfolk, who figures in the play
Richard II.)   **29 see** saw   **30 Scoggin** (Perhaps John Scogan, court jester
to Edward IV and protagonist of an Elizabethan jestbook known as
"Scogan's Jests.")   **31 crack** pert little boy   **33 Gray's Inn** one of the
Inns of Court   **38–39 Death . . . die** (See Psalm 89:48.)   **39 How** how
much (is the asking price for)

SILENCE By my troth, I was not there.

SHALLOW Death is certain. Is old Double of your town living yet?

SILENCE Dead, sir.

SHALLOW Jesu, Jesu, dead! 'A drew a good bow; and dead? 'A shot a fine shoot. John o' Gaunt loved him 45 well, and betted much money on his head. Dead? 'A would have clapped i' the clout at twelve score, and 47 carried you a forehand shaft a fourteen and fourteen 48 and a half, that it would have done a man's heart good 49 to see. How a score of ewes now?

SILENCE Thereafter as they be; a score of good ewes 51 may be worth ten pounds.

SHALLOW And is old Double dead?

SILENCE Here come two of Sir John Falstaff's men, as I think.

Enter Bardolph and one with him.

SHALLOW Good morrow, honest gentlemen.

BARDOLPH I beseech you, which is Justice Shallow?

SHALLOW I am Robert Shallow, sir, a poor esquire of 58 this county, and one of the King's justices of the peace. What is your good pleasure with me?

BARDOLPH My captain, sir, commends him to you, my 61 captain, Sir John Falstaff, a tall gentleman, by heaven, 62 and a most gallant leader.

SHALLOW He greets me well, sir. I knew him a good backsword man. How doth the good knight? May I 65 ask how my lady his wife doth?

BARDOLPH Sir, pardon; a soldier is better accommo- 67 dated than with a wife. 68

SHALLOW It is well said, in faith, sir, and it is well said indeed too. "Better accommodated"! It is good, yea, indeed is it. Good phrases are surely, and ever were,

---

45 John o' Gaunt (Father of Henry IV.) **47 clapped . . . score** hit the bull's-eye at 240 yards **48–49 carried . . . half** i.e., could shoot a heavy arrow in a straight line rather than in a curved trajectory for a distance of 280 to 290 yards **51 Thereafter . . . be** according to their quality **58 esquire** (A social rank between gentleman and knight.) **61 commends him** sends his respects **62 tall** valiant **65 backsword** stick with a basket hilt used for fencing practice. (See 2.4.129, note.) **67–68 accommodated** furnished equipped. (A bit of fine language on Bardolph's part.)

very commendable. "Accommodated"! It comes of *ac-commodo*. Very good, a good phrase.

BARDOLPH Pardon, sir, I have heard the word. Phrase
call you it? By this day, I know not the phrase. But I
will maintain the word with my sword to be a soldier-
like word, and a word of exceeding good command, 77
by heaven. Accommodated; that is, when a man is, as
they say, accommodated; or when a man is being
whereby 'a may be thought to be accommodated,
which is an excellent thing.

Enter Falstaff.

SHALLOW It is very just.—Look, here comes good Sir 82
John. Give me your good hand, give me your worship's good hand. By my troth, you like well and bear 84
your years very well. Welcome, good Sir John.

FALSTAFF I am glad to see you well, good Master Robert
Shallow. Master Surecard, as I think?

SHALLOW No, Sir John, it is my cousin Silence, in com- 88
mission with me. 89

FALSTAFF Good Master Silence, it well befits you should
be of the peace. 91

SILENCE Your good worship is welcome.

FALSTAFF Fie, this is hot weather, gentlemen. Have you
provided me here half a dozen sufficient men? 94

SHALLOW Marry, have we, sir. Will you sit?

[They sit at a table.]

FALSTAFF Let me see them, I beseech you.

SHALLOW Where's the roll? Where's the roll? Where's
the roll? Let me see, let me see, let me see. So, so, so,
so, so, so, so; yea, marry, sir. Ralph Moldy! Let them
appear as I call; let them do so, let them do so. Let me
see, where is Moldy?

[Enter Moldy.]

MOLDY Here, an 't please you. 102

---

77 a word . . . command a perfectly good military term   82 just true
84 like well are in good condition, thrive   88–89 in . . . me a fellow
justice of the peace   91 of the peace i.e., a magistrate (with a play on
the name *Silence*, peace)   94 sufficient fit for service   102 an 't if it
(also in l. 106)

SHALLOW What think you, Sir John? A good-limbed fellow, young, strong, and of good friends.   104

FALSTAFF Is thy name Moldy?

MOLDY Yea, an 't please you.

FALSTAFF 'Tis the more time thou wert used.

SHALLOW Ha, ha, ha! Most excellent, i' faith! Things
that are moldy lack use. Very singular good, in faith,
well said, Sir John, very well said.

FALSTAFF Prick him.   111

[*Shallow writes on the muster roll.*]

MOLDY I was pricked well enough before, an you   112
could have let me alone. My old dame will be undone 113
now for one to do her husbandry and her drudgery.   114
You need not to have pricked me. There are other men
fitter to go out than I.

FALSTAFF Go to. Peace, Moldy, you shall go, Moldy,
it is time you were spent.   118

MOLDY Spent?

SHALLOW Peace, fellow, peace. Stand aside. Know you
where you are? For th' other, Sir John, let me see: Si- 121
mon Shadow!

[*Enter Shadow.*]

FALSTAFF Yea, marry, let me have him to sit under. He's
like to be a cold soldier.   124

SHALLOW Where's Shadow?

SHADOW Here, sir.

FALSTAFF Shadow, whose son art thou?

SHADOW My mother's son, sir.

FALSTAFF Thy mother's son! Like enough, and thy fa- 129
ther's shadow. So the son of the female is the shadow 130
of the male. It is often so, indeed; but much of the
father's substance.

---

104 of good friends well connected by family **111 Prick** mark him
down on the list **112 pricked** i.e., (1) goaded by nagging (2) turning
sour or moldy (with sexual suggestion also, continued in *undone,
husbandry,* and *spent,* sexually used up) **113 dame** mother, or, more
probably in view of the sexual punning, "wife" **114 husbandry** farm
work. (But see note at l. 112.) **118 spent** used up (But see note at
l. 112.) **121 other** others **124 like** likely. **cold** (1) cool, deliberate
(2) cowardly **129 son** (with play on "sun") **130 shadow** i.e., image,
copy. (But, Falstaff jests, the father is only dimly copied in a bastard
son who lacks the true substance of his purported father.)

SHALLOW   Do you like him, Sir John?

FALSTAFF   Shadow will serve for summer. Prick him, 134
for we have a number of shadows fill up the muster 135
book.

SHALLOW   Thomas Wart!

[*Enter Wart.*]

FALSTAFF   Where's he?

WART   Here, sir.

FALSTAFF   Is thy name Wart?

WART   Yea, sir.

FALSTAFF   Thou art a very ragged wart.

SHALLOW   Shall I prick him, Sir John?

FALSTAFF   It were superfluous, for his apparel is built
upon his back and the whole frame stands upon pins. 145
Prick him no more.

SHALLOW   Ha, ha, ha! You can do it, sir, you can do it. 147
I commend you well. Francis Feeble!

[*Enter Feeble.*]

FEEBLE   Here, sir.

SHALLOW   What trade art thou, Feeble?

FEEBLE   A woman's tailor, sir. 151

SHALLOW   Shall I prick him, sir?

FALSTAFF   You may. But if he had been a man's tailor,
he'd a' pricked you.—Wilt thou make as many holes in 154
an enemy's battle as thou hast done in a woman's pet- 155
ticoat?

FEEBLE   I will do my good will, sir. You can have no
more.

FALSTAFF   Well said, good woman's tailor! Well said,
courageous Feeble! Thou wilt be as valiant as the
wrathful dove or most magnanimous mouse. Prick the 161

---

134 serve (1) suffice (2) be inducted   **135 shadows** i.e., fictitious names
for which the officer in charge receives pay.   **fill** to fill   **145 the whole
. . . pins** i.e., he's pinned together, badly made physically, and therefore
needs no more pinpricks. (In a carpentry metaphor, the *pins* are also
pegs for joining timber.)   **147 can** know how to.   **do it** i.e., make a
joke   **151 woman's tailor** (Often regarded as an effeminate occupa-
tion.)   **154 a' pricked** (1) have attired (2) have thrust you through. (The
word has a sexual suggestion also.) *Tailor* could mean the male or
female sex organ.   **155 battle** army   **161 magnanimous** stouthearted

woman's tailor. Well, Master Shallow; deep, Master
Shallow.

FEEBLE   I would Wart might have gone, sir.

FALSTAFF   I would thou wert a man's tailor, that thou
mightst mend him and make him fit to go. I cannot
put him to a private soldier that is the leader of so   167
many thousands. Let that suffice, most forcible Feeble.   168

FEEBLE   It shall suffice, sir.

FALSTAFF   I am bound to thee, reverend Feeble. Who is   170
next?

SHALLOW   Peter Bullcalf o' the green!

[*Enter Bullcalf.*]

FALSTAFF   Yea, marry, let's see Bullcalf.

BULLCALF   Here, sir.

FALSTAFF   'Fore God, a likely fellow! Come, prick me
Bullcalf till he roar again.

BULLCALF   O Lord! Good my lord Captain—

FALSTAFF   What, dost thou roar before thou art pricked?

BULLCALF   O Lord, sir! I am a diseased man.

FALSTAFF   What disease hast thou?

BULLCALF   A whoreson cold, sir, a cough, sir, which I
caught with ringing in the King's affairs upon his   182
coronation day, sir.   183

FALSTAFF   Come, thou shalt go to the wars in a gown.   184
We will have away thy cold, and I will take such order   185
that thy friends shall ring for thee. Is here all?   186

SHALLOW   Here is two more called than your number;
you must have but four here, sir. And so, I pray you,
go in with me to dinner.

FALSTAFF   Come, I will go drink with you, but I cannot
tarry dinner. I am glad to see you, by my troth, Master   191
Shallow.

SHALLOW   O, Sir John, do you remember since we lay   193
all night in the Windmill in Saint George's Field?   194

---

167 put him to enlist him as   **168 thousands** i.e., of vermin, lice
170 bound obliged   **182-183 ringing . . . day** i.e., ringing the church bells to
celebrate the anniversary of the King's coronation   **184 gown** dressing
gown   **185 have away** do away with.   **take such order** provide   **186 for
thee** (1) in your place (2) at your death   **191 tarry** wait for   **193 since**
when   **194 the Windmill** a brothel, or an inn in a brothel district.   **Saint
George's Field** a popular place of resort on the south bank of the Thames

FALSTAFF No more of that, good Master Shallow, no more of that.

SHALLOW Ha! 'Twas a merry night. And is Jane Nightwork alive?

FALSTAFF She lives, Master Shallow.

SHALLOW She never could away with me. 200

FALSTAFF Never, never; she would always say she could not abide Master Shallow.

SHALLOW By the Mass, I could anger her to the heart. She was then a bona-roba. Doth she hold her own well?

FALSTAFF Old, old, Master Shallow.

SHALLOW Nay, she must be old. She cannot choose but be old. Certain she's old, and had Robin Nightwork by old Nightwork before I came to Clement's Inn.

SILENCE That's fifty-five year ago.

SHALLOW Ha, cousin Silence, that thou hadst seen that that this knight and I have seen! Ha, Sir John, said I well?

FALSTAFF We have heard the chimes at midnight, Master Shallow.

SHALLOW That we have, that we have, that we have, in faith, Sir John, we have. Our watchword was "Hem 217 boys!" Come, let's to dinner, come, let's to dinner. Je- 218 sus, the days that we have seen! Come, come.

Exeunt [Falstaff and the Justices].

BULLCALF Good Master Corporate Bardolph, stand my 220 friend, and here's four Harry ten shillings in French 221 crowns for you. [*He gives money.*] In very truth, sir, I had as lief be hanged, sir, as go. And yet for mine own 223 part, sir, I do not care, but rather because I am unwilling, and for mine own part have a desire to stay with my friends. Else, sir, I did not care, for mine own part, so much.

BARDOLPH Go to, stand aside.

---

200 away with tolerate **217–218 Hem boys** i.e., down the hatch
220 Corporate (For *Corporal.*) **stand** be, act as **221 Harry ten shillings**
i.e., money coined in the reign of Henry VII, current in late Elizabethan
times at half the face value. The reference is anachronistic. Four such
coins would be worth 20 shillings, or 1 pound. Bullcalf gives his bribe
in *French crowns*, worth 4 shillings each; presumably he gives five such
coins **223 lief** willingly

MOLDY   And, good Master Corporal Captain, for my old dame's sake, stand my friend. She has nobody to do anything about her when I am gone, and she is old and cannot help herself. [*He gives money.*] You shall have forty, sir.   233

BARDOLPH   Go to, stand aside.

FEEBLE   By my troth, I care not. A man can die but once. We owe God a death. I'll ne'er bear a base mind. An 't be my destiny, so; an 't be not, so. No man's too good to serve 's prince. And let it go which way it will, he that dies this year is quit for the next.   239

BARDOLPH   Well said. Thou'rt a good fellow.

FEEBLE   Faith, I'll bear no base mind.   241

Enter Falstaff and the Justices.

FALSTAFF   Come, sir, which men shall I have?

SHALLOW   Four of which you please.

BARDOLPH [*To Falstaff*] Sir, a word with you. [*Aside.*] I have three pound to free Moldy and Bullcalf.

FALSTAFF   Go to, well.

SHALLOW   Come, Sir John, which four will you have?

FALSTAFF   Do you choose for me.

SHALLOW   Marry, then, Moldy, Bullcalf, Feeble, and Shadow.

FALSTAFF   Moldy and Bullcalf: for you, Moldy, stay at home till you are past service; and for your part, Bullcalf, grow till you come unto it. I will none of you.   251 252 253

SHALLOW   Sir John, Sir John, do not yourself wrong. They are your likeliest men, and I would have you served with the best.

FALSTAFF   Will you tell me, Master Shallow, how to choose a man? Care I for the limb, the thews, the stature, bulk, and big assemblance of a man? Give me the spirit, Master Shallow. Here's Wart; you see what a ragged appearance it is. 'A shall charge you and discharge you with the motion of a pewterer's hammer,   258 259 261 262

---

233 forty i.e., 40 shillings   **239 quit** free, clear   **241 bear** have   **251 for** as for   **252 past service** (1) too old to serve militarily (2) too old for sexual functioning   **253 come unto it** (1) are a man old enough to fight (2) have arrived at sexual maturity   **258 thews** strength   **259 assemblance** appearance, frame   **261–262 charge . . . discharge you** load and fire   **262 motion . . . hammer** i.e., precise, quick motion

come off and on swifter than he that gibbets on the   263
brewer's bucket. And this same half-faced fellow,   264
Shadow; give me this man. He presents no mark to
the enemy; the foeman may with as great aim level at   266
the edge of a penknife. And for a retreat, how swiftly
will this Feeble the woman's tailor run off! O, give me
the spare men, and spare me the great ones. Put me a
caliver into Wart's hand, Bardolph.   270

BARDOLPH [*Giving Wart a musket*]   Hold, Wart, traverse.   271
Thus, thus, thus.

FALSTAFF   Come, manage me your caliver. So. [*Wart
performs maneuvers with the musket.*] Very well. Go to.
Very good, exceeding good. O, give me always a little,
lean, old, chapped, bald shot. Well said, i' faith, Wart,   276
thou'rt a good scab. Hold, there's a tester for thee.   277
                         [*He gives sixpence.*]

SHALLOW   He is not his craft's master; he doth not do it
right. I remember at Mile End Green, when I lay at   279
Clement's Inn—I was then Sir Dagonet in Arthur's   280
show—there was a little quiver fellow, and 'a would   281
manage you his piece thus [*Shallow demonstrates*], and   282
'a would about and about, and come you in and come   283
you in. "Rah, tah, tah," would 'a say, "Bounce,"   284
would 'a say, and away again would 'a go, and again
would 'a come. I shall ne'er see such a fellow.

FALSTAFF   These fellows will do well, Master Shallow.
God keep you, Master Silence. I will not use many
words with you. Fare you well, gentlemen both. I

263–264 come . . . bucket raise and lower his musket quicker than a
brewer's man raises and lowers the beam (*bucket*) of the brewer's yoke
across his shoulders   264 half-faced thin-faced. (Alludes to the profile
portraits on coins.)   266 as great aim as much likelihood of hitting the
target.   level aim   270 caliver light musket   271 traverse march, or,
perhaps, perform the manual of arms, an exercise drill with a
musket   276 shot marksman   277 scab rascal (punning on the name *Wart*).
tester sixpence   279 Mile End Green a drilling ground for citizen
soldiers, to the east of London.   lay lodged   280–281 Sir . . . show (An
exhibition of archery was held annually at Mile End Green called
"Arthur's show," in which each archer took the name of one of King
Arthur's knights; Shallow played the part of Sir Dagonet, Arthur's
fool.)   281 quiver nimble   282 piece firearm   283–284 'a would . . . you
in i.e., he was skillful at firing and then running around to the rear rank
of musketeers to reload while the next rank fired, and so on
284 Bounce bang

thank you. I must a dozen mile tonight. Bardolph, give
the soldiers coats.

SHALLOW   Sir John, the Lord bless you! God prosper
your affairs! God send us peace! At your return, visit
our house; let our old acquaintance be renewed. Peradventure I will with ye to the court.

FALSTAFF   'Fore God, would you would.

SHALLOW   Go to; I have spoke at a word. God keep you.   297

FALSTAFF   Fare you well, gentle gentlemen. *Exeunt
[Justices.]* On, Bardolph; lead the men away. [*Exeunt
Bardolph, recruits, etc.*] As I return, I will fetch off   300
these justices. I do see the bottom of Justice Shallow.
Lord, Lord, how subject we old men are to this vice of
lying! This same starved justice hath done nothing but
prate to me of the wildness of his youth and the feats
he hath done about Turnbull Street, and every third   305
word a lie, duer paid to the hearer than the Turk's   306
tribute. I do remember him at Clement's Inn like a   307
man made after supper of a cheese paring. When 'a
was naked, he was, for all the world, like a forked rad-
ish, with a head fantastically carved upon it with a
knife. 'A was so forlorn that his dimensions to any   311
thick sight were invisible. 'A was the very genius of   312
famine, yet lecherous as a monkey, and the whores
called him mandrake. 'A came ever in the rearward of   314
the fashion, and sung those tunes to the overscutched   315
huswives that he heard the carmen whistle, and sware   316
they were his fancies or his good-nights. And now is   317
this Vice's dagger become a squire, and talks as famil-   318
iarly of John o' Gaunt as if he had been sworn brother   319

---

297 I have . . . word I mean what I say   **300 fetch off** get the better of
305 Turnbull Street a street in Clerkenwell, ill-reputed   **306 duer** more
promptly   **306–307 Turk's tribute** tribute money paid annually to the
Sultan of Turkey by merchants and others   **311 forlorn** meager, thin
312 thick imperfect.   **invisible** (Some editors retain the reading of the
quarto and the Folio, *invincible*, as meaning "invisible.")   **genius** spirit,
personification   **314 mandrake** root of a plant, said to resemble the
body of a man   **315–316 overscutched huswives** outworn and often-
whipped prostitutes   **316 carmen** wagoners   **317 fancies . . . good-
nights** fantasies and serenades (of which he claimed authorship)
318 Vice's dagger (The Vice, or comic character of the morality plays,
was armed with a wooden dagger.)   **319 sworn brother** companion in
arms who has taken a chivalric oath to share his fortunes

to him, and I'll be sworn 'a ne'er saw him but once in
the tilt-yard, and then he burst his head for crowding   321
among the marshal's men. I saw it, and told John o'
Gaunt he beat his own name, for you might have   323
thrust him and all his apparel into an eelskin; the case   324
of a treble hautboy was a mansion for him, a court.   325
And now has he land and beefs. Well, I'll be ac-   326
quainted with him if I return, and 't shall go hard but
I'll make him a philosopher's two stones to me. If the   328
young dace be a bait for the old pike, I see no reason   329
in the law of nature but I may snap at him. Let time
shape, and there an end.   [Exit.]

❧

321 tilt-yard arena for jousting at Westminster. **he burst his head** he,
Shallow, had his head beaten so that he bled **323 beat his own name**
i.e., was thrashing a gaunt person **324 case** instrument case
325 hautboy ancestor of the oboe. (The *treble hautboy* was the smallest
and narrowest of this family of instruments.) **326 beefs** oxen **328 a
philosopher's two stones** i.e., as valuable as the philosopher's stones
that supposedly changed ordinary metal into gold and preserved youth
and health. (*Two stones* also suggests "testicles.") **329 dace** small fish
used for live bait

4.1   *Enter the Archbishop [of York], Mowbray,*
         [Lord] Bardolph, Hastings, [and others,] within
         the Forest of Gaultree.

ARCHBISHOP   What is this forest called?
HASTINGS
  'Tis Gaultree Forest, an 't shall please Your Grace.   2
ARCHBISHOP
  Here stand, my lords, and send discoverers forth   3
  To know the numbers of our enemies.   4
HASTINGS
We have sent forth already.
ARCHBISHOP   'Tis well done.
  My friends and brethren in these great affairs,
  I must acquaint you that I have received
  New-dated letters from Northumberland,   8
  Their cold intent, tenor, and substance, thus: 9
  Here doth he wish his person, with such powers   10
  As might hold sortance with his quality,   11
  The which he could not levy. Whereupon
  He is retired, to ripe his growing fortunes,   13
  To Scotland, and concludes in hearty prayers
  That your attempts may overlive the hazard   15
  And fearful meeting of their opposite.   16
MOWBRAY
  Thus do the hopes we have in him touch ground   17
  And dash themselves to pieces.

         Enter Messenger.

HASTINGS   Now, what news?
MESSENGER
  West of this forest, scarcely off a mile,
  In goodly form comes on the enemy,   20
  And by the ground they hide, I judge their number
  Upon or near the rate of thirty thousand.   22

4.1. Location: Yorkshire. Gaultree Forest.
2 an 't if it **3 discoverers** scouts **4 know** learn **8 New** recently
9 cold dispiriting, gloomy **10 powers** forces **11 hold sortance** ac-
cord. **quality** rank **13 ripe** make ripe **15 overlive** outlive
16 opposite adversary **17 touch ground** hit bottom **20 form** military
formation **22 rate** estimate

MOWBRAY

   The just proportion that we gave them out.   23

   Let us sway on and face them in the field.   24

ARCHBISHOP

   What well-appointed leader fronts us here?   25

   Enter Westmorland.

MOWBRAY

   I think it is my lord of Westmorland.

WESTMORLAND

   Health and fair greeting from our general,

   The Prince, Lord John and Duke of Lancaster.

ARCHBISHOP

   Say on, my lord of Westmorland, in peace,

   What doth concern your coming.

WESTMORLAND   Then, my lord,   30

   Unto Your Grace do I in chief address

   The substance of my speech. If that rebellion

   Came like itself, in base and abject routs,   33

   Led on by bloody youth, guarded with rags,   34

   And countenanced by boys and beggary,   35

   I say, if damned commotion so appeared   36

   In his true, native, and most proper shape,

   You, reverend father, and these noble lords

   Had not been here to dress the ugly form

   Of base and bloody insurrection

   With your fair honors. You, Lord Archbishop,

   Whose see is by a civil peace maintained,   42

   Whose beard the silver hand of peace hath touched,

   Whose learning and good letters peace hath tutored,   44

   Whose white investments figure innocence,   45

   The dove and very blessèd spirit of peace,

   Wherefore do you so ill translate yourself   47

   Out of the speech of peace that bears such grace

   Into the harsh and boisterous tongue of war,

---

23 just . . . out precise number that we estimated **24 sway on** advance **25 well-appointed** well-armed. **fronts** confronts **30 What . . . coming** what your coming means **33 routs** mobs **34 bloody** passionate. **guarded** adorned, trimmed **35 countenanced** supported. **beggary** beggars **36 commotion** tumult, sedition **42 see** diocese. **civil** orderly, law-abiding **44 good letters** scholarship **45 investments** vestments. **figure** symbolize **47 translate** (1) change from one language to another (2) transform

Turning your books to graves, your ink to blood,
Your pens to lances, and your tongue divine
To a loud trumpet and a point of war?   52

ARCHBISHOP
Wherefore do I this? So the question stands.
Briefly to this end: we are all diseased,
And with our surfeiting and wanton hours   55
Have brought ourselves into a burning fever,
And we must bleed for it; of which disease   57
Our late King Richard, being infected, died.
But, my most noble lord of Westmorland,
I take not on me here as a physician,   60
Nor do I as an enemy to peace
Troop in the throngs of military men,
But rather show awhile like fearful war   63
To diet rank minds sick of happiness   64
And purge th' obstructions which begin to stop
Our very veins of life. Hear me more plainly.
I have in equal balance justly weighed   67
What wrongs our arms may do, what wrongs we suffer,
And find our griefs heavier than our offenses.   69
We see which way the stream of time doth run,
And are enforced from our most quiet there   71-
By the rough torrent of occasion,   72
And have the summary of all our griefs,
When time shall serve, to show in articles;   74
Which long ere this we offered to the King,
And might by no suit gain our audience.
When we are wronged and would unfold our griefs,
We are denied access unto his person
Even by those men that most have done us wrong.   79
The dangers of the days but newly gone,
Whose memory is written on the earth
With yet-appearing blood, and the examples

52 **point of war** trumpet signal of war   55–79 **And . . . wrong** (Omitted
from the quarto probably because of censorship, since these lines plead
the cause of rebellion; also ll. 103–139.)   55 **wanton** self-indulgent
57 **bleed** be bled (as a medical treatment)   60 **take . . . as** do not now
undertake the role of   63 **show** appear   64 **rank** swollen, bloated
67 **equal balance** balanced scales.   **justly** exactly   69 **griefs** grievances   71 **our . . . there** our greatest quiet therein, i.e., in the stream of
time   72 **occasion** circumstances   74 **articles** specified items

Of every minute's instance, present now,   83
Hath put us in these ill-beseeming arms,
Not to break peace or any branch of it,
But to establish here a peace indeed,
Concurring both in name and quality.   87

WESTMORLAND
Whenever yet was your appeal denied?
Wherein have you been gallèd by the King?   89
What peer hath been suborned to grate on you,   90
That you should seal this lawless bloody book   91
Of forged rebellion with a seal divine   92
And consecrate commotion's bitter edge?

ARCHBISHOP
My brother general, the commonwealth,   94
To brother born an household cruelty,   95
I make my quarrel in particular.   96

WESTMORLAND
There is no need of any such redress;
Or if there were, it not belongs to you.

MOWBRAY
Why not to him in part, and to us all
That feel the bruises of the days before,
And suffer the condition of these times
To lay a heavy and unequal hand   102
Upon our honors?

WESTMORLAND   O my good Lord Mowbray,
Construe the times to their necessities,   104
And you shall say indeed it is the time,
And not the King, that doth you injuries.
Yet for your part, it not appears to me
Either from the King or in the present time

---

83 Of . . . instance presented every minute   **87 Concurring . . . quality**
i.e., a peace that will be both in name and in fact   **89 gallèd** injured,
made sore with chafing   **90 suborned . . . on** induced to annoy, harass
91–92 That . . . divine i.e., that you should put your seal of approval on
this lawless and forged rebellion, much as if a bishop were to license a
troublesome book   **94–96 My brother . . . particular** (The text is perhaps corrupt here, but the general sense seems to be: The grievances of
my brother-Englishmen, and the cruelty shown to my blood brother
Scroop [who was executed at Bristol by Henry IV; see *1 Henry IV*,
1.3.269], provoke me to make this cause my own.)   **102 unequal** un-
just   **104 to** according to.   **their necessities** i.e., that which is necessary
in a time of disorder and civil strife

That you should have an inch of any ground
To build a grief on. Were you not restored
To all the Duke of Norfolk's seigniories,   111
Your noble and right well remembered father's?

MOWBRAY
What thing, in honor, had my father lost,
That need to be revived and breathed in me?   114
The King that loved him, as the state stood then,   115
Was force perforce compelled to banish him;   116
And then that Henry Bolingbroke and he,
Being mounted and both rousèd in their seats,   118
Their neighing coursers daring of the spur,   119
Their armed staves in charge, their beavers down,   120
Their eyes of fire sparkling through sights of steel,   121
And the loud trumpet blowing them together,
Then, then, when there was nothing could have stayed
My father from the breast of Bolingbroke,
O, when the King did throw his warder down—   125
His own life hung upon the staff he threw—
Then threw he down himself and all their lives
That by indictment and by dint of sword   128
Have since miscarried under Bolingbroke.   129

WESTMORLAND
You speak, Lord Mowbray, now you know not what.
The Earl of Hereford was reputed then   131
In England the most valiant gentleman.
Who knows on whom fortune would then have smiled?
But if your father had been victor there,
He ne'er had borne it out of Coventry;   135
For all the country in a general voice
Cried hate upon him, and all their prayers and love
Were set on Hereford, whom they doted on,
And blessed, and graced, indeed more than the King.

---

111 seigniories properties, estates   **114 breathed** given the breath of life
115 state condition of things   **116 force perforce** willy-nilly. (For the
banishment of Mowbray by Richard II, see *Richard II*, 1.1 and 1.3.)
118 rousèd raised.   **seats** saddles   **119 daring of the spur** i.e., eager to be
urged on   **120 armèd . . . charge** lances ready for the charge.   **beavers**
movable visors of helmets   **121 sights** eye slits   **125 warder** staff of
command   **128 dint** force   **129 miscarried** died   **131 Earl of Hereford**
i.e., Bolingbroke, later King Henry IV   **135 borne . . . Coventry** i.e., carried away the prize from the site of the intended trial by combat

But this is mere digression from my purpose.
Here come I from our princely general
To know your griefs, to tell you from His Grace
That he will give you audience; and wherein   143
It shall appear that your demands are just,
You shall enjoy them, everything set off   145
That might so much as think you enemies.   146

MOWBRAY
But he hath forced us to compel this offer,
And it proceeds from policy, not love.

WESTMORLAND
Mowbray, you overween to take it so.   149
This offer comes from mercy, not from fear.
For, lo, within a ken our army lies,   151
Upon mine honor, all too confident
To give admittance to a thought of fear.
Our battle is more full of names than yours,   154
Our men more perfect in the use of arms,
Our armor all as strong, our cause the best.
Then reason will our hearts should be as good.   157
Say you not then our offer is compelled.

MOWBRAY
Well, by my will we shall admit no parley.   159

WESTMORLAND
That argues but the shame of your offense.
A rotten case abides no handling.   161

HASTINGS
Hath the Prince John a full commission,
In very ample virtue of his father,   163
To hear and absolutely to determine
Of what conditions we shall stand upon?   165

WESTMORLAND
That is intended in the General's name.   166
I muse you make so slight a question.   167

---

143 wherein wherever   **145 set off** put out of consideration, removed
146 think you make you seem   **149 overween** are arrogant or presumptu-
ous   **151 ken** seeing distance   **154 battle** army.   **names** noble names
157 reason will i.e., it is reasonable that   **159 by my will** i.e., as far as I'm
concerned.   **admit no parley** accept no conference   **161 abides** tolerates
163 virtue authority   **165 what** whatever.   **stand** insist   **166 intended**
understood, implied.   **name** i.e., title   **167 muse** wonder

ARCHBISHOP [*Giving a document*]
    Then take, my lord of Westmorland, this schedule,
    For this contains our general grievances.
    Each several article herein redressed,   170
    All members of our cause, both here and hence,
    That are insinewed to this action,   172
    Acquitted by a true substantial form   173
    And present execution of our wills   174
    To us and to our purposes confined,   175
    We come within our awful banks again   176
    And knit our powers to the arm of peace.

WESTMORLAND
    This will I show the General. Please you, lords,
    In sight of both our battles we may meet,   179
    And either end in peace—which God so frame!—   180
    Or to the place of difference call the swords   181
    Which must decide it.

ARCHBISHOP   My lord, we will do so.
                            Exit Westmorland.

MOWBRAY
    There is a thing within my bosom tells me
    That no conditions of our peace can stand.

HASTINGS
    Fear you not that. If we can make our peace
    Upon such large terms and so absolute   186
    As our conditions shall consist upon,   187
    Our peace shall stand as firm as rocky mountains.

MOWBRAY
    Yea, but our valuation shall be such   189
    That every slight and false-derivèd cause,
    Yea, every idle, nice, and wanton reason,   191
    Shall to the King taste of this action,
    That, were our royal faiths martyrs in love,   193
    We shall be winnowed with so rough a wind

170 Each . . . herein provided that each separate article herein is
172 insinewed joined as by strong sinews   **173 substantial form** formal
agreement   **174 present . . . wills** immediate fulfillment of our desires
175 To . . . confined i.e., as regards us and our plans   **176 awful banks**
banks or bounds of respect   **179 battles** armies   **180 frame** bring about
181 difference conflict   **186 large** liberal   **187 consist** insist   **189 our . . .
such** i.e., we shall be so considered by the King   **191 idle . . . wanton**
foolish, petty, and frivolous   **193 That . . . love** i.e., so that even if our
allegiance to the King were as strong as the devotion of martyrs

That even our corn shall seem as light as chaff   195
And good from bad find no partition.   196

ARCHBISHOP
No, no, my lord. Note this: the King is weary
Of dainty and such picking grievances;   198
For he hath found to end one doubt by death   199
Revives two greater in the heirs of life,   200
And therefore will he wipe his tables clean   201
And keep no telltale to his memory
That may repeat and history his loss   203
To new remembrance. For full well he knows
He cannot so precisely weed this land   205
As his misdoubts present occasion.   206
His foes are so enrooted with his friends
That, plucking to unfix an enemy,
He doth unfasten so and shake a friend.
So that this land, like an offensive wife
That hath enraged him on to offer strokes,
As he is striking, holds his infant up
And hangs resolved correction in the arm   213
That was upreared to execution.

HASTINGS
Besides, the King hath wasted all his rods   215
On late offenders, that he now doth lack   216
The very instruments of chastisement,
So that his power, like to a fangless lion,
May offer, but not hold.

ARCHBISHOP   'Tis very true.   219
And therefore be assured, my good Lord Marshal,
If we do now make our atonement well,   221
Our peace will, like a broken limb united,
Grow stronger for the breaking.

MOWBRAY   Be it so.
Here is returned my lord of Westmorland.

---

195 corn grain, wheat **196 partition** distinction **198 picking** fastidi-
ous, trivial **199 doubt** danger, source of fear **200 of life** still living
201 tables tablets, notebooks **203 history** record, chronicle
205 precisely thoroughly **206 misdoubts** suspicions **213 hangs** sus-
pends in midaction. **resolved correction** the punishment that was
intended **215 wasted** exhausted, spent. **rods** whipping rods **216 late**
(other) recent **219 offer . . . hold** offer violence, but not hold fast
221 atonement reconciliation

Enter Westmorland.

WESTMORLAND
  The Prince is here at hand. Pleaseth your lordship   225
  To meet His Grace just distance 'tween our armies.   226
MOWBRAY
  Your Grace of York, in God's name then set forward.
ARCHBISHOP
  Before, and greet His Grace.—My lord, we come.   228

4.2   *Enter Prince John [of Lancaster] and his army.*

PRINCE JOHN
  You are well encountered here, my cousin Mowbray.   1
  Good day to you, gentle Lord Archbishop,   2
  And so to you, Lord Hastings, and to all.
  My lord of York, it better showed with you   4
  When that your flock, assembled by the bell,
  Encircled you to hear with reverence
  Your exposition on the holy text
  Than now to see you here an iron man,   8
  Cheering a rout of rebels with your drum,   9
  Turning the word to sword and life to death.   10
  That man that sits within a monarch's heart
  And ripens in the sunshine of his favor,
  Would he abuse the countenance of the King,   13
  Alack, what mischiefs might he set abroach   14
  In shadow of such greatness! With you, Lord Bishop,
  It is even so. Who hath not heard it spoken   16
  How deep you were within the books of God,   17

---

225 Pleaseth may it please **226 just distance** i.e., halfway **228 Before**
i.e., go before

**4.2. Location: This scene is apparently continuous with the previous
scene. In the quarto, Prince John and his army enter before the last two
lines of 4.1.**
1 cousin (Normal address of royal family to a duke.) **2 gentle** noble **4 it
. . . you** it showed you to better advantage **8 iron man** (1) warrior clad in
armor (2) merciless fighter **9 rout** mob **10 the word** i.e., the word of God,
the Scripture **13 Would he** if he should choose to. **countenance** favor
14 set abroach set aflowing, begin **16 even** just **17 within . . . God**
(1) versed in works of divinity (2) in God's good graces

To us the speaker in his parliament,   18
To us th' imagined voice of God himself,
The very opener and intelligencer   20
Between the grace, the sanctities, of heaven
And our dull workings? O, who shall believe   22
But you misuse the reverence of your place,
Employ the countenance and grace of heaven
As a false favorite doth his prince's name,
In deeds dishonorable? You have ta'en up,   26
Under the counterfeited zeal of God,
The subjects of his substitute, my father,   28
And both against the peace of heaven and him
Have here up-swarmed them.
ARCHBISHOP   Good my lord of Lancaster,   30
I am not here against your father's peace;
But, as I told my lord of Westmorland,
The time misordered doth, in common sense,   33
Crowd us and crush us to this monstrous form
To hold our safety up. I sent Your Grace
The parcels and particulars of our grief,   36
The which hath been with scorn shoved from the court,
Whereon this Hydra son of war is born,   38
Whose dangerous eyes may well be charmed asleep   39
With grant of our most just and right desires,
And true obedience, of this madness cured,
Stoop tamely to the foot of majesty.
MOWBRAY
   If not, we ready are to try our fortunes
   To the last man.
HASTINGS   And though we here fall down,   44
   We have supplies to second our attempt;   45
   If they miscarry, theirs shall second them,

---

18 speaker i.e., spokesman for God, just as the Speaker of Parliament
spoke in the name of the King   **20 opener** revealer.   **intelligencer**
interpreter, agent   **22 dull workings** imperfect human perceptions
26 ta'en up enlisted   **28 his substitute** God's deputy   **30 up-swarmed**
raised up in swarms   **33 time misordered** disorders of the time.   **in
common sense** i.e., as anyone can see   **36 parcels** items, details.   **grief**
grievances   **38 Hydra** (The Lernaean Hydra was a fabulous monster
with several heads; when one was cut off, others grew in its place.)
39 eyes (The image here conflates Hydra with Argus, Juno's watchful
guard with one hundred eyes, who was charmed asleep by Mercury's
music.)   **44 though** even if   **45 supplies** forces in reserve

And so success of mischief shall be born   47
And heir from heir shall hold this quarrel up
Whiles England shall have generation.   49

PRINCE JOHN
You are too shallow, Hastings, much too shallow,
To sound the bottom of the aftertimes.   51

WESTMORLAND
Pleaseth Your Grace to answer them directly   52
How far forth you do like their articles.

PRINCE JOHN
I like them all, and do allow them well,   54
And swear here, by the honor of my blood,
My father's purposes have been mistook,
And some about him have too lavishly   57
Wrested his meaning and authority.   58
My lord, these griefs shall be with speed redressed,
Upon my soul, they shall. If this may please you,
Discharge your powers unto their several counties,   61
As we will ours; and here between the armies
Let's drink together friendly and embrace,
That all their eyes may bear those tokens home
Of our restorèd love and amity.

ARCHBISHOP
I take your princely word for these redresses.

PRINCE JOHN
I give it you, and will maintain my word,
And thereupon I drink unto Your Grace.
                    [*They drink together, and embrace.*]

HASTINGS
Go, Captain, and deliver to the army
This news of peace. Let them have pay, and part.   70
I know it will well please them. Hie thee, Captain.
                    [*Exit a Captain.*]

ARCHBISHOP
To you, my noble lord of Westmorland.

---

47 success succession   **49 generation** issue, offspring   **51 sound . . .
aftertimes** predict what the future will bring.   **sound the bottom** plumb
the depths   **52 Pleaseth** may it please   **54 allow** approve, sanction
57 lavishly loosely, negligently   **58 Wrested** twisted   **61 powers**
forces.   **several** respective   **70 part** depart

WESTMORLAND
  I pledge Your Grace; and, if you knew what pains
  I have bestowed to breed this present peace,
  You would drink freely. But my love to ye
  Shall show itself more openly hereafter.
ARCHBISHOP
  I do not doubt you.
WESTMORLAND   I am glad of it.
  Health to my lord and gentle cousin, Mowbray.
MOWBRAY
  You wish me health in very happy season,   79
  For I am on the sudden something ill.   80
ARCHBISHOP
  Against ill chances men are ever merry,   81
  But heaviness foreruns the good event.   82
WESTMORLAND
  Therefore be merry, coz, since sudden sorrow   83
  Serves to say thus, "Some good thing comes tomorrow."
ARCHBISHOP
  Believe me, I am passing light in spirit.   85
MOWBRAY
  So much the worse, if your own rule be true.
                                    Shout [*within*].
PRINCE JOHN
  The word of peace is rendered. Hark, how they shout!   87
MOWBRAY
  This had been cheerful after victory.   88
ARCHBISHOP
  A peace is of the nature of a conquest,
  For then both parties nobly are subdued,
  And neither party loser.
PRINCE JOHN   Go, my lord,
  And let our army be dischargèd too.
                              [*Exit Westmorland.*]
  And, good my lord, so please you, let our trains   93

---

79 **in . . . season** at an opportune moment   **80 something** somewhat
81 **Against** when about to face   **82 heaviness . . . event** sadness comes
over men prior to a happy outcome   **83 coz** cousin, kinsman
85 **passing** surpassingly   **87 rendered** proclaimed   **88 had been** would
have been   **93 trains** followers, armies

March by us, that we may peruse the men
We should have coped withal.
ARCHBISHOP   Go, good Lord Hastings, 95
And, ere they be dismissed, let them march by.

[*Exit Hastings.*]

PRINCE JOHN
I trust, lords, we shall lie tonight together.

Enter Westmorland.

Now, cousin, wherefore stands our army still?   98
WESTMORLAND
The leaders, having charge from you to stand,
Will not go off until they hear you speak.
PRINCE JOHN   They know their duties.

Enter Hastings.

HASTINGS
My lord, our army is dispersed already.
Like youthful steers unyoked, they take their courses
East, west, north, south, or, like a school broke up,
Each hurries toward his home and sporting-place.   105
WESTMORLAND
Good tidings, my lord Hastings, for the which
I do arrest thee, traitor, of high treason.
And you, Lord Archbishop, and you, Lord Mowbray,
Of capital treason I attach you both.   109
MOWBRAY
Is this proceeding just and honorable?
WESTMORLAND   Is your assembly so?
ARCHBISHOP
Will you thus break your faith?
PRINCE JOHN   I pawned thee none. 112
I promised you redress of these same grievances
Whereof you did complain, which, by mine honor,
I will perform with a most Christian care.
But for you rebels, look to taste the due   116
Meet for rebellion.   117
Most shallowly did you these arms commence,   118

95 **coped withal** encountered, fought with   98 **wherefore** why
105 **sporting-place** playground   109 **capital** punishable by death.
attach arrest   112 **pawned** pledged   116 **for** as for.   **look** expect
117 **Meet** fitting   118 **arms** hostilities

Fondly brought here and foolishly sent hence.   119
Strike up our drums; pursue the scattered stray.   120
God, and not we, hath safely fought today.
Some guard these traitors to the block of death,
Treason's true bed and yielder-up of breath.

                                                    [*Exeunt.*]

4.3   *Alarum. Excursions. Enter Falstaff [and Sir*
            John Coleville].

FALSTAFF   What's your name, sir? Of what condition are   1
you, and of what place?

COLEVILLE   I am a knight, sir, and my name is Coleville of
the Dale.

FALSTAFF   Well, then, Coleville is your name, a knight is
your degree, and your place the Dale. Coleville shall be
still your name, a traitor your degree, and the dungeon
your place, a place deep enough; so shall you be still
Coleville of the Dale.

COLEVILLE   Are not you Sir John Falstaff?

FALSTAFF   As good a man as he, sir, whoe'er I am. Do
ye yield, sir, or shall I sweat for you? If I do sweat,
they are the drops of thy lovers, and they weep for thy   13
death. Therefore rouse up fear and trembling, and do
observance to my mercy.   15

COLEVILLE   I think you are Sir John Falstaff, and in that
thought yield me.

FALSTAFF   I have a whole school of tongues in this belly   18
of mine, and not a tongue of them all speaks any other
word but my name. An I had but a belly of any indif-   20
ferency, I were simply the most active fellow in Eu-   21
rope. My womb, my womb, my womb undoes me.   22
Here comes our general.

---

119 Fondly foolishly   **120 stray** stragglers

4.3. Location: Gaultree Forest, as before. The scene is continuous.
s.d. Alarum trumpet call to battle.   **Excursions** sallies, sudden move-
ments of troops   **1 condition** rank   **13 drops** tears.   **lovers** friends
15 observance reverence, homage   **18 school** crowd (i.e., his belly
eloquently identifies him)   **20 An** if   **20–21 indifferency** moderate
size   **22 womb** belly

Enter [Prince] John [of Lancaster], Westmorland,
[Blunt,] and the rest.

PRINCE JOHN
The heat is past; follow no further now.   24
Call in the powers, good cousin Westmorland.   25
              [Exit Westmorland. Sound] retreat.
Now, Falstaff, where have you been all this while?
When everything is ended, then you come.
These tardy tricks of yours will, on my life,
One time or other break some gallows' back.

FALSTAFF I would be sorry, my lord, but it should be   30
thus. I never knew yet but rebuke and check was the   31
reward of valor. Do you think me a swallow, an arrow,
or a bullet? Have I, in my poor and old motion, the
expedition of thought? I have speeded hither with the   34
very extremest inch of possibility. I have foundered   35
nine score and odd posts, and here, travel-tainted as I   36
am, have in my pure and immaculate valor taken Sir
John Coleville of the Dale, a most furious knight and
valorous enemy. But what of that? He saw me and
yielded, that I may justly say, with the hook-nosed fel-   40
low of Rome, "I came, saw, and overcame."   41

PRINCE JOHN   It was more of his courtesy than your de-
serving.

FALSTAFF   I know not. Here is he, and here I yield him.
And I beseech Your Grace, let it be booked with the   45
rest of this day's deeds, or, by the Lord, I will have it
in a particular ballad else, with mine own picture on   47
the top on 't, Coleville kissing my foot. To the which   48
course if I be enforced, if you do not all show like gilt   49
twopences to me, and I in the clear sky of fame   50
o'ershine you as much as the full moon doth the cin-   51
ders of the element, which show like pins' heads to   52

24 heat pursuit, race   **25 powers** forces   **30–31 but . . . thus** if it were
not thus. (It is fitting, Falstaff wryly says, that valor is never properly
recognized, because that is how the world goes.)   **31 check** reprimand
34 expedition speed   **35 very extremest inch** fullest extent.   **foundered**
made lame   **36 posts** post horses   **40–41 hook-nosed . . . Rome** i.e.,
Julius Caesar   **45 booked** recorded by the chroniclers   **47 a particular
ballad** a broadside ballad written and published for the particular
occasion.   **else** otherwise   **48 on 't** of it   **49 show** look   **49–50 gilt
twopences** coins gilded to pass for half-crowns of the same size   **50 to**
compared to (also in l. 52)   **51–52 cinders . . . element** i.e., stars

her, believe not the word of the noble. Therefore let
me have right, and let desert mount.   54
PRINCE JOHN Thine's too heavy to mount.
FALSTAFF Let it shine, then.
PRINCE JOHN Thine's too thick to shine.   57
FALSTAFF Let it do something, my good lord, that may
do me good, and call it what you will.
PRINCE JOHN Is thy name Coleville?
COLEVILLE It is, my lord.
PRINCE JOHN A famous rebel art thou, Coleville.
FALSTAFF And a famous true subject took him.
COLEVILLE
I am, my lord, but as my betters are
That led me hither. Had they been ruled by me,   65
You should have won them dearer than you have.   66
FALSTAFF I know not how they sold themselves. But
thou, like a kind fellow, gavest thyself away gratis, and
I thank thee for thee.

    Enter Westmorland.

PRINCE JOHN Now, have you left pursuit?
WESTMORLAND
Retreat is made and execution stayed.   71
PRINCE JOHN
Send Coleville with his confederates
To York, to present execution.   73
Blunt, lead him hence, and see you guard him sure.
                    [Exit Blunt with Coleville.]
And now dispatch we toward the court, my lords.   75
I hear the King my father is sore sick.
Our news shall go before us to His Majesty,
Which, cousin, you shall bear to comfort him,   78
And we with sober speed will follow you.   79
FALSTAFF My lord, I beseech you give me leave to go
through Gloucestershire, and, when you come to
court, stand my good lord in your good report.   82

54 desert mount merit be promoted   **57 thick** (1) opaque (2) heavy
65 been ruled by me listened to my advice   **66 dearer** i.e., at greater
military cost   **71 Retreat . . . stayed** the order for withdrawal has been
sounded and the slaughter has been stopped   **73 present** immediate
75 dispatch we let us hasten   **78 cousin** i.e., Westmorland   **79 sober**
controlled, dignified   **82 stand my good lord** act as my patron

PRINCE JOHN

  Fare you well, Falstaff. I, in my condition,   83
  Shall better speak of you than you deserve.

                              [*Exeunt all but Falstaff.*]

FALSTAFF I would you had but the wit; 'twere better
than your dukedom. Good faith, this same young
sober-blooded boy doth not love me, nor a man cannot make him laugh. But that's no marvel; he drinks
no wine. There's never none of these demure boys
come to any proof, for thin drink doth so overcool   90
their blood, and making many fish meals, that they
fall into a kind of male greensickness, and then, when   92
they marry, they get wenches. They are generally fools   93
and cowards, which some of us should be too, but for
inflammation. A good sherris sack hath a twofold op-   95
eration in it. It ascends me into the brain, dries me   96
there all the foolish and dull and crudy vapors which   97
environ it, makes it apprehensive, quick, forgetive,   98
full of nimble, fiery, and delectable shapes, which, delivered o'er to the voice, the tongue, which is the birth,
becomes excellent wit. The second property of your   101
excellent sherris is the warming of the blood, which,
before cold and settled, left the liver white and pale, 103
which is the badge of pusillanimity and cowardice.
But the sherris warms it and makes it course from the   105
innards to the parts' extremes. It illumineth the face, 106
which as a beacon gives warning to all the rest of this
little kingdom, man, to arm; and then the vital com-   108
moners and inland petty spirits muster me all to their   109
captain, the heart, who, great and puffed up with this
retinue, doth any deed of courage; and this valor
comes of sherris. So that skill in the weapon is nothing

---

83 condition i.e., function as commander **90 come to any proof** stand
up well under testing, turn out well. **thin drink** i.e., beer **92 greensickness** a kind of anemia thought to affect young women **93 get
wenches** beget girls **95 inflammation** passions excited by liquor.
sherris sack sherry **96 ascends me** i.e., ascends. (*Me* is used colloqui-
ally, as also in l. 109.) **97 crudy** curded **98 environ** surround.
apprehensive quick to perceive. **forgetive** inventive **101 wit** mental
capacity **103 liver** (Thought to be the seat of courage.) **105 course**
run **106 extremes** extremities **108–109 vital . . . spirits** vital spirits of
man's internal region **109 muster me** assemble

without sack, for that sets it a-work, and learning a 113
mere hoard of gold kept by a devil till sack com- 114
mences it and sets it in act and use. Hereof comes it 115
that Prince Harry is valiant, for the cold blood he did
naturally inherit of his father, he hath, like lean, ster- 117
ile, and bare land, manured, husbanded, and tilled 118
with excellent endeavor of drinking good and good
store of fertile sherris, that he is become very hot and
valiant. If I had a thousand sons, the first human 121
principle I would teach them should be to forswear
thin potations and to addict themselves to sack. 123

Enter Bardolph.

How now, Bardolph?
BARDOLPH   The army is discharged all and gone.
FALSTAFF   Let them go. I'll through Gloucestershire, and
there will I visit Master Robert Shallow, Esquire. I have
him already tempering between my finger and my 128
thumb, and shortly will I seal with him. Come away. 129
                                    [*Exeunt.*]

❖

4.4   *Enter the King; Warwick; Thomas, Duke of
Clarence; Humphrey, [Duke] of Gloucester;
[and others].*

KING
Now, lords, if God doth give successful end
To this debate that bleedeth at our doors, 2
We will our youth lead on to higher fields 3

---

113 learning learning is   **114 kept by a devil** guarded by an evil
spirit, like a dragon   **114–115 commences it** transforms its poten-
tial into actuality (as at a commencement)   **117 lean** barren
118 husbanded cultivated   **121 human** secular   **123 potations** drinks
128 tempering softening (like a piece of wax)   **129 seal with** i.e., shape
him to my purposes; seal a bargain with (continuing the metaphor of
sealing wax)

4.4. Location: King Henry's court at Westminster. The Jerusalem
Chamber (adjoining Westminster Abbey); so called for its various
inscriptions concerning Jerusalem.
2 debate strife   **3 higher fields** i.e., a crusade to Palestine

And draw no swords but what are sanctified. 4
Our navy is addressed, our power collected, 5
Our substitutes in absence well invested, 6
And everything lies level to our wish. 7
Only we want a little personal strength, 8
And pause us till these rebels now afoot
Come underneath the yoke of government.

WARWICK
Both which we doubt not but Your Majesty
Shall soon enjoy.

KING　　　　　　　　Humphrey, my son of Gloucester,
Where is the Prince your brother?

GLOUCESTER
I think he's gone to hunt, my lord, at Windsor.

KING
And how accompanied?

GLOUCESTER　　　　　　　　I do not know, my lord.

KING
Is not his brother Thomas of Clarence with him?

GLOUCESTER
No, my good lord, he is in presence here. 17

CLARENCE　What would my lord and father? 18

KING
Nothing but well to thee, Thomas of Clarence.
How chance thou art not with the Prince thy brother?
He loves thee, and thou dost neglect him, Thomas;
Thou hast a better place in his affection
Than all thy brothers. Cherish it, my boy,
And noble offices thou mayst effect 24
Of mediation, after I am dead,
Between his greatness and thy other brethren.
Therefore omit him not, blunt not his love, 27
Nor lose the good advantage of his grace 28
By seeming cold or careless of his will.
For he is gracious, if he be observed. 30
He hath a tear for pity and a hand
Open as day for melting charity. 32

---

4 what those that　**5 addressed** ready, prepared　**6 substitutes** deputies.
invested empowered　**7 level** conformable　**8 want** lack　**17 in presence**
present at court　**18 would** wishes　**24 offices** functions.　**effect** perform,
accomplish　**27 omit** neglect　**28 grace** favor　**30 observed** paid proper
respect, humored　**32 melting** tender, compassionate

Yet notwithstanding, being incensed, he is flint,   33
As humorous as winter, and as sudden   34
As flaws congealèd in the spring of day.   35
His temper, therefore, must be well observed.   36
Chide him for faults, and do it reverently,
When you perceive his blood inclined to mirth;
But, being moody, give him time and scope,   39
Till that his passions, like a whale on ground,
Confound themselves with working. Learn this,
    Thomas,   41
And thou shalt prove a shelter to thy friends,
A hoop of gold to bind thy brothers in,
That the united vessel of their blood,
Mingled with venom of suggestion—   45
As, force perforce, the age will pour it in—
Shall never leak, though it do work as strong
As aconitum or rash gunpowder.   48

CLARENCE
I shall observe him with all care and love.

KING
Why art thou not at Windsor with him, Thomas?

CLARENCE
He is not there today; he dines in London.

KING   And how accompanied?

CLARENCE
With Poins and other his continual followers.

KING
Most subject is the fattest soil to weeds,   54
And he, the noble image of my youth,
Is overspread with them. Therefore my grief
Stretches itself beyond the hour of death.
The blood weeps from my heart when I do shape
In forms imaginary th' unguided days
And rotten times that you shall look upon

---

33 flint i.e., in emitting fire   **34 humorous** unpredictable in mood
35 flaws congealèd snow squalls.   **spring of day** early morning
36 temper disposition   **39 moody** angry   **41 Confound** exhaust, consume.   **working** struggling   **45 suggestion** insinuation, suspicion. (The
image in ll. 43–48 is of a vessel of the brothers' combined blood, held
together with golden hoops of affection and loyalty but threatened by
the poison of mutual mistrust their enemies will try to foment in
them.)   **48 aconitum** a strong poison extracted from monkshood.   **rash**
quick-acting   **54 fattest** richest

When I am sleeping with my ancestors.
For when his headstrong riot hath no curb,
When rage and hot blood are his counselors,
When means and lavish manners meet together,   64
O, with what wings shall his affections fly   65
Towards fronting peril and opposed decay!   66

WARWICK
My gracious lord, you look beyond him quite.   67
The Prince but studies his companions
Like a strange tongue, wherein, to gain the language,   69
'Tis needful that the most immodest word
Be looked upon and learned, which, once attained,
Your Highness knows, comes to no further use
But to be known and hated. So, like gross terms,   73
The Prince will in the perfectness of time
Cast off his followers, and their memory
Shall as a pattern or a measure live
By which His Grace must mete the lives of other,   77
Turning past evils to advantages.

KING
'Tis seldom when the bee doth leave her comb   79
In the dead carrion.

    Enter Westmorland.

                    Who's here? Westmorland?   80

WESTMORLAND
Health to my sovereign, and new happiness
Added to that that I am to deliver!
Prince John your son doth kiss Your Grace's hand.
Mowbray, the Bishop Scroop, Hastings, and all
Are brought to the correction of your law.
There is not now a rebel's sword unsheathed,
But Peace puts forth her olive everywhere.
The manner how this action hath been borne

---

64 lavish unrestrained, licentious   **65 affections** inclinations
66 fronting . . . decay danger and ruin that confront him   **67 look
beyond** go too far in judging   **69 strange** foreign   **73 like gross terms**
just as with coarse expressions   **77 mete** measure, appraise.   **other**
others   **79–80 'Tis . . . carrion** rarely does the bee that has placed her
comb in dead carrion leave her honeycomb; i.e., the Prince will not
forsake his corrupt delights

Here at more leisure may Your Highness read,
With every course in his particular.   90

> [*He gives a document.*]

KING

O Westmorland, thou art a summer bird,
Which ever in the haunch of winter sings   92
The lifting up of day.

> *Enter Harcourt.*

Look, here's more news.   93

HARCOURT

From enemies heaven keep Your Majesty,
And, when they stand against you, may they fall
As those that I am come to tell you of!
The Earl Northumberland and the Lord Bardolph,
With a great power of English and of Scots,
Are by the sheriff of Yorkshire overthrown.
The manner and true order of the fight
This packet, please it you, contains at large.   101

> [*He gives letters.*]

KING

And wherefore should these good news make me sick?
Will Fortune never come with both hands full,
But write her fair words still in foulest letters?   104
She either gives a stomach and no food—   105
Such are the poor, in health; or else a feast
And takes away the stomach—such are the rich,
That have abundance and enjoy it not.
I should rejoice now at this happy news,
And now my sight fails and my brain is giddy.
O, me! Come near me. Now I am much ill.

> [*The King swoons. Several come to his aid.*]

GLOUCESTER

Comfort, Your Majesty!

CLARENCE   O my royal father!

WESTMORLAND

My sovereign lord, cheer up yourself, look up.

---

90 course . . . particular event or phase set forth in detail   **92 haunch**
latter end   **93 lifting up** dawn   **101 at large** in full   **104 still** always
105 stomach appetite

WARWICK
  Be patient, princes. You do know these fits
  Are with His Highness very ordinary.
  Stand from him; give him air. He'll straight be well.
CLARENCE
  No, no, he cannot long hold out these pangs.   117
  Th' incessant care and labor of his mind
  Hath wrought the mure that should confine it in   119
  So thin that life looks through.
GLOUCESTER
  The people fear me, for they do observe   121
  Unfathered heirs and loathly births of nature.   122
  The seasons change their manners, as the year   123
  Had found some months asleep and leapt them over.
CLARENCE
  The river hath thrice flowed, no ebb between,   125
  And the old folk, time's doting chronicles,
  Say it did so a little time before
  That our great-grandsire, Edward, sicked and died.   128
WARWICK
  Speak lower, princes, for the King recovers.
GLOUCESTER
  This apoplexy will certain be his end.
KING
  I pray you, take me up and bear me hence
  Into some other chamber.

4.5   [*The King is borne to another part of the stage,
      to bed.*]

[KING]
  Let there be no noise made, my gentle friends,
  Unless some dull and favorable hand   2
  Will whisper music to my weary spirit.

---

117 hold out endure   **119 wrought the mure** made the wall   **121 fear**
frighten   **122 Unfathered heirs** persons believed to be supernaturally
conceived.   **loathly births** monstrous offspring   **123 as** as if   **125 river**
i.e., Thames. (Holinshed records this event as having happened on
October 12, 1412.)   **128 Edward** Edward III.   **sicked** fell sick

4.5. Location: The scene is continuous.
2 dull soft, soothing.   **favorable** kindly

WARWICK
  Call for the music in the other room.
                    [*Exit one or more. Soft music within.*]
KING
  Set me the crown upon my pillow here.
CLARENCE
  His eye is hollow, and he changes much.   6
WARWICK
  Less noise, less noise!
                    [*The crown is placed on the King's pillow.*]

      Enter [*Prince*] *Harry.*

PRINCE   Who saw the Duke of Clarence?
CLARENCE
  I am here, brother, full of heaviness.   8
PRINCE
  How now, rain within doors, and none abroad?   9
  How doth the King?
GLOUCESTER   Exceeding ill.
PRINCE
  Heard he the good news yet? Tell it him.
GLOUCESTER
  He altered much upon the hearing it.
PRINCE If he be sick with joy, he'll recover without
  physic.
WARWICK
  Not so much noise, my lords. Sweet Prince, speak low.
  The King your father is disposed to sleep.
CLARENCE
  Let us withdraw into the other room.
WARWICK
  Will 't please Your Grace to go along with us?
PRINCE
  No, I will sit and watch here by the King.
                    [*Exeunt all but the Prince.*]
  Why doth the crown lie there upon his pillow,
  Being so troublesome a bedfellow?
  O polished perturbation! Golden care!   23
  That keep'st the ports of slumber open wide   24

---

6 changes changes color, turns pale   **8 heaviness** sadness   **9 rain** i.e.,
tears   **23 perturbation** cause of perturbation   **24 ports** gates

To many a watchful night! Sleep with it now!   25
Yet not so sound and half so deeply sweet   26
As he whose brow with homely biggen bound   27
Snores out the watch of night. O majesty!
When thou dost pinch thy bearer, thou dost sit   29
Like a rich armor worn in heat of day,
That scald'st with safety. By his gates of breath   31
There lies a downy feather which stirs not.
Did he suspire, that light and weightless down   33
Perforce must move. My gracious lord! My Father!
This sleep is sound indeed. This is a sleep
That from this golden rigol hath divorced   36
So many English kings. Thy due from me
Is tears and heavy sorrows of the blood,   38
Which nature, love, and filial tenderness
Shall, O dear Father, pay thee plenteously.
My due from thee is this imperial crown,
Which, as immediate from thy place and blood,   42
Derives itself to me. [*He puts on the crown.*] Lo, where
  it sits,   43
Which God shall guard. And put the world's whole
  strength
Into one giant arm, it shall not force
This lineal honor from me. This from thee   46
Will I to mine leave, as 'tis left to me.   *Exit.*
KING [*Awaking*]   Warwick! Gloucester! Clarence!

  *Enter Warwick, Gloucester, Clarence, [and
  others].*

CLARENCE
  Doth the King call?
WARWICK   What would Your Majesty?
KING
  Why did you leave me here alone, my lords?

25 **watchful** wakeful.   **Sleep with it** i.e., may you (King Henry) sleep
with this symbol of care beside you   26 **Yet not** i.e., yet your sleep will
nonetheless not be   27 **biggen** nightcap   29 **pinch** torment   31 **scald'st
with safety** burns while providing safety.   **gates of breath** lips   33 **suspire** breathe   36 **rigol** circle, i.e., crown   38 **blood** (1) heart (2) kinship
42 **as immediate from** as I am next in line to   43 **Derives itself** descends
46 **lineal** inherited

CLARENCE
　We left the Prince my brother here, my liege,
　Who undertook to sit and watch by you.

KING
　The Prince of Wales? Where is he? Let me see him.
　He is not here.

WARWICK
　This door is open; he is gone this way.

GLOUCESTER
　He came not through the chamber where we stayed.

KING
　Where is the crown? Who took it from my pillow?

WARWICK
　When we withdrew, my liege, we left it here.

KING
　The Prince hath ta'en it hence. Go seek him out.
　Is he so hasty that he doth suppose
　My sleep my death?
　Find him, my lord of Warwick; chide him hither.
　　　　　　　　　　　　　　　　[Exit Warwick.]
　This part of his conjoins with my disease　　　　　　63
　And helps to end me. See, sons, what things you are!
　How quickly Nature falls into revolt
　When gold becomes her object!
　For this the foolish overcareful fathers
　Have broke their sleep with thoughts,　　　　　　68
　Their brains with care, their bones with industry;
　For this they have engrossèd and piled up　　　　　　70
　The cankered heaps of strange-achievèd gold;　　　　71
　For this they have been thoughtful to invest　　　　72
　Their sons with arts and martial exercises—
　When, like the bee, tolling from every flower　　　　74
　The virtuous sweets,
　Our thighs packed with wax, our mouths with honey,
　We bring it to the hive, and like the bees
　Are murdered for our pains. This bitter taste　　　　78
　Yields his engrossments to the ending father.　　　　79

63 **part** act.　**conjoins** unites, joins　68 **thoughts** cares　70 **engrossèd** amassed　71 **cankered** rusting and malignant.　**strange-achievèd** won by unusual effort or means, or in distant lands　72 **thoughtful** careful 74 **tolling** taking as toll, collecting　78–79 **This . . . father** his storing up of treasures yields this bitter taste to the dying father

Enter Warwick.

Now, where is he that will not stay so long
Till his friend sickness have determined me?   81

WARWICK
My lord, I found the Prince in the next room,
Washing with kindly tears his gentle cheeks,   83
With such a deep demeanor in great sorrow   84
That tyranny, which never quaffed but blood,   85
Would, by beholding him, have washed his knife
With gentle eyedrops. He is coming hither.

KING
But wherefore did he take away the crown?

Enter [Prince] Harry [with the crown].

Lo, where he comes. Come hither to me, Harry.—
Depart the chamber; leave us here alone.
                              Exeunt [Warwick and the rest].

PRINCE
I never thought to hear you speak again.

KING
Thy wish was father, Harry, to that thought.
I stay too long by thee; I weary thee.
Dost thou so hunger for mine empty chair   94
That thou wilt needs invest thee with my honors   95
Before thy hour be ripe? O foolish youth,
Thou seek'st the greatness that will overwhelm thee.
Stay but a little, for my cloud of dignity   98
Is held from falling with so weak a wind   99
That it will quickly drop. My day is dim.
Thou hast stol'n that which after some few hours
Were thine without offense, and at my death
Thou hast sealed up my expectation.   103
Thy life did manifest thou lovedst me not,
And thou wilt have me die assured of it.
Thou hid'st a thousand daggers in thy thoughts,

81 determined ended, put an end to   **83 kindly** natural   **84 deep** intense
85 tyranny cruelty.   **quaffed** drank   **94 chair** throne   **95 wilt needs** must
98 my cloud of dignity the fragile substance of my high estate   **99 so weak
a wind** i.e., the King's failing breath, compared to the wind that was
thought to hold up the clouds   **103 sealed up** confirmed

Which thou hast whetted on thy stony heart,   107
To stab at half an hour of my life.
What, canst thou not forbear me half an hour?   109
Then get thee gone and dig my grave thyself,
And bid the merry bells ring to thine ear
That thou art crownèd, not that I am dead.
Let all the tears that should bedew my hearse
Be drops of balm to sanctify thy head.   114
Only compound me with forgotten dust;   115
Give that which gave thee life unto the worms.
Pluck down my officers, break my decrees,
For now a time is come to mock at form.   118
Harry the Fifth is crowned. Up, vanity!   119
Down, royal state! All you sage counselors, hence!   120
And to the English court assemble now,
From every region, apes of idleness!
Now, neighbor confines, purge you of your scum.   123
Have you a ruffian that will swear, drink, dance,
Revel the night, rob, murder, and commit
The oldest sins the newest kind of ways?
Be happy; he will trouble you no more.
England shall double gild his treble guilt;
England shall give him office, honor, might;
For the fifth Harry from curbed license plucks
The muzzle of restraint, and the wild dog
Shall flesh his tooth on every innocent.   132
O my poor kingdom, sick with civil blows!
When that my care could not withhold thy riots,   134
What wilt thou do when riot is thy care?   135
O, thou wilt be a wilderness again,   136
Peopled with wolves, thy old inhabitants!
PRINCE [*Kneeling and returning the crown*]
　　O, pardon me, my liege! But for my tears,   138

---

107 whetted sharpened　**109 forbear** spare　**114 balm** consecrated oil
used in anointing the king at his coronation　**115 compound** mix
118 form ceremony, orderly usages　**119 vanity** folly　**120 state** ceremony　**123 neighbor confines** territories of neighboring countries
132 flesh his tooth on i.e., plunge his teeth into the flesh of. (To *flesh*
means to initiate into bloodshed, to make an animal eager for prey by
the taste of blood.)　**134 When that** when.　**care** careful maintenance of
discipline　**135 care** concern　**136 thou** i.e., the Prince and his kingdom　**138 But for** were it not for

The moist impediments unto my speech,
I had forestalled this dear and deep rebuke   140
Ere you with grief had spoke and I had heard
The course of it so far. There is your crown;
And He that wears the crown immortally
Long guard it yours! If I affect it more   144
Than as your honor and as your renown,
Let me no more from this obedience rise,   146
Which my most inward true and duteous spirit
Teacheth this prostrate and exterior bending.
God witness with me, when I here came in,
And found no course of breath within Your Majesty,   150
How cold it struck my heart! If I do feign,
O, let me in my present wildness die
And never live to show th' incredulous world
The noble change that I have purposèd!
Coming to look on you, thinking you dead,
And dead almost, my liege, to think you were,
I spake unto this crown as having sense,   157
And thus upbraided it: "The care on thee depending
Hath fed upon the body of my father;
Therefore, thou best of gold art worst of gold.
Other, less fine in carat, is more precious,
Preserving life in med'cine potable;   162
But thou, most fine, most honored, most renowned,
Hast eat thy bearer up." Thus, my most royal liege,   164
Accusing it, I put it on my head,
To try with it, as with an enemy   166
That had before my face murdered my father,
The quarrel of a true inheritor.   168
But if it did infect my blood with joy
Or swell my thoughts to any strain of pride,   170
If any rebel or vain spirit of mine
Did with the least affection of a welcome   172

140 had would have.   **dear** severe (because deeply felt emotionally)
144 affect desire   **146 obedience** obeisance   **150 course** current
157 as having sense as if it were capable of sense impressions
162 med'cine potable potable gold, an elixir, thought from Galen's time
to possess magical power to cure   **164 eat** eaten. (Pronounced "et.")
166 try struggle   **168 The quarrel . . . inheritor** (The Prince, as the son
and heir of a murdered man, has a quarrel to settle with the mur-
derer.)   **170 strain** feeling, tendency   **172 affection** inclination

Give entertainment to the might of it,
Let God forever keep it from my head
And make me as the poorest vassal is
That doth with awe and terror kneel to it!
KING O my son,
    God put it in thy mind to take it hence,
    That thou mightst win the more thy father's love,
    Pleading so wisely in excuse of it!
    Come hither, Harry, sit thou by my bed,
            [*The Prince rises and sits by the bed*]
    And hear, I think, the very latest counsel   182
    That ever I shall breathe. God knows, my son,
    By what bypaths and indirect crook'd ways
    I met this crown, and I myself know well
    How troublesome it sat upon my head.
    To thee it shall descend with better quiet,
    Better opinion, better confirmation,   188
    For all the soil of the achievement goes   189
    With me into the earth. It seemed in me
    But as an honor snatched with boisterous hand,   191
    And I had many living to upbraid
    My gain of it by their assistances,
    Which daily grew to quarrel and to bloodshed,
    Wounding supposèd peace. All these bold fears   195
    Thou seest with peril I have answerèd,
    For all my reign hath been but as a scene
    Acting that argument. And now my death   198
    Changes the mood, for what in me was purchased   199
    Falls upon thee in a more fairer sort;   200
    So thou the garland wear'st successively.   201
    Yet, though thou stand'st more sure than I could do,
    Thou art not firm enough, since griefs are green.   203
    And all my friends, which thou must make thy friends,
    Have but their stings and teeth newly ta'en out,
    By whose fell working I was first advanced   206
    And by whose power I well might lodge a fear   207

182 latest last **188 opinion** public support, reputation **189 soil** stain
191 boisterous violent **195 fears** objects of fear **198 argument**
theme **199 mood** state of mind; mode, musical key. **purchased** i.e.,
gained by transaction **200 sort** manner, way **201 So** thus. **garland**
crown. **successively** by right of succession **203 griefs are green**
grievances are fresh **206 fell working** fierce effort **207 lodge** harbor

To be again displaced. Which to avoid,
I cut them off, and had a purpose now
To lead out many to the Holy Land,
Lest rest and lying still might make them look   211
Too near unto my state. Therefore, my Harry,   212
Be it thy course to busy giddy minds
With foreign quarrels, that action, hence borne out,   214
May waste the memory of the former days.   215
More would I, but my lungs are wasted so
That strength of speech is utterly denied me.
How I came by the crown, O God forgive,
And grant it may with thee in true peace live!
PRINCE   My gracious liege,
You won it, wore it, kept it, gave it me.
Then plain and right must my possession be,
Which I with more than with a common pain   223
'Gainst all the world will rightfully maintain.

Enter [Prince John of] Lancaster [and Warwick].

KING
Look, look, here comes my John of Lancaster.
PRINCE JOHN
Health, peace, and happiness to my royal father!
KING
Thou bring'st me happiness and peace, son John;
But health, alack, with youthful wings is flown
From this bare withered trunk. Upon thy sight   229
My worldly business makes a period.   230
Where is my lord of Warwick?
PRINCE   My lord of Warwick!

[Warwick comes forward.]

KING
Doth any name particular belong
Unto the lodging where I first did swoon?   233
WARWICK
'Tis called Jerusalem, my noble lord.

211–212 look . . . state examine too painstakingly my regal status, my
claim   **214 action . . . out** military action, conducted in other lands
215 waste efface, obliterate   **223 pain** effort   **229 Upon thy sight** at the
very moment of my seeing you   **230 makes a period** comes to an end,
rounds out a whole   **233 lodging** room, chamber

KING
Laud be to God! Even there my life must end.
It hath been prophesied to me many years
I should not die but in Jerusalem,
Which vainly I supposed the Holy Land.
But bear me to that chamber; there I'll lie.
In that Jerusalem shall Harry die.   [*Exeunt.*]

❖

5.1 *Enter Shallow, Falstaff, and Bardolph [and Page].*

SHALLOW By Cock and pie, sir, you shall not away to- 1
night.—What, Davy, I say!

FALSTAFF You must excuse me, Master Robert Shallow.

SHALLOW I will not excuse you, you shall not be
excused, excuses shall not be admitted, there is no excuse shall serve, you shall not be excused.—Why, Davy!

[*Enter Davy.*]

DAVY Here, sir.

SHALLOW Davy, Davy, Davy, Davy, let me see, Davy,
let me see, Davy, let me see. Yea, marry, William cook, 9
bid him come hither.—Sir John, you shall not be excused.

DAVY Marry, sir, thus, those precepts cannot be served. 12
And again, sir, shall we sow the hade land with 13
wheat?

SHALLOW With red wheat, Davy. But for William 15
cook—are there no young pigeons?

DAVY Yes, sir. Here is now the smith's note for shoeing 17
and plow irons.   [*He gives a paper.*]

SHALLOW Let it be cast and paid.—Sir John, you shall not 19
be excused.

DAVY Now, sir, a new link to the bucket must needs be 21
had. And, sir, do you mean to stop any of William's
wages about the sack he lost the other day at Hinckley 23
fair?

SHALLOW 'A shall answer it. Some pigeons, Davy, a 25
couple of short-legged hens, a joint of mutton, and any
pretty little tiny kickshaws, tell William cook. 27

[*Davy and Shallow confer privately.*]

5.1. Location: Gloucestershire. Shallow's house.
1 By Cock and pie (A mild oath, meaning "By God and the ordinal or
book of services for the Church.") 9 William cook William the cook
12 precepts writs, summonses 13 hade land strip of unplowed land
between two plowed fields 15 red wheat a variety of red-tinged wheat
planted late in the summer 17 note bill 19 cast added up 21 link
chain. bucket yoke or pail 23 Hinckley market town not far from
Coventry, famous for its fairs 25 answer pay for 27 kickshaws fancy
dishes. (From French *quelque chose*.)

DAVY Doth the man of war stay all night, sir?

SHALLOW Yea, Davy. I will use him well. A friend i' the
court is better than a penny in purse. Use his men
well, Davy, for they are arrant knaves, and will back-
bite.

DAVY No worse than they are backbitten, sir, for they 33
have marvelous foul linen.   34

SHALLOW Well conceited, Davy. About thy business, 35
Davy.

DAVY I beseech you, sir, to countenance William Visor 37
of Woncot against Clement Perkes o' the hill.

SHALLOW There is many complaints, Davy, against that
Visor. That Visor is an arrant knave, on my knowledge.

DAVY I grant your worship that he is a knave, sir; but
yet, God forbid, sir, but a knave should have some
countenance at his friend's request. An honest man,
sir, is able to speak for himself, when a knave is not.
I have served your worship truly, sir, this eight years;
an I cannot once or twice in a quarter bear out a knave 47
against an honest man, I have little credit with your
worship. The knave is mine honest friend, sir; therefore, I beseech you, let him be countenanced.

SHALLOW Go to, I say he shall have no wrong. Look 51
about, Davy. [*Exit Davy.*] Where are you, Sir John? 52
Come, come, come, off with your boots. Give me your
hand, Master Bardolph.

BARDOLPH I am glad to see your worship.

SHALLOW I thank thee with all my heart, kind Master
Bardolph. And welcome, my tall fellow [*To the Page*]. 57
Come, Sir John.

FALSTAFF I'll follow you, good Master Robert Shallow.
[*Exit Shallow.*] Bardolph, look to our horses. [*Exeunt
Bardolph and Page.*] If I were sawed into quantities, I 61
should make four dozen of such bearded hermits'
staves as Master Shallow. It is a wonderful thing to see

---

33 backbitten (with pun on "bitten by vermin") **34 marvelous** marvel-
ously **35 Well conceited** ingeniously punned **37 countenance** favor
47 bear out support **51–52 Look about** look sharp, be on the alert
57 tall brave (but also with an ironic witticism about the page's small
stature) **61 quantities** pieces

the semblable coherence of his men's spirits and his. 64
They, by observing of him, do bear themselves like
foolish justices; he, by conversing with them, is turned 66
into a justice-like servingman. Their spirits are so married in conjunction with the participation of society 68
that they flock together in consent, like so many wild 69
geese. If I had a suit to Master Shallow, I would humor
his men with the imputation of being near their mas- 71
ter; if to his men, I would curry with Master Shallow 72
that no man could better command his servants. It is
certain that either wise bearing or ignorant carriage is 74
caught, as men take diseases, one of another. Therefore let men take heed of their company. I will devise
matter enough out of this Shallow to keep Prince
Harry in continual laughter the wearing out of six
fashions, which is four terms, or two actions, and 'a 79
shall laugh without intervallums. O, it is much that a 80
lie with a slight oath and a jest with a sad brow will 81
do with a fellow that never had the ache in his shoul- 82
ders! O, you shall see him laugh till his face be like a 83
wet cloak ill laid up. 84

SHALLOW [*Within*]   Sir John!

FALSTAFF   I come, Master Shallow, I come, Master
Shallow.   [*Exit.*]

✣

5.2   *Enter Warwick [and the] Lord Chief Justice*
        [meeting].

WARWICK
  How now, my Lord Chief Justice, whither away?   1

64 semblable coherence similar or complete agreement   **66 conversing**
associating   **68 with . . . society** by close association   **69 consent**
agreement   **71 with . . . near** implying that I am friendly with
72 curry with employ flattery with   **74 carriage** demeanor, behavior
79 four terms i.e., of court, Michaelmas, Hilary, Easter, and Trinity, all
in all comprising one legal year.   **actions** lawsuits   **80 intervallums**
intervals between terms of court   **81 sad** serious   **82–83 a fellow . . .
shoulders** i.e., someone who is inexperienced in the troubles and complexities of this world and hence gullible   **84 ill laid up** carelessly put
away so that it wrinkles

5.2. Location: Westminster. The royal court.
1 whither away where are you going

CHIEF JUSTICE   How doth the King?

WARWICK
Exceeding well. His cares are now all ended.

CHIEF JUSTICE
I hope, not dead.

WARWICK   He's walked the way of nature,   4
And to our purposes he lives no more.

CHIEF JUSTICE
I would His Majesty had called me with him.
The service that I truly did his life   7
Hath left me open to all injuries.

WARWICK
Indeed I think the young King loves you not.

CHIEF JUSTICE
I know he doth not, and do arm myself
To welcome the condition of the time,
Which cannot look more hideously upon me
Than I have drawn it in my fantasy.

    Enter [Prince] John [of Lancaster], Thomas [of
    Clarence], and Humphrey [of Gloucester, with]
    Westmorland, [and others].

WARWICK
Here comes the heavy issue of dead Harry.   14
O, that the living Harry had the temper   15
Of he, the worst of these three gentlemen!   16
How many nobles then should hold their places
That must strike sail to spirits of vile sort!   18

CHIEF JUSTICE
O God, I fear all will be overturned.

PRINCE JOHN
Good morrow, cousin Warwick, good morrow.

GLOUCESTER, CLARENCE   Good morrow, cousin.

PRINCE JOHN
We meet like men that had forgot to speak.   22

WARWICK
We do remember, but our argument   23
Is all too heavy to admit much talk.

---

4 walked . . . nature i.e., died   **7 truly** loyally   **14 heavy issue** grieving
sons   **15 temper** disposition   **16 he, the worst** the least worthy
18 strike sail i.e., salute as a token of submission. (A naval custom.)
22 forgot forgotten how   **23 argument** subject

PRINCE JOHN
  Well, peace be with him that hath made us heavy!
CHIEF JUSTICE
  Peace be with us, lest we be heavier!
GLOUCESTER
  O good my lord, you have lost a friend indeed,
  And I dare swear you borrow not that face
  Of seeming sorrow; it is sure your own.
PRINCE JOHN
  Though no man be assured what grace to find,   30
  You stand in coldest expectation.   31
  I am the sorrier; would 'twere otherwise.   32
CLARENCE
  Well, you must now speak Sir John Falstaff fair,   33
  Which swims against your stream of quality.   34
CHIEF JUSTICE
  Sweet princes, what I did I did in honor,
  Led by th' impartial conduct of my soul,
  And never shall you see that I will beg
  A ragged and forestalled remission.   38
  If truth and upright innocency fail me,
  I'll to the King my master that is dead
  And tell him who hath sent me after him.
WARWICK   Here comes the Prince.

      Enter the Prince [as King Henry the Fifth] and
      Blunt.

CHIEF JUSTICE
  Good morrow, and God save Your Majesty!
KING
  This new and gorgeous garment, majesty,
  Sits not so easy on me as you think.
  Brothers, you mix your sadness with some fear.
  This is the English, not the Turkish court;
  Not Amurath an Amurath succeeds,   48

30 grace to find favor he will find   **31 coldest** most comfortless
32 would I wish   **33 speak . . . fair** speak courteously to Sir John
Falstaff   **34 swims . . . quality** runs counter to your natural inclination
and position   **38 A . . . remission** a half-hearted (beggarly) pardon,
which is sure to be refused, or whose effect is gone before it is
granted   **48 Amurath** a Turkish sultan who, upon succeeding his father,
had his brothers strangled

But Harry Harry. Yet be sad, good brothers,
For, by my faith, it very well becomes you.
Sorrow so royally in you appears
That I will deeply put the fashion on
And wear it in my heart. Why then, be sad,
But entertain no more of it, good brothers,
Than a joint burden laid upon us all.
For me, by heaven, I bid you be assured,　　56
I'll be your father and your brother too.
Let me but bear your love, I'll bear your cares.
Yet weep that Harry's dead, and so will I;
But Harry lives that shall convert those tears
By number into hours of happiness.　　61

PRINCES
We hope no otherwise from Your Majesty.

KING
You all look strangely on me. [*To the Chief Justice.*]
　And you most.
You are, I think, assured I love you not.

CHIEF JUSTICE
I am assured, if I be measured rightly,
Your Majesty hath no just cause to hate me.

KING　No?
How might a prince of my great hopes forget
So great indignities you laid upon me?
What? Rate, rebuke, and roughly send to prison　　70
Th' immediate heir of England? Was this easy?　　71
May this be washed in Lethe and forgotten?　　72

CHIEF JUSTICE
I then did use the person of your father;　　73
The image of his power lay then in me.
And in th' administration of his law,
Whiles I was busy for the commonwealth,
Your Highness pleasèd to forget my place,
The majesty and power of law and justice,
The image of the King whom I presented,　　79
And struck me in my very seat of judgment;

---

56 For as for　**61 By number** i.e., for each of our many tears there will
be an hour of happiness　**70 Rate** chide　**71 immediate heir** next heir
in succession.　**easy** of small importance, easily forgotten　**72 Lethe** the
river of forgetfulness in Hades　**73 use the person** act as representative　**79 presented** represented

Whereon, as an offender to your father,
I gave bold way to my authority
And did commit you. If the deed were ill,   83
Be you contented, wearing now the garland,   84
To have a son set your decrees at naught,
To pluck down justice from your awful bench,   86
To trip the course of law and blunt the sword
That guards the peace and safety of your person,
Nay, more, to spurn at your most royal image
And mock your workings in a second body?   90
Question your royal thoughts, make the case yours;
Be now the father and propose a son,   92
Hear your own dignity so much profaned,
See your most dreadful laws so loosely slighted,
Behold yourself so by a son disdained,
And then imagine me taking your part
And in your power soft silencing your son.   97
After this cold considerance sentence me,   98
And, as you are a king, speak in your state   99
What I have done that misbecame my place,
My person, or my liege's sovereignty.

KING
You are right justice, and you weigh this well.   102
Therefore still bear the balance and the sword;   103
And I do wish your honors may increase,
Till you do live to see a son of mine
Offend you and obey you, as I did.
So shall I live to speak my father's words:
"Happy am I that have a man so bold
That dares do justice on my proper son;   109
And not less happy, having such a son
That would deliver up his greatness so
Into the hands of justice." You did commit me;
For which I do commit into your hand
Th' unstainèd sword that you have used to bear,   114
With this remembrance, that you use the same   115

___

83 commit i.e., to prison **84 garland** crown **86 awful** inspiring awe
90 second body representative, deputy **92 propose** imagine, suppose
97 soft gently **98 cold considerance** calm reflection **99 state** royal
capacity **102 right** true, ideal **103 balance** scale (which along with the
sword was an emblem of justice) **109 proper** own **114 have used** were
accustomed **115 remembrance** reminder, admonition

With the like bold, just, and impartial spirit
As you have done 'gainst me. There is my hand.
You shall be as a father to my youth.
My voice shall sound as you do prompt mine ear,   119
And I will stoop and humble my intents
To your well-practiced wise directions.
And, princes all, believe me, I beseech you:
My father is gone wild into his grave,   123
For in his tomb lie my affections,   124
And with his spirits sadly I survive   125
To mock the expectation of the world,
To frustrate prophecies, and to rase out   127
Rotten opinion, who hath writ me down   128
After my seeming. The tide of blood in me   129
Hath proudly flowed in vanity till now;   130
Now doth it turn and ebb back to the sea,
Where it shall mingle with the state of floods   132
And flow henceforth in formal majesty.
Now call we our high court of Parliament.
And let us choose such limbs of noble counsel
That the great body of our state may go
In equal rank with the best-governed nation;
That war, or peace, or both at once, may be
As things acquainted and familiar to us,
[*To Chief Justice*] In which you, father, shall have
   foremost hand.
Our coronation done, we will accite,   141
As I before remembered, all our state.   142
And, God consigning to my good intents,   143
No prince nor peer shall have just cause to say,
God shorten Harry's happy life one day!   *Exeunt.*

❖

119 **sound** speak   123–124 **My . . . affections** i.e., my wildness, having
disappeared with my father's death, is buried along with my father
124 **affections** (wild) inclinations   125 **sadly** soberly   127 **rase out**
erase   128 **who** which   129 **After my seeming** according to what I
appeared to be.   **blood** passion   130 **vanity** folly   132 **state of floods**
majesty of the ocean   141 **accite** summon   142 **remembered** mentioned.   **state** peers, nobility   143 **consigning to** sanctioning

5.3   *Enter Sir John [Falstaff], Shallow, Silence,*
           Davy, Bardolph, [and the] Page. [Davy provides
           food and wine.]

SHALLOW   Nay, you shall see my orchard, where, in an
arbor, we will eat a last year's pippin of mine own   2
grafting, with a dish of caraways, and so forth. Come,   3
cousin Silence. And then to bed.

FALSTAFF   'Fore God, you have here a goodly dwelling
and a rich.

SHALLOW   Barren, barren, barren. Beggars all, beggars
all, Sir John. Marry, good air.—Spread, Davy, spread,   8
Davy. Well said, Davy.   9

FALSTAFF   This Davy serves you for good uses. He is
your servingman and your husband.   11

SHALLOW   A good varlet, a good varlet, a very good var-   12
let, Sir John. By the Mass, I have drunk too much sack
at supper. A good varlet. Now sit down, now sit
down. Come, cousin.   [*They sit.*]

SILENCE   Ah, sirrah, quoth 'a, we shall   16
[*Sings.*] "Do nothing but eat, and make good cheer,
            And praise God for the merry year,
            When flesh is cheap and females dear,   19
            And lusty lads roam here and there
                        So merrily,
            And ever among so merrily."   22

FALSTAFF   There's a merry heart! Good Master Silence,
I'll give you a health for that anon.   24

SHALLOW   Give Master Bardolph some wine, Davy.

DAVY   Sweet sir, sit, I'll be with you anon. Most sweet
sir, sit. Master page, good master page, sit. Proface!   27
What you want in meat, we'll have in drink. But you   28
must bear; the heart's all.   [*Exit.*]   29

SHALLOW   Be merry, Master Bardolph, and, my little
soldier there, be merry.

5.3. Location: Gloucestershire. Shallow's orchard.
2 pippin a kind of apple   **3 caraways** caraway seeds (often eaten with
apples)   **8 Spread** spread the cloth   **9 said** done   **11 husband** manager
of the household   **12 varlet** servant   **16 quoth 'a** said he   **19 flesh** meat
(with sexual suggestion)   **22 ever among** all the while   **24 give you a
health** drink you a toast   **27 Proface** (Formula of welcome to a meal,
meaning "May it do you good.")   **28 want** lack.   **meat** food   **29 bear**
be forbearing

SILENCE [*Sings*]
>"Be merry, be merry, my wife has all,
>   For women are shrews, both short and tall.
>'Tis merry in hall when beards wags all,   34
>   And welcome merry Shrovetide.   35
>Be merry, be merry."

FALSTAFF   I did not think Master Silence had been a man of this mettle.   38

SILENCE   Who, I? I have been merry twice and once   39 ere now.

Enter Davy.

DAVY [*To Bardolph*]   There's a dish of leather-coats   41 for you.

SHALLOW   Davy!

DAVY   Your worship? I'll be with you straight. [*To Bardolph*.*] A cup of wine, sir?

SILENCE [*Sings*]
>"A cup of wine that's brisk and fine,
>   And drink unto thee, leman mine,   47
>   And a merry heart lives long-a."

FALSTAFF   Well said, Master Silence.

SILENCE   And we shall be merry; now comes in the sweet o' the night.

FALSTAFF   Health and long life to you, Master Silence.

SILENCE [*Sings*]
>"Fill the cup, and let it come,   53
>   I'll pledge you a mile to the bottom."   54

SHALLOW   Honest Bardolph, welcome. If thou want'st anything, and wilt not call, beshrew thy heart. Welcome, my little tiny thief [*To the Page*], and welcome indeed, too. I'll drink to Master Bardolph, and to all the cabileros about London.   59

DAVY   I hope to see London once ere I die.   60

BARDOLPH   An I might see you there, Davy!

SHALLOW   By the Mass, you'll crack a quart together, ha,   62 will you not, Master Bardolph?

---

34 beards wags all all the beards wag up and down (as men talk and laugh)   **35 Shrovetide** a season of merrymaking before Lent   **38 mettle** spirit   **39 twice and once** i.e., now and again   **41 leather-coats** russet apples   **47 leman** sweetheart   **53 let it come** i.e., pass it around   **54 a mile** i.e., even if it were a mile   **59 cabileros** cavaliers, gallants   **60 once** one day   **62 crack** consume

BARDOLPH   Yea, sir, in a pottle pot.   64
SHALLOW   By God's liggens, I thank thee. The knave   65
   will stick by thee, I can assure thee that. 'A will not   66
   out, 'a; 'tis true bred.   67
BARDOLPH   And I'll stick by him, sir.
SHALLOW   Why, there spoke a king. Lack nothing; be
   merry. (*One knocks at door.*) Look who's at door there,
   ho! Who knocks?   [*Davy goes to the door.*]
FALSTAFF [*To Silence, seeing him drinking*]   Why, now
   you have done me right.   73
SILENCE [*Sings*]
         "Do me right,
            And dub me knight,
               Samingo."
Is 't not so?   76
FALSTAFF   'Tis so.
SILENCE   Is 't so? Why then, say an old man can do
   somewhat.   80
DAVY [*Returning*]   An 't please your worship, there's
   one Pistol come from the court with news.
FALSTAFF   From the court? Let him come in.

         Enter Pistol.

How now, Pistol?
PISTOL   Sir John, God save you!
FALSTAFF   What wind blew you hither, Pistol?
PISTOL   Not the ill wind which blows no man to good.
   Sweet knight, thou art now one of the greatest men in
   this realm.
SILENCE   By 'r Lady, I think 'a be, but goodman Puff of   90
   Barson.
PISTOL   Puff?
   Puff i' thy teeth, most recreant coward base!   93
   Sir John, I am thy Pistol and thy friend,
   And helter-skelter have I rode to thee,

---

64 pottle pot two-quart tankard   **65 liggens** (Unexplained.)   **66–67 'A
will not out** he won't drop out of the drinking, or won't pass out (?)
73 done me right i.e., kept up with me in drinking   **76 Samingo** Sir
Mingo (from the Latin *mingo*, I urinate), the hero of the song
80 somewhat something   **90 but** except. (Silence interprets *greatest* in
the sense of "heaviest.")   **goodman** yeoman   **93 recreant** faithless

And tidings do I bring, and lucky joys,
And golden times, and happy news of price.   97
FALSTAFF I pray thee now, deliver them like a man of   98
this world.   99
PISTOL
A foutre for the world and worldlings base!   100
I speak of Africa and golden joys.   101
FALSTAFF
O base Assyrian knight, what is thy news?   102
Let King Cophetua know the truth thereof.   103
SILENCE [*Sings*]
    "And Robin Hood, Scarlet, and John."   104
PISTOL
Shall dunghill curs confront the Helicons?   105
And shall good news be baffled?   106
Then, Pistol, lay thy head in Furies' lap.
SHALLOW Honest gentleman, I know not your breed-   108
ing.   109
PISTOL Why then, lament therefor.   110
SHALLOW Give me pardon, sir. If, sir, you come with
news from the court, I take it there's but two ways,
either to utter them or conceal them. I am, sir, under
the King, in some authority.
PISTOL
Under which king, Besonian? Speak, or die.   115
SHALLOW
Under King Harry.
PISTOL   Harry the Fourth, or Fifth?
SHALLOW
Harry the Fourth.
PISTOL   A foutre for thine office!
Sir John, thy tender lambkin now is king;
Harry the Fifth's the man. I speak the truth.

---

97 price great value **98–99 man of this world** ordinary man **100 foutre**
(From the French *foutre*, fornicate; a very insulting phrase.) **101 Africa**
(Fabled for wealth.) **102 Assyrian** (Falstaff adopts Pistol's highflown style
and metrics.) **103 Cophetua** (King Cophetua married a beggar maid, according to the popular ballad "King Cophetua and the Beggar Maid.")
104 And . . . John (A scrap from another ballad.) **105 Helicons** i.e., poets.
(Mount Helicon was the abode of the Muses.) **106 baffled** disgraced
108–109 breeding parentage, rank **110 therefor** for that **115 Besonian**
low, beggarly rascal. (From Italian *bisogno*, need.)

When Pistol lies, do this, and fig me like   120
The bragging Spaniard.   [*Pistol makes a fig.*]

FALSTAFF What, is the old King dead?

PISTOL
As nail in door. The things I speak are just.   123

FALSTAFF Away, Bardolph! Saddle my horse. Master
Robert Shallow, choose what office thou wilt in the
land, 'tis thine. Pistol, I will double-charge thee with   126
dignities.

BARDOLPH O joyful day! I would not take a knighthood
for my fortune.

PISTOL What, I do bring good news?

FALSTAFF Carry Master Silence to bed. [*Exit Davy,
carrying Silence.*] Master Shallow, my lord Shallow—
be what thou wilt, I am fortune's steward—get on
thy boots. We'll ride all night. O sweet Pistol! Away,
Bardolph! [*Exit Bardolph.*] Come, Pistol, utter more to
me, and withal devise something to do thyself good.
Boot, boot, Master Shallow! I know the young King is
sick for me. Let us take any man's horses; the laws of
England are at my commandment. Blessed are they
that have been my friends, and woe to my Lord Chief
Justice!

PISTOL
Let vultures vile seize on his lungs also!
"Where is the life that late I led?" say they.   143
Why, here it is. Welcome these pleasant days!

                                        Exeunt.

✤

5.4 *Enter Beadle and three or four officers
[dragging in Hostess Quickly and Doll
Tearsheet].*

HOSTESS No, thou arrant knave! I would to God that I

---

120 fig insult with a vulgar gesture consisting in thrusting the thumb
between the index and middle fingers. (The gesture originated in Spain,
as l. 121 suggests. It means much the same as *foutre*, ll. 100 and 117.)
123 just true   **126 double-charge** (with a play on Pistol's name)
143 Where . . . led (Fragment of a ballad.)

5.4. Location: London. A street.

might die, that I might have thee hanged. Thou hast
drawn my shoulder out of joint.

BEADLE   The constables have delivered her over to me,
and she shall have whipping cheer, I warrant her. 5
There hath been a man or two lately killed about her. 6

DOLL   Nuthook, nuthook, you lie! Come on, I'll tell thee 7
what, thou damned tripe-visaged rascal, an the child I 8
go with do miscarry, thou wert better thou hadst
struck thy mother, thou paper-faced villain! 10

HOSTESS   O the Lord, that Sir John were come! He would
make this a bloody day to somebody. But I pray God
the fruit of her womb miscarry!

BEADLE   If it do, you shall have a dozen of cushions
again; you have but eleven now. Come, I charge you 15
both, go with me, for the man is dead that you and
Pistol beat amongst you.

DOLL   I'll tell you what, you thin man in a censer, I will 18
have you as soundly swinged for this—you bluebottle 19
rogue, you filthy famished correctioner, if you be not
swinged, I'll forswear half-kirtles. 21

BEADLE   Come, come, you she knight-errant, come. 22

HOSTESS   O God, that right should thus overcome 23
might! Well, of sufferance comes ease. 24

DOLL   Come, you rogue, come, bring me to a justice.

HOSTESS   Ay, come, you starved bloodhound.

DOLL   Goodman death, goodman bones!

HOSTESS   Thou atomy, thou! 28

DOLL   Come, you thin thing, come, you rascal! 29

BEADLE   Very well.   [*Exeunt.*]

❧

5 whipping cheer i.e., a whipping for supper   **6 about her** (1) in her company (2) on her account   **7 Nuthook** hook for pulling down branches in
nutting; here, a constable   **8, 10 tripe-visaged, paper-faced** (Allusions to the
pockmarked and sallow complexion of the Beadle.)   **15 eleven now** (The
Beadle accuses Doll of using one of the cushions to make her appear
pregnant; pregnant women were spared execution.)   **18 thin . . . censer** i.e.,
figure of a man on the lid of a censer or incense burner, embossed in low
relief   **19 swinged** thrashed.   **bluebottle** (An allusion to the Beadle's blue
coat.)   **21 half-kirtles** skirts   **22 she knight-errant** i.e., a woman who wan-
ders about and sins at night   **23–24 right . . . might** (The hostess gets this
backward.)   **24 sufferance** suffering. (Suffering now promises a better
future, since one's luck is bound to change.)   **28 atomy** (For *anatomy*,
skeleton; an *atomy* is an atom, speck.)   **29 rascal** lean deer

5.5   *Enter [Grooms as] strewers of rushes.*

FIRST GROOM   More rushes, more rushes!   1
SECOND GROOM   The trumpets have sounded twice.
THIRD GROOM   'Twill be two o'clock ere they come from
the coronation. Dispatch, dispatch.   [*Exeunt.*]   4

> *Trumpets sound, and the King and his train pass*
> *over the stage. After them enter Falstaff, Shallow,*
> *Pistol, Bardolph, and the Boy [Page].*

FALSTAFF   Stand here by me, Master Shallow; I will
make the King do you grace. I will leer upon him as   6
'a comes by, and do but mark the countenance that he
will give me.
PISTOL   God bless thy lungs, good knight!
FALSTAFF   Come here, Pistol, stand behind me.—O, if I
had had time to have made new liveries, I would have 11
bestowed the thousand pound I borrowed of you. But   12
'tis no matter; this poor show doth better. This doth 13
infer the zeal I had to see him.   14
SHALLOW   It doth so.
FALSTAFF   It shows my earnestness of affection—
SHALLOW   It doth so.
FALSTAFF   My devotion—
SHALLOW   It doth, it doth, it doth.
FALSTAFF   As it were, to ride day and night, and not to
deliberate, not to remember, not to have patience to
shift me—   22
SHALLOW   It is best, certain.
FALSTAFF   But to stand stained with travel, and sweating
with desire to see him, thinking of nothing else, put-
ting all affairs else in oblivion, as if there were nothing
else to be done but to see him.

5.5. Location: A public place near Westminster Abbey.
1 rushes floor coverings, here used for strewing the streets in the King's
path   4 Dispatch hurry   6 grace honor.   leer glance sideways and
invitingly   11 liveries uniforms of a noble or royal household
12 bestowed spent.   you i.e., Justice Shallow   13 poor show appearing
in inferior garments   14 infer imply   22 shift me change my apparel

PISTOL   'Tis *semper idem*, for *obsque hoc nihil est.*   28
'Tis all in every part.   29
SHALLOW   'Tis so, indeed.
PISTOL
My knight, I will inflame thy noble liver   31
And make thee rage.
Thy Doll, and Helen of thy noble thoughts,   33
Is in base durance and contagious prison,   34
Haled thither   35
By most mechanical and dirty hand.   36
Rouse up revenge from ebon den with fell Alecto's snake,   37
For Doll is in. Pistol speaks naught but truth.   38
FALSTAFF   I will deliver her.
          [*Shouts within, and the trumpets sound.*]
PISTOL
There roared the sea, and trumpet-clangor sounds.

          *Enter the King and his train, [the Lord Chief
          Justice among them].*

FALSTAFF
God save Thy Grace, King Hal, my royal Hal!
PISTOL
The heavens thee guard and keep, most royal imp of
fame!   42
FALSTAFF   God save thee, my sweet boy!
KING
My Lord Chief Justice, speak to that vain man.   44
CHIEF JUSTICE [*To Falstaff*]
Have you your wits? Know you what 'tis you speak?
FALSTAFF
My King! My Jove! I speak to thee, my heart!
KING
I know thee not, old man. Fall to thy prayers.

---

28 semper . . . est "always the same," for "without this there is nothing." (Pistol approvingly rephrases Falstaff's dedication to put his
loyalty to the Prince above all else.) *Obsque* is an error for *absque.*
29 'Tis . . . part (Perhaps a very free translation of the Latin.)   **31 liver**
(The seat of the passions.)   **33 Helen** i.e., Helen of Troy, the type of
womanly beauty   **34 durance** imprisonment.   **contagious** pestilential
35 Haled dragged   **36 mechanical** menial, base   **37 ebon** black.   **Alecto**
one of the Furies, who were depicted with snakes twined in their hair
38 in i.e., in prison   **42 imp** scion   **44 vain** foolish

How ill white hairs becomes a fool and jester!
I have long dreamt of such a kind of man,
So surfeit-swelled, so old, and so profane,   50
But being awaked I do despise my dream.
Make less thy body hence, and more thy grace;   52
Leave gormandizing. Know the grave doth gape   53
For thee thrice wider than for other men.
Reply not to me with a fool-born jest.
Presume not that I am the thing I was,
For God doth know, so shall the world perceive,
That I have turned away my former self;
So will I those that kept me company.
When thou dost hear I am as I have been,
Approach me, and thou shalt be as thou wast,
The tutor and the feeder of my riots.
Till then I banish thee, on pain of death,
As I have done the rest of my misleaders,
Not to come near our person by ten mile.
For competence of life I will allow you,   66
That lack of means enforce you not to evils.
And, as we hear you do reform yourselves,
We will, according to your strengths and qualities,
Give you advancement.—Be it your charge, my lord,
To see performed the tenor of our word.
Set on.   [*Exeunt King and his train.*]

FALSTAFF Master Shallow, I owe you a thousand
pound.

SHALLOW Yea, marry, Sir John, which I beseech you to
let me have home with me.

FALSTAFF That can hardly be, Master Shallow. Do not
you grieve at this. I shall be sent for in private to him.
Look you, he must seem thus to the world. Fear not
your advancements; I will be the man yet that shall
make you great.

SHALLOW I cannot well perceive how, unless you
should give me your doublet and stuff me out with
straw. I beseech you, good Sir John, let me have five
hundred of my thousand.

---

50 surfeit-swelled swollen from gluttony **52 hence** henceforth
53 gormandizing gluttonous eating **66 competence of life** modest
allowance

FALSTAFF   Sir, I will be as good as my word. This that
you heard was but a color.   87
SHALLOW   A color that I fear you will die in, Sir John.   88
FALSTAFF   Fear no colors. Go with me to dinner. Come,   89
Lieutenant Pistol, come, Bardolph. I shall be sent for
soon at night.   91

    Enter [the Lord Chief] Justice and Prince John [of
    Lancaster, with officers].

CHIEF JUSTICE
Go, carry Sir John Falstaff to the Fleet.   92
Take all his company along with him.
FALSTAFF   My lord, my lord—
CHIEF JUSTICE
I cannot now speak. I will hear you soon.
Take them away.
PISTOL
Si fortuna me tormenta, spero me contenta.   97
                Exeunt [all but Prince John
                  and the Chief Justice].

PRINCE JOHN
I like this fair proceeding of the King's.
He hath intent his wonted followers
Shall all be very well provided for,
But all are banished till their conversations   101
Appear more wise and modest to the world.
CHIEF JUSTICE   And so they are.
PRINCE JOHN
The King hath called his Parliament, my lord.
CHIEF JUSTICE   He hath.
PRINCE JOHN
I will lay odds that, ere this year expire,
We bear our civil swords and native fire   107
As far as France. I heard a bird so sing,

---

87 color pretense. (But Shallow uses the word to mean *collar*, hang-
man's noose.)   **88 die** (1) be hanged (2) be dyed   **89 colors** standards or
flags (of the enemy)   **91 soon at night** early in the evening   **92 Fleet** a
famous London prison   **97 Si . . . contenta** (See note on 2.4.179,
above.)   **101 conversations** conduct   **107 civil . . . fire** i.e., our weapons
used recently in civil war

Whose music, to my thinking, pleased the King.
Come, will you hence?   [*Exeunt.*]

❖

Epilogue

[*Enter Epilogue.*]

EPILOGUE

First, my fear; then, my curtsy; last, my speech. My 1
fear is your displeasure; my curtsy, my duty; and my
speech, to beg your pardons. If you look for a good
speech now, you undo me, for what I have to say is of
mine own making, and what indeed I should say will,
I doubt, prove mine own marring. But to the purpose, 6
and so to the venture. Be it known to you, as it is very
well, I was lately here in the end of a displeasing play, 8
to pray your patience for it and to promise you a better. I meant indeed to pay you with this, which, if like
an ill venture it come unluckily home, I break, and 11
you, my gentle creditors, lose. Here I promised you I
would be, and here I commit my body to your mer-
cies. Bate me some and I will pay you some and, as 14
most debtors do, promise you infinitely. And so I
kneel down before you—but, indeed, to pray for the
Queen.

If my tongue cannot entreat you to acquit me, will
you command me to use my legs? And yet that were
but light payment, to dance out of your debt. But a
good conscience will make any possible satisfaction,
and so would I. All the gentlewomen here have for-
given me. If the gentlemen will not, then the gentlemen do not agree with the gentlewomen, which was
never seen in such an assembly.

One word more, I beseech you. If you be not too
much cloyed with fat meat, our humble author will
continue the story, with Sir John in it, and make you 28
merry with fair Katharine of France. Where, for anything I know, Falstaff shall die of a sweat, unless al- 30

Epilogue
1 curtsy bow, obeisance **6 doubt** fear **8 displeasing play** (No satisfac-
tory identification has ever been made.) **11 ill venture** unlucky sending
out of merchant vessels. **break** (1) break my promise (2) become bank-
rupt **14 Bate me some** let me off from some portion of the debt
28 Sir John in it (Shakespeare evidently originally intended to introduce
Falstaff into *Henry V*; instead, only his death is reported there in 2.1 and
2.3.) **30 sweat** i.e., plague, fever, or venereal disease

ready 'a be killed with your hard opinions; for Oldcas- 31
tle died a martyr, and this is not the man. My tongue 32
is weary; when my legs are too, I will bid you good
night.   [*Dance, and exit Epilogue.*]

31–32 Oldcastle . . . man i.e., Falstaff was not intended to resemble Sir
John Oldcastle, the Lollard venerated by sixteenth-century Puritans as a
martyr for their beliefs. (This statement may have been intended to
placate Lord Cobham, descendant of Oldcastle, whose resentment of
Shakespeare's use of the Oldcastle name in an earlier version of the
Henry IV plays may have led to the change of the name to Falstaff.)

Date and Text

"The second parte of the history of Kinge Henry the iiijth with the humours of Sir John Fallstaff: Wrytten by master Shakespere" was entered in the Stationers' Register, the official record book of the London Company of Stationers (booksellers and printers), by Andrew Wise and William Aspley on August 23, 1600. (This is the first time Shakespeare's name appeared in the Stationers' Register.) The quarto was published later that year as

> THE Second part of Henrie the fourth, continuing to his death, *and coronation of Henrie* the fift. With the humours of sir Iohn Fal*staffe, and swaggering* Pistoll. *As it hath been sundrie times publikely* acted by the right honourable, the Lord Chamberlaine his seruants. *Written by William Shakespeare*. LONDON Printed by V. S. [Valentine Sims] for Andrew Wise, and William Aspley. 1600.

One scene, 3.1, was omitted from Sims's first printing [Qa] of this quarto, whereupon Sims reset two leaves as four new leaves [Qb] including not only the omitted 3.1, but 2.4.340–389 and 3.2.1–104. Qb is therefore the best copy text for 3.1 and Qa for those portions that were reset. In addition, still other passages were omitted from both versions of the 1600 quarto; they were later restored in or added to the First Folio. No further quartos appeared prior to the First Folio of 1623—an odd fact in view of *1 Henry IV*'s continued popularity, but perhaps the result of a large printing of *2 Henry IV* in anticipation of heavy sales. At any rate, this quarto text seems to have been based on Shakespeare's papers and was a reliable one except for some substantial omissions and for some misreadings owing to the compositors' difficulty in reading an authorial manuscript that may have been unfinished. Speech prefixes are at times quite irregular, indicative of author's papers before they have received the attentions of the prompter. Of the omitted passages, some may have been the result of shortening for performance, but some suggest political censorship. Others suggest authorial revision. The Folio text restores or adds the omitted readings.

The relationship of Folio to quarto text is extraordinarily

difficult to determine. Perhaps the Folio compositors were using a manuscript that had been transcribed either from an extensively annotated copy of the quarto or from a quarto and a manuscript source jointly compared. Another hypothesis is that the copy for the Folio was made up from actors' parts. The Folio copy was in any case a strange transcript, showing perhaps some stage influence and possibly used as a promptbook but less adequately provided with stage directions than most promptbooks; perhaps the scribe imposed certain literary features. It seems to have been a special case. George Walton Williams (*Shakespeare Studies* 9:173) speculates that it was an edited transcript of a promptbook prepared for Lord Cobham. Whatever its identity, it embodied tendencies toward sophistication and regularization that frequently render the Folio readings less authoritative than those of the quarto. The Folio text does restore the passages excised from the quarto, however, and on other occasions as well it provides what appear to be authentic corrections of and authorial additions to the quarto. The quarto text is generally the most authoritative when it is not manifestly in error or lacking material found in the Folio, but the Folio corrections and additions have to be regarded with close attention.

Like *1 Henry IV, Part Two* shows signs of revision in the use of characters' names, most notably that of Falstaff. Plainly the original version of both plays called him Sir John Oldcastle, after one of the prince's companions in the anonymous *Famous Victories of Henry the Fifth* (c. 1588). The speech prefix "Old." is left standing at 1.2.119 in the quarto of *2 Henry IV*, and in *1 Henry IV* Falstaff is jokingly referred to as "my old lad of the castle" (1.2.41). Moreover, there are several contemporary allusions to a play about a fat knight named Oldcastle. Apparently Henry Brooke, Lord Cobham, a living descendant of the Lollard martyr Oldcastle of Henry V's reign, took umbrage at the profane use Shakespeare had made of this revered name, whereupon Shakespeare's company shifted to another less controversial name from the chronicles, Sir John Fastolfe (called "Falstaffe" in the Folio text of Shakespeare's *1 Henry VI* and assigned a cowardly role in the French wars of that play). The revision also changed the names of Oldcastle's cronies from Harvey and Russell to Peto and Bardolph.

Cobham was Lord Chamberlain from July 1596 until his death in March 1597, during which interval Shakespeare's company bore the name of Lord Hunsdon's men. Quite possibly the difficulty over the name Oldcastle erupted during that period, for *1 Henry IV* seems to have been written and performed in late 1596 and early 1597, not long after Shakespeare had finished *Richard II* (c. 1595–1596). *2 Henry IV* must have been written before the end of 1598, so that Shakespeare could then begin *Henry V* in early 1599. Since *2 Henry IV* was originally written using the names Oldcastle, Harvey, and Russell, however, there is reason to date it somewhat earlier, in 1597, before the squabble over the names broke out. Scholars who prefer a date in 1597 for *The Merry Wives* also date *2 Henry IV* early in 1597, since it appears to have introduced Shallow and Pistol before they appeared in *The Merry Wives*. Francis Meres refers in 1598 to "*Henry the* 4" without specifying one or two parts. Publication of *1 Henry IV* in 1598 assured the Elizabethan public that the changes in names to Falstaff, Peto, and Bardolph had taken place; a revised epilogue to the 1600 quarto of *2 Henry IV* protests that "Oldcastle died a martyr, and this [Falstaff] is not the man," as though by way of apology or disclaimer. A play defending the reputation of the Lollard Oldcastle and attacking Falstaff, called *The History of the Life of Sir John Oldcastle, Lord Cobham, with his Martyrdom*, had been performed by the rival Admiral's men in 1599.

Textual Notes

These textual notes are not a historical collation, either of the early quarto and the early folios or of more recent editions; they are simply a record of departures in this edition from the copy text. The reading adopted in this edition appears in boldface, followed by the rejected reading from the copy text, i.e., the quarto of 1600. Only major alterations in punctuation are noted. Changes in lineation are not indicated, nor are some minor and obvious typographical errors.

Abbreviations used:
F the First Folio
Q the quarto of 1600
s.d. stage direction
s.p. speech prefix

Copy text: the quarto of 1600, of which 2.4.340 through 3.2.104 exists in two states: the original printing by Valentine Sims [Qa], and a second version with six reset pages [Qb] that had been expanded to include 3.1, inadvertently omitted from Qa. Qa is the copy text for those portions that were reset, Qb for 3.1 itself. In addition, the First Folio is copy text for certain passages excised from Q, as indicated below.

The Actors' Names [taken from F, at the end of the play]

Induction.1. s.p. Rumor [not in Q]   **35 hold** hole   **36 Where** [F] When
40 s.d. Rumor Rumours

1.1. 7 s.d. [and elsewhere] **Northumberland** Earle   **27 s.d.** [at l. 25 in Q]
41 ill [F] bad   **96 slain, say so** [F] slain   **161 s.p. Lord Bardolph** Vmfr
162 [assigned to Bard. in Q and F]   **164 Lean on your** [F] Leaue on you
166–179; 189–209 [F; not in Q]   **178 brought** bring [F]   **183 ventured, for . . .
proposed** ventured for . . . proposed,

1.2. 1 s.p. [and elsewhere] **Falstaff** Iohn [or sir Iohn]   **21 one of** [F] one off
31 s.p. [and elsewhere] **Page** Boy   **36 rascally** [F] rascall   **48 Where's Bardolph** [F; in Q, follows "through it" in l. 47]   **49 into** [F] in   **96 age** [F] an
ague   **119 s.p. Falstaff** [F] Old   **142 slenderer** [F] slender   **159 on** [F] in
171 this [F] his   **171–172 them, are** [F] the one   **177 s.p.** [and elsewhere]
Chief Justice Lo   **192 ear** yeere   **201–202 you and Prince Harry** [F] you

1.3. s.d. Hastings Hastings, Fauconbridge   **1 s.p.** [and elsewhere] **Archbishop**
Bishop   **5 s.p. Mowbray** Marsh   **21–24, 36–55, 85–108** [F; not in Q]   **26 case**
[F] cause   **28 on** [F] and   **58 one** [F] on   **59 through** [F] thorough   **66 a** [F]
so   **71 Are** [F] And   **79 To French** French   **84 'gainst** [F] against
109 s.p. Mowbray [F] Bish

2.1. 21 vice [F] view   **25 continuantly** [F] continually   **43 Sir John, I** [F] I
71–72 all, all [F] all   **102 mad** [F] made   **117 done** [F] done with
143 German Iarman   **145 tapestries** [F] tapestrie   **163 s.d. Exeunt** exit [at
l. 160 in Q]   **167, 171 s.p. Gower** Mess   **167 Basingstoke** [F] Billingsgate

2.2. s.d. Poins Poynes, sir Iohn Russel   **others** other   **15 viz.** [F] with
16 ones [F] once   **21–22 made a shift to eat** [F] eate   **75 e'en now** enow

81 rabbit rabble   **90 him be** [F] him   **109 borrower's** borrowed
119 s.p. Prince [Reads] [not in Q or F]   **125 familiars** [F] family

2.3. 5 s.p. [and elsewhere] Lady Northumberland Wife   **9 s.p. [and else-
where] Lady Percy** Kate   **11 endeared** [F] endeere   **23–45 He . . . grave**
[F; not in Q]

2.4. 4 s.p. Second Drawer Draw   **12 s.d.** [at l. 18 in Q]   **13 s.p. Third Drawer**
Dra [also at l. 19]   **21 s.p. Second Drawer** [F] Francis   **22 s.p. [and else-
where] Hostess** Quickly   **30 s.p. [and elsewhere] Doll** Tere   **42–43 them; I**
[F] I   **49 know; to** know to   **62 s.p. Doll** Dorothy   **83 swagger, 'a** swaggrer
107 s.d. Boy Bardolfes boy   **172 Die men** [F] Men   **189 Quoit** Quaite
196 Untwine vntwinde   **215 Ah, rogue** a rogue   **219 A rascally** Ah rascally
252 the scales [F] scales   **253 avoirdupois** haber de poiz   **257 poll** poule
265 master's [F] master   **275 It** [F] a   **278 so** [F] to   **300 even now** [F] now
313 Not? To Not to   **340–389** [copy text for this passage is Qa]   **381 s.d. Exit**
[Qb; not in Qa]

3.1 [this scene appears in Qb, not in Qa]   **18 mast** [F] masse   **22 billows** [F]
pillowes   **26 thy** [F] them   **27 sea-boy** [F] season   **36 letters** letter   **59 years**
[F] yeare   **81 nature of** [F] natures or   **85 beginnings** [F] beginning   **87 of**
[F] or

3.2. 1–104 [copy text for this passage is Qa]   **23 bona-robas** [F] bona robes
39 Stamford [F] Samforth   **45 fine** [Qb, F] fiue   **56 s.p. Shallow** [F] Bardolfe
[Qa uncorr.; not in Qa corr. or Qb]   **67–68 accommodated** [F] accommodate
82 s.p. Shallow Iust [Qa]   **87 Surecard** [F] Soccard   **111 s.p. and text Falstaff Prick him** [Q prints as s.d.: "Iohn prickes him"]   **144 for his** [F] for
175 prick me [F] prick   **195–196 good . . . that** [F] master Shallow
209 Clement's Inn [F] Clemham   **229–230 old dame's** [F] dames
250 Shadow Sadow   **271 traverse** trauers   **272 Thus, thus, thus** thas, thas,
thas   **287 will** wooll   **298 s.d. Exeunt** Exit   **299–331 On . . . end** [this speech
assigned in Q to Shallow]   **312 invisible** inuincible   **genius** gemies
314 ever [F] ouer   **324 eelskin** [F, Q corr.] eele-shin [Q uncorr.]   **326 be** [F]
he

4.1. 1 s.p. [and elsewhere] Archbishop Bish   **9 tenor** tenure   **12 could** [F, Q
corr.] would [Q uncorr.]   **30 Then, my lord** [F, Q corr.; not in Q uncorr.]
34 rags rage   **36 appeared** appeare   **45 figure** [F, Q corr.] figures [Q uncorr.]
55–79 [F; not in Q]   **103–139 O my . . . King** [F; not in Q]   **93, 95 And . . .
edge, To . . . cruelty** [Q uncorr.; not in Q corr. or F]   **116 force** forc'd [F]
139 indeed and did [F]   **175 to our** [F] our   **180 And** At

4.2. s.d. [appears at 4.1.226 in Q]   **8 Than** [F] That   **man** [F] man talking
19 imagined imagine   **24 Employ** [F] Imply   **48 this** [F] his   **67 s.p. Prince
John** [F; not in Q]   **69 s.p. Hastings** [F] Prince   **97 s.d.** [at l. 96 in Q]
122 these traitors [F] this traitour

4.3. s.d. [Q: "Alarum. Enter Falstaffe. excursions"]   **25 s.d. retreat** [at l. 23 in
Q]   **41 I came** [F] there cosin, I came   **85 had but** had

4.4. s.d. Warwick Warwike, Kent   **32 melting** [F] meeting   **51 s.p. [and
elsewhere] Clarence** Tho   **80 s.d. Enter Westmorland** [after l. 80 in Q]
94 heaven [F] heauens   **104 write** [F] wet   **letters** [F] termes   **112 s.p. [and
elsewhere] Gloucester** Hum

4.5. 13 altered [F, Q corr.] vttred [Q uncorr.] **75 The virtuous sweets** [F; not in Q] **76 thighs** [F] thigh **79 s.d.** [at l. 81 in Q] **81 have** hands [Q] hath [F] **88 s.d.** [at l. 87 in Q] **91 s.p. Prince** Harry **107 Which** [F] Whom **160 worst of** [F] worse then **161 carat, is** [F] karrat **177 O my son** [F; not in Q] **178 it in** [F] in **204 my** thy **220 My gracious liege** [F; not in Q] **226 s.p. [and elsewhere] Prince John** Lanc

5.1. 23 lost the other day [F] lost **Hinckley** [F] Hunkly **56 all my** [F] my **65 of him** [F] him

5.2. s.d. [Q: "Enter Warwike, duke Humphrey, L. chiefe Iustice, Thomas Clarence, Prince, Iohn Westmarland"] **13 s.d. Westmorland** [at o.s.d. in Q] **21 s.p. Gloucester, Clarence** Prin. ambo **44 s.p. [and elsewhere] King** Prince **46 mix** mixt **62 s.p. Princes** Bro **127 rase** race **145 s.d. Exeunt** exit

5.3. 5–6 a goodly . . . a rich goodly . . . rich **47 thee** the **70 s.d.** [at l. 68 in Q] **83 s.d.** [after l. 82 in Q] **93 i' thy** ith thy **103 Cophetua** Couetua **128 knighthood** [F] Knight **144 s.d. Exeunt** exit

5.4. s.d. Beadle Sincklo **4 s.p. [and throughout scene] Beadle** Sincklo **6 lately killed** [F] kild **7 s.p. [and throughout scene] Doll** [F] Whoore **11 He** [F] I

5.5. 1 s.p. First Groom 1 [and similarly in ll. 2 and 3] **15 s.p. Shallow** [F] Pist **17, 19 s.p. Shallow** Pist [Q, F] **24 s.p. Falstaff** [F; not in Q] **29 all in** in **71 our** [F] my **82 cannot well** [F] cannot **83 should give** [F] giue **97 me** [F; not in Q]

Epilogue 32 died a [F] died

Shakespeare's Sources

As in the case of *1 Henry IV*, Shakespeare's chief historical source for *2 Henry IV* is the 1587 edition of Raphael Holinshed's *Chronicles*. Samuel Daniel's *Civil Wars* provides less pertinent material here than for *1 Henry IV*, so that Shakespeare is particularly indebted to Holinshed for historical information about the rebels' grievances, negotiations with the rebel leaders, King Henry IV's illness and death, and the Prince's succession to the throne. Changes are nonetheless prominent and telling. Shakespeare condenses time, giving an impression of failing health on the part of King Henry IV almost immediately after Shrewsbury, whereas historically the King reigned vigorously for ten years after that battle. The Earl of Northumberland is presented as more "crafty-sick" than in Holinshed, and Prince John, too, is shown in a disagreeable light by his cold-blooded handling of negotiations that in Holinshed are the responsibility of the Earl of Westmorland; Shakespeare thus tarnishes the integrity of both sides, accentuating (as he does also in the Induction spoken by Rumor) a mood of cynicism and world-weariness. The theme of nemesis for Henry IV's usurpation is touched upon in *2 Henry IV*, as in Daniel, and Henry is accordingly plagued by sleeplessness and mournful reflection.

Like Shakespeare's first play about Prince Hal, *2 Henry IV* makes extensive use of legends of Hal's wild youth. Some are from John Stow's *Chronicles of England* (1588) and *Annals of England* (1592). Sir Thomas Elyot's *The Governor* (1531) is the ultimate source of an account of Hal's boxing the ear of the Lord Chief Justice. Shakespeare evidently knew *The Governor* at first hand, though he could also have found the story reproduced almost verbatim in Stow; by the 1590s it was widely circulated. Shakespeare certainly used the anonymous play (usually attributed to Richard Tarleton or Samuel Rowley) called *The Famous Victories of Henry the Fifth*, usually dated around 1587–1588, a selection of which follows. He had already used parts of this play for *1 Henry IV*. In *Famous Victories* Shakespeare found a dramatization of the famous blow to the Lord Chief Justice's

ear, interpreted there as a blow for freedom and against authority. He found also a vivid account of Hal's entry into his
father's death chamber and the final reconciliation of
father and son, followed by the coronation and the young
king's rejection of his disreputable companions, Sir John
Oldcastle, Tom, and Ned; they are banished beyond a ten-
mile limit, though the new king will assist them if they behave. The anonymous play then goes on to King Henry's
successful campaign against the French, as dramatized in
Henry V.

Shakespeare's changes are as significant as his extensive
borrowings. He mutes the parricidal suggestions of Hal's
interview with his dying father; in the anonymous play Hal
can hardly wait to see his father in the grave. Shakespeare
greatly expands the tavern scenes, with an added emphasis
on Falstaff's age and dissipation; new characters such as
Pistol and Doll Tearsheet, with their rowdiness and colorful
vituperation, surround Falstaff with signs of his increasing
isolation from Hal. The venal country justices, Shallow and
Silence, have no counterparts in *Famous Victories*, though
that play does show a scene of farcical recruitment. Most of
all, Shakespeare has immeasurably added to the humor
and pathos of his chief comic character. Sir John Oldcastle
of the anonymous play is a minor figure whose banishment
at King Henry V's coronation is simply an appropriate gesture of the new king's reform. The characterization of Falstaff owes something to many traditional stage types,
including the Vice of the morality play and the cowardly
braggart soldier of classical comedy, but the richness and
complexity are Shakespeare's own.

The Third Volume of Chronicles (1587 edition)
Compiled by Raphael Holinshed

HENRY THE FOURTH

[After the defeat of the rebel forces and the death of Hotspur at the Battle of Shrewsbury in 1403, the Earl of Northumberland withdraws to Warkworth Castle to consider his next moves. A new conspiracy against King Henry surfaces in 1405.]

But at the same time, to his further disquieting, there was a conspiracy put in practice against him at home by the Earl of Northumberland, who had conspired with Richard Scroop, Archbishop of York; Thomas Mowbray, Earl Marshal, son to Thomas, Duke of Norfolk, who for the quarrel betwixt him and King Henry had been banished, as ye have heard; the Lords Hastings, Faulconbridge, Bardolph, and divers others. It was appointed that they should meet all together with their whole power upon Yorkswold, at a day assigned, and that the Earl of Northumberland should be chieftain, promising to bring with him a great number of Scots. The Archbishop, accompanied with the Earl Marshal, devised certain articles of such matters as it was supposed that not only the commonalty of the realm but also the nobility found themselves grieved with, which articles they showed first unto such of their adherents as were near about them and after sent them abroad to their friends further off, assuring them that for redress of such oppressions they would shed the last drop of blood in their bodies, if need were.

The Archbishop, not meaning to stay after he saw himself accompanied with a great number of men that came flocking to York to take his part in this quarrel, forthwith discovered[1] his enterprise, causing the articles aforesaid to be set up in the public streets of the city of York and upon the gates of the monasteries, that each man might understand the cause that moved him to rise in arms against the King,

---

1 discovered made public

the reforming whereof did not yet appertain unto him. Hereupon knights, esquires, gentlemen, yeomen, and other of the commons as well of the city, towns, and countries about, being allured either for desire of change or else for desire to see a reformation in such things as were mentioned in the articles, assembled together in great numbers. And the Archbishop, coming forth amongst them clad in armor, encouraged, exhorted, and by all means he could pricked them forth to take the enterprise in hand and manfully to continue in their begun purpose, promising forgiveness of sins to all them whose hap it was to die in the quarrel. And thus not only all the citizens of York but all other in the countries about that were able to bear weapon came to the Archbishop and the Earl Marshal. Indeed, the respect that men had to the Archbishop caused them to like the better of the cause, since the gravity of his age, his integrity of life and incomparable learning, with the reverent aspect of his amiable personage, moved all men to have him in no small estimation.

The King, advertised[2] of these matters, meaning to prevent them, left his journey into Wales and marched with all speed towards the north parts. Also, Ralph Neville, Earl of Westmorland, that was not far off, together with the Lord John of Lancaster, the King's son, being informed of this rebellious attempt, assembled together such power as they might make and, together with those which were appointed to attend on the said Lord John to defend the borders against the Scots (as the Lord Henry Fitzhugh, the Lord Ralph Evers, the Lord Robert Umfrevile, and others), made forward against the rebels and, coming into a plain within the forest of Gaultree, caused their standards to be pitched down in like sort as the Archbishop had pitched his, over against them,[3] being far stronger in number of people than the other, for, as some write, there were of the rebels at the least twenty thousand men.

When the Earl of Westmorland perceived the force of the adversaries, and that they lay still and attempted not to

---

2 advertised advised, informed   **3 caused . . . them** had their ensigns or banners erected on flagpoles stuck in the ground in the same manner as the Archbishop had erected his, facing opposite

come forward upon him, he subtly devised how to quail[4] their purpose and forthwith dispatched messengers unto the Archbishop to understand the cause, as it were, of that great assembly and for what cause, contrary to the King's peace, they came so in armor. The Archbishop answered that he took nothing in hand against the King's peace,[5] but that whatsoever he did tended rather to advance the peace and quiet of the commonwealth than otherwise. And where he and his company were in arms, it was for fear of the King, to whom he could have no free access by reason of such a multitude of flatterers as were about him. And therefore he maintained that his purpose[6] to be good and profitable, as well for the King himself as for the realm, if men were willing to understand a truth. And herewith he showed forth a scroll in which the articles were written whereof before ye have heard.

The messengers, returning to the Earl of Westmorland, showed him[7] what they had heard and brought from the Archbishop. When he had read the articles, he showed in word and countenance outwardly that he liked of[8] the Archbishop's holy and virtuous intent and purpose, promising that he and his would prosecute[9] the same in assisting the Archbishop, who, rejoicing hereat, gave credit to[10] the Earl and persuaded the Earl Marshal (against his will, as it were) to go with him to a place appointed for them to commune[11] together. Here, when they were met with like number on either part,[12] the articles were read over, and without any more ado, the Earl of Westmorland and those that were with him agreed to do their best to see that a reformation might be had according to the same.

The Earl of Westmorland, using more policy[13] than the rest,[14] "Well," said he, "then our travail is come to the wished end; and where[15] our people have been long in armor, let them depart home to their wonted trades and occu-

---

4 quail destroy, frustrate. (Possibly *quell*, crush, though the text reads "quaile.")   **5 took . . . peace** had no business in hand inimical to the peace of the realm   **6 that his purpose** that purpose of his   **7 showed him** revealed to him   **8 liked of** liked   **9 prosecute** pursue, follow up   **10 gave credit to** believed   **11 commune** talk   **12 part** side   **13 policy** cunning   **14 the rest** i.e., the others who were there   **15 where** whereas

pations. In the meantime, let us drink together in sign of
agreement, that the people on both sides may see it and
know that it is true that we be light at a point."[16] They had
no sooner shaken hands together but that a knight was sent
straightways from the Archbishop to bring word to the people that there was peace concluded, commanding each man
to lay aside his arms and to resort home to their houses.
The people, beholding such tokens of peace as shaking of
hands, and drinking together of the lords in loving manner,
they, being already wearied with the unaccustomed travail
of war, brake up their field[17] and returned homewards. But
in the meantime, whilst the people of the Archbishop's side
withdrew away, the number of the contrary part increased,
according to order given by the Earl of Westmorland. And
yet the Archbishop perceived not that he was deceived until
the Earl of Westmorland arrested both him and the Earl
Marshal with divers other. Thus saith Walsingham.[18]

But others write somewhat otherwise of this matter, affirming that the Earl of Westmorland, indeed, and the Lord
Ralph Evers procured[19] the Archbishop and the Earl Marshal to come to a communication with them upon a ground
just in the midway betwixt both the armies, where the Earl
of Westmorland in talk declared to them how perilous[20] an
enterprise they had taken in hand so to raise the people and
to move[21] war against the King, advising them therefore to
submit themselves without further delay unto the King's
mercy and his son the Lord John, who was present there in
the field with banners spread, ready to try the matter by
dint of sword if they refused this counsel. And therefore he
willed them to remember themselves well, and, if they
would not yield and crave the King's pardon, he bade them
do their best to defend themselves.

Hereupon as well the Archbishop as[22] the Earl Marshal
submitted themselves unto the King and to his son the Lord
John that was there present and returned not to their army.
Whereupon their troops skailed[23] and fled their ways, but

---

16 **be light at a point** have come to an agreement   17 **field** order of
battle   18 **Walsingham** Thomas Walsingham, historian, author of
Historia Anglicana, 1418   19 **procured** induced   20 **perilous** (with the
suggestion also of *parlous*, harmful and mischievous as well as dangerous)   21 **move** urge   22 **as well ... as** both ... and   23 **skailed** scattered, dispersed

being pursued, many were taken, many slain, and many spoiled[24] of that that they had about them and so permitted to go their ways. Howsoever the matter was handled, true it is that the Archbishop and the Earl Marshal were brought to Pomfret to the King, who in this meanwhile was advanced thither with his power, and from thence he went to York, whither the prisoners were also brought, and there beheaded the morrow after Whitsunday[25] in a place without[26] the city; that is to understand, the Archbishop himself, the Earl Marshal, Sir John Lampley, and Sir Robert Plumpton. Unto all which persons though indemnity were promised, yet was the same to none of them at any hand performed. By the issue hereof,[27] I mean the death of the foresaid, but specially of the Archbishop, the prophecy of a sickly canon[28] of Bridlington in Yorkshire fell out to be true, who darkly enough foretold this matter and the infortunate event thereof in these words hereafter following, saying:

> Pacem tractabunt, sed fraudem subter arabunt,
> Pro nulla marca, salvabitur ille hierarcha.[29]

The Archbishop suffered death very constantly,[30] insomuch as the common people took it he died a martyr, affirming that certain miracles were wrought as well in the field where he was executed as also in the place where he was buried. And immediately upon such bruits,[31] both men and women began to worship his dead carcass, whom they loved so much when he was alive, till they were forbidden by the King's friends and for fear gave over to visit the place of his sepulture. The Earl Marshal's body, by the King's leave, was buried in the cathedral church, many lamenting his destiny. But his head was set on a pole aloft on the walls for a certain space, till by the King's permission (after the same had suffered many a hot, sunny day and many a wet shower of rain) it was taken down and buried together with the body.

---

24 spoiled plundered   **25 Whitsunday** the seventh Sunday after Easter
26 without outside of   **27 issue hereof** consequence of this   **28 canon** a
clergyman living in a clergy house and abiding by the canons of the
Church   **29 Pacem . . . hierarcha** they will sue for peace but foster
secret deceit; that bishop will not be saved for all his distinction
30 constantly resolutely   **31 bruits** rumors

After the King, accordingly as seemed to him good, had ransomed and punished by grievous fines the citizens of York which had borne armor on their Archbishop's side against him, he departed from York with an army of thirty-and-seven thousand fighting men furnished with all provision necessary, marching northwards against the Earl of Northumberland. At his coming to Durham, the Lord Hastings, the Lord Falconbridge, Sir John Coleville of the Dale, and Sir John Griffith, being convicted of the conspiracy, were there beheaded.

[The Earl of Northumberland and the Lord Bardolph rise against King Henry again in 1408. Northumberland is slain in battle and Bardolph is so wounded that he dies shortly thereafter. Glendower dies in 1409. King Henry and his son are reconciled in 1412, in a scene that Shakespeare uses primarily for *1 Henry IV* rather than for *2 Henry IV*. That same year, troubled and in ill health, Henry unsuccessfully plans a crusade to the Holy Land.]

In this fourteenth and last year of King Henry's reign, a council was holden in the Whitefriars in London, at the which, among other things, order was taken for ships and galleys to be builded and made ready and all other things necessary to be provided for a voyage which he meant to make into the Holy Land, there to recover the city of Jerusalem from the infidels. For it grieved him to consider the great malice of Christian princes that were bent upon a mischievous purpose to destroy one another, to the peril of their own souls, rather than to make war against the enemies of the Christian faith, as in conscience (it seemed to him) they were bound. He held his Christmas this year at Eltham, being sore vexed with sickness, so that it was thought sometimes that he had been dead. Notwithstanding, it pleased God that he somewhat recovered his strength again and so passed that Christmas with as much joy as he might.

The morrow after Candlemas Day[32] began a Parliament, which he had called at London, but he departed this life be-

---

fore the same Parliament was ended, for now that his provisions were ready and that he was furnished with sufficient treasure, soldiers, captains, victuals, munitions, tall ships, strong galleys, and all things necessary for such a royal journey as he pretended[33] to take into the Holy Land, he was eftsoons[34] taken with a sore sickness, which was not a leprosy stricken[35] by the hand of God (saith Master Hall),[36] as foolish friars imagined, but a very apoplexy of the which he languished till his appointed hour and had none other grief nor malady; so that what man ordaineth, God altereth at his good will and pleasure, not giving place more to the prince than to the poorest creature living, when He seeth His time to dispose of him this way or that, as to His omnipotent power and divine providence seemeth expedient. During this his last sickness, he caused his crown, as some write, to be set on a pillow at his bed's head, and suddenly his pangs so sore troubled him that he lay as though all his vital spirits had been from him departed. Such as were about him, thinking verily that he had been departed, covered his face with a linen cloth.

The Prince, his son, being hereof advertised, entered into the chamber, took away the crown, and departed. The father, being suddenly revived out of that trance, quickly perceived the lack of his crown and, having knowledge that the Prince his son had taken it away, caused him to come before his presence, requiring of him what he meant, so to misuse himself. The Prince with a good audacity answered, "Sir, to mine and all men's judgments you seemed dead in this world, wherefore I, as your next heir apparent, took that as mine own and not as yours." "Well, fair son," said the King with a great sigh, "what right I had to it, God knoweth." "Well," said the Prince, "if you die king, I will have the garland and trust to keep it with the sword against all mine enemies, as you have done." "Then," said the King, "I commit all to God, and remember you to do well." With that he turned himself in his bed and shortly after departed to God in a chamber of the Abbot's of Westminster

---

33 pretended intended   **34 eftsoons** again   **35 stricken** inflicted
36 Master Hall Edward Hall, author of *The Union of the Two Noble and Illustre Families of Lancaster and York* (1542)

called "Jerusalem." .... He was so suddenly and grievously taken that such as were about him feared lest he would have died presently,[37] wherefore to relieve him (if it were possible) they bare him into a chamber that was next at hand, belonging to the Abbot of Westminster, where they laid him on a pallet before the fire and used all remedies to revive him. At length he recovered his speech, and understanding and perceiving himself in a strange place which he knew not, he willed to know if the chamber had any particular name, whereunto answer was made that it was called "Jerusalem." "Then," said the King, "lauds be given to the Father of Heaven, for now I know that I shall die here in this chamber, according to the prophecy of me declared that I should depart this life in Jerusalem."

Whether this was true that so he spake, as one that gave too much credit to foolish prophecies and vain tales, or whether it was feigned, as in such cases it commonly happeneth, we leave it to the advised reader to judge.

[King Henry's son and heir, Henry V, receives the homage of his new subjects.]

He was crowned the ninth of April, being Passion Sunday, which was a sore, ruggy,[38] and tempestuous day, with wind, snow, and sleet, that men greatly marveled thereat, making divers interpretations what the same might signify. But this King, even at first appointing with himself to show that in his person princely honors should change public manners, he determined to put on him the shape of a new man. For whereas aforetime he had made himself a companion unto misruly mates of dissolute order and life, he now banished them all from his presence (but not unrewarded or else unpreferred), inhibiting[39] them upon a great pain not once to approach, lodge, or sojourn within ten miles of his court or presence; and in their places he chose men of gravity, wit, and high policy, by whose wise counsel he might at all times rule to his honor and dignity, calling to mind how once, to

37 presently immediately   **38 ruggy** stormy, wild   **39 inhibiting** prohibiting

high offense of the King his father, he had with his fist
stricken the Chief Justice for sending one of his minions
(upon desert) to prison, when the Justice stoutly com-
manded himself also straight to ward, and he (then Prince)
obeyed.

The second edition of Raphael Holinshed's *Chronicles* was published in
1587. This selection is based on that edition, Volume 3, folios 529–543.

The Famous Victories of Henry the Fifth, Containing the Honorable Battle of Agincourt

[The play's first two scenes, in which Prince Henry takes part in a robbery and carouses with Sir John Oldcastle and other tavern mates, are materials for *1 Henry IV* and are printed as sources for that play.]

[Scene 3]   *Enter Henry the Fourth, with the Earl of Exeter and the Lord of Oxford.*

OXFORD   An[1] please Your Majesty, here is my Lord Mayor and the Sheriff of London to speak with Your Majesty.

KING   Admit them to our presence.

   Enter the Mayor and the Sheriff.

Now, my good Lord Mayor of London, the cause of my sending for you at this time is to tell you of a matter which I have learned of my Council. Herein I understand that you have committed my son to prison without our leave and license. What? Although he be a rude youth and likely to give occasion, yet you might have considered that he is a prince, and my son, and not to be haled[2] to prison by every subject.

MAYOR   May it please Your Majesty to give us leave to tell our tale?

KING   Or else God forbid! Otherwise, you might think me an unequal judge, having more affection to my son than to any rightful judgment.

MAYOR   Then I do not doubt but we shall rather deserve commendations at Your Majesty's hands than any anger.

KING   Go to. Say on.

MAYOR   Then, if it please Your Majesty, this night betwixt two and three of the clock in the morning my lord the young Prince, with a very disordered company, came to the old tavern in Eastcheap. And whether it was that their music

Scene 3. Location: The royal court of England.
1 An if it   2 haled dragged

liked[3] them not, or whether they were overcome with wine, I know not, but they drew their swords, and into the street they went; and some took my lord the young Prince's part, and some took the other, but betwixt them there was such a bloody fray for the space of half an hour that neither watchmen nor any other could stay[4] them, till my brother, the Sheriff of London, and I were sent for. And at the last, with much ado, we stayed them. But it was long first, which was a great disquieting to all your loving subjects thereabouts. And then, my good lord, we knew not whether Your Grace had sent them to try us whether we would do justice, or whether it were of their own voluntary will or not, we cannot tell. And therefore, in such a case, we knew not what to do; but for our own safeguard, we sent him to ward,[5] where he wanteth[6] nothing that is fit for His Grace and Your Majesty's son. And thus, most humbly beseeching Your Majesty to think of our answer—

KING   Stand aside until we have further deliberated on your answer.   *Exit Mayor [with Sheriff].*
Ah, Harry, Harry, now thrice-accursed Harry, that hath gotten a son which with grief will end his father's days! Oh, my son, a prince thou art, ay, a prince indeed—and to deserve imprisonment! And well have they done, and like faithful subjects.—Discharge them and let them go.

EXETER   I beseech Your Grace, be good to my lord the young Prince.

KING   Nay, nay, 'tis no matter. Let him alone.

OXFORD   Perchance the Mayor and the Sheriff have been too precise[7] in this matter.

KING   No, they have done like faithful subjects. I will go myself to discharge them and let them go.   *Exit omnes.*[8]

[Scene 4]   *Enter Lord Chief Justice, Clerk of the Office, Jailer, John Cobbler, Derick, and the Thief. [The Chief Justice sits.]*

CHIEF JUSTICE   Jailer, bring the prisoner to the bar.

---

3 **liked** pleased   4 **stay** stop   5 **ward** prison   6 **wanteth** lacks
7 **precise** strict in the observance of rule   8 **omnes** all

Scene 4. Location: A court of justice.

DERICK Hear you, my lord: I pray you, bring the bar[1] to the prisoner.

CHIEF JUSTICE Hold thy hand up at the bar.

THIEF Here it is, my lord.

CHIEF JUSTICE Clerk of the Office, read his indictment.

CLERK What is thy name?

THIEF My name was known before I came here and shall be when I am gone, I warrant you.

CHIEF JUSTICE Ay, I think so, but we will know it better before thou go.

DERICK Zounds, an[2] you do but send to the next jail, we are sure to know his name, for this is not the first prison he hath been in, I'll warrant you.

CLERK What is thy name?

THIEF What need you to ask, and have it in writing?

CLERK Is not thy name Cutbert Cutter?

THIEF What the devil need you ask, and know it so well?

CLERK Why then, Cutbert Cutter, I indict thee, by the name of Cutbert Cutter, for robbing a poor carrier the twentieth day of May last past, in the fourteen year of the reign of our sovereign lord King Henry the Fourth, for setting upon a poor carrier upon Gad's Hill, in Kent, and having beaten and wounded the said carrier, and taken his goods from him—

DERICK Oh, masters, stay there! Nay, let's never belie the man, for he hath not beaten and wounded me also, but he hath beaten and wounded my pack, and hath taken the great race[3] of ginger that Bouncing Bess with the jolly buttocks should have had. That grieves me most.

CHIEF JUSTICE Well, what sayest thou? Art thou guilty, or not guilty?

THIEF Not guilty, my lord.

CHIEF JUSTICE By whom wilt thou be tried?

THIEF By my lord the young Prince, or by myself, whether[4] you will.

Enter the young Prince, with Ned and Tom.

PRINCE Come away, my lads.—Gog's wounds,[5] ye villain,

---

1 bar (Derick may understand *bar* to mean an iron bar used in breaking criminals on the wheel, or some such instrument of punishment.)
2 Zounds, an by His (God's) wounds, if   **3 race** root   **4 whether** whichever   **5 Gog's wounds** by God's wounds

what make you here? I must go about my business myself,
and you must stand loitering here?

THIEF   Why, my lord, they have bound me and will not let me
go.

PRINCE   Have they bound thee, villain?—Why, how now, my
lord?

CHIEF JUSTICE   I am glad to see Your Grace in good health.

PRINCE   Why, my lord, this is my man. 'Tis marvel you knew
him not long before this. I tell you he is a man of his hands.[6]

THIEF   Ay, Gog's wounds, that I am! Try me who dare.

CHIEF JUSTICE   Your Grace shall find small credit by acknowl-
edging him to be your man.

PRINCE   Why, my lord, what hath he done?

CHIEF JUSTICE   An it please Your Majesty, he hath robbed a
poor carrier.

DERICK   Hear you, sir: marry, it was one Derick, goodman
Hobling's man, of Kent.

PRINCE   What? Was 't you, buttonbreech?[7] Of[8] my word, my
lord, he did it but in jest.

DERICK   Hear you, sir, is it your man's quality[9] to rob folks in
jest? In faith, he shall be hanged in earnest.

PRINCE   Well, my lord, what do you mean to do with my man?

CHIEF JUSTICE   An please Your Grace, the law must pass on
him according to justice. Then he must be executed.*

PRINCE   Why, then, belike you mean to hang my man?

CHIEF JUSTICE   I am sorry that it falls out so.

PRINCE   Why, my lord, I pray ye, who am I?

CHIEF JUSTICE   An please Your Grace, you are my lord the
young Prince, our king that shall be after the decease of our
sovereign lord King Henry the Fourth, whom God grant long
to reign!

PRINCE   You say true, my lord. And you will hang my man?

CHIEF JUSTICE   An like Your Grace, I must needs do justice.

PRINCE   Tell me, my lord, shall I have my man?

CHIEF JUSTICE   I cannot, my lord.

PRINCE   But will you not let him go?

CHIEF JUSTICE   I am sorry that his case is so ill.

PRINCE   Tush, case me no casings! Shall I have my man?

---

6 man of his hands man of valor   **7 buttonbreech** (A condescending
term for one who dresses in rustic fashion as Derick does.)   **8 Of** on
9 quality nature, disposition

CHIEF JUSTICE   I cannot nor I may not, my lord.

PRINCE   Nay, and "I shall not," say—and then I am answered?

CHIEF JUSTICE   No.

PRINCE   No? Then I will have him.

He giveth him a box on the ear.

NED   Gog's wounds, my lord, shall I cut off his head?

PRINCE   No, I charge you, draw not your swords, but get you hence. Provide a noise of musicians. Away, begone!

*Exeunt Ned and Tom.**

CHIEF JUSTICE   Well, my lord, I am content to take it at your hands.

PRINCE   Nay, an you be not, you shall have more.

CHIEF JUSTICE   Why, I pray you, my lord, who am I?

PRINCE   You, who knows not you? Why, man, you are Lord Chief Justice of England.

CHIEF JUSTICE   Your Grace hath said truth. Therefore, in striking me in this place you greatly abuse me, and not me only but also your father, whose lively person here in this place I do represent. And therefore, to teach you what prerogatives mean, I commit you to the Fleet[10] until we have spoken with your father.

PRINCE   Why, then, belike you mean to send me to the Fleet?

CHIEF JUSTICE   Ay, indeed, and therefore carry him away.

Exeunt Henry V with the officers.

Jailer, carry the prisoner to Newgate again until the next 'sizes.[11]

JAILER   At your commandment, my lord, it shall be done.

*[Exeunt all except] Derick and John Cobbler.**

[Scene 5]

DERICK   Zounds, masters, here's ado when princes must go to prison! Why, John, didst ever see the like?

JOHN   O Derick, trust me, I never saw the like.

DERICK   Why, John, thou mayst see what princes be in choler. A judge a box on the ear! I'll tell thee, John, O John, I would not have done it for twenty shillings.

10 the Fleet a London prison   **11 'sizes** assizes, court sessions

Scene 5. Location: The scene continues at the court of justice.

JOHN   No, nor I. There had been no way but one with us—we should have been hanged.

DERICK   Faith, John, I'll tell thee what: thou shalt be my Lord Chief Justice, and thou shalt sit in the chair, and I'll be the young Prince and hit thee a box on the ear. And then thou shalt say, "To teach you what prerogatives mean, I commit you to the Fleet."

JOHN   Come on, I'll be your judge. But thou shalt not hit me hard?

DERICK   No, no.

                    [*John Cobbler takes the Chief Justice's seat.*]

JOHN   What hath he done?

DERICK   Marry, he hath robbed Derick.

JOHN   Why, then, I cannot let him go.

DERICK   I must needs have my man.

JOHN   You shall not have him.

DERICK   Shall I not have my man? Say no, an you dare! How say you? Shall I not have my man?

JOHN   No, marry, shall you not.

DERICK   Shall I not, John?

JOHN   No, Derick.

DERICK   Why, then, take you that [*boxing his ear*] till more come! Zounds, shall I not have him?

JOHN   Well, I am content to take this at your hand. But, I pray you, who am I?

DERICK   Who art thou? Zounds, dost not know thyself?

JOHN   No.

DERICK   Now away, simple fellow. Why, man, thou art John the Cobbler.

JOHN   No, I am my Lord Chief Justice of England.

DERICK   Oh, John, Mass,[1] thou sayst true, thou art indeed.

JOHN   Why, then, to teach you what prerogatives mean, I commit you to the Fleet.

DERICK   Well, I will go. But i'faith, you graybeard knave, I'll course[2] you.   *Exit. And straight enters again.*
Oh, John, come, come out of thy chair. Why, what a clown wert thou to let me hit thee a box on the ear! And now thou seest they will not take me to the Fleet. I think that thou art one of these worenday[3] clowns.

1 **Mass** by the Mass   2 **course** chase or drive with blows, thrash
3 **worenday** ordained (often spelled *wordeyned*), destined (? Derick may mean that John Cobbler is a born clown.)

JOHN   But I marvel what will become of thee.

DERICK   Faith, I'll be no more a carrier.

JOHN   What wilt thou do, then?

DERICK   I'll dwell with thee and be a cobbler.

JOHN   With me? Alas, I am not able to keep thee. Why, thou wilt eat me out of doors.

DERICK   Oh, John! No, John, I am none of these great slouching fellows that devour these great pieces of beef and brewis.[4] Alas, a trifle serves me—a woodcock, a chicken, or a capon's leg, or any such little thing serves me.

JOHN   A capon! Why, man, I cannot get a capon once a year, except it be at Christmas, at some other man's house; for we cobblers be glad of a dish of roots.

DERICK   Roots? Why, are you so good at rooting? Nay, cobbler, we'll have you ringed.[5]

JOHN   But Derick,

> Though we be so poor,
> Yet will we have in store
> A crab[6] in the fire,
> With nut-brown ale
> That is full stale,[7]
> Which will a man quail
> And lay in the mire.

DERICK   A bots[8] on you! An be but for[9] your ale, I'll dwell with you. Come, let's away as fast as we can.   *Exeunt.*

[Scene 6]   *Enter the young Prince, with Ned and Tom.*

PRINCE   Come away, sirs. Gog's wounds, Ned, didst thou not see what a box on the ear I took[1] my Lord Chief Justice?

---

4 brewis beef broth   **5 ringed** i.e., ringed through the nose, like a pig (since pigs *root* or dig with their snouts in search of food)   **6 crab** crabapple   **7 stale** old and strong   **8 bots** (Literally, an intestinal maggot disease affecting horses; here, used as an execration.)   **9 An be but for** if only for the sake of

Scene 6. Location: somewhere in London. At one point the Prince and his companions proceed to the court.
1 took gave

TOM   By Gog's blood, it did me good to see it. It made his teeth jar in his head!

Enter Sir John Oldcastle.

PRINCE   How now, Sir John Oldcastle, what news with you?

SIR JOHN OLDCASTLE   I am glad to see Your Grace at liberty. I was come, I, to visit you in prison.

PRINCE   To visit me? Didst thou not know that I am a prince's son? Why, 'tis enough for me to look into a prison, though I come not in myself. But here's such ado nowadays—here's prisoning, here's hanging, whipping, and the devil and all. But I tell you, sirs, when I am king we will have no such things. But, my lads, if the old King, my father, were dead, we would be all kings.

SIR JOHN OLDCASTLE   He is a good old man. God take him to his mercy the sooner!

PRINCE   But, Ned, so soon as I am king, the first thing I will do shall be to put my Lord Chief Justice out of office, and thou shalt be my Lord Chief Justice of England.

NED   Shall I be Lord Chief Justice? By Gog's wounds, I'll be the bravest[2] Lord Chief Justice that ever was in England!

PRINCE   Then, Ned, I'll turn all these prisons into fence schools, and I will endue[3] thee with them, with lands to maintain them withal. Then I will have a bout with my Lord Chief Justice. Thou shalt hang none but pickpurses, and horse stealers, and such base-minded villains; but that fellow that will stand by the highway side courageously with his sword and buckler and take a purse—that fellow, give him commendations! Beside that, send him to me and I will give him an annual pension out of my exchequer to maintain him all the days of his life.

SIR JOHN OLDCASTLE   Nobly spoken, Harry! We shall never have a merry world till the old King be dead.

NED   But whither are you going now?

PRINCE   To the court, for I hear say my father lies very sick.

TOM   But I doubt[4] he will not die.

PRINCE   Yet will I go thither. For the breath shall be no sooner out of his mouth but I will clap the crown on my head.

2 bravest most splendid   **3 endue** invest, bestow   **4 doubt** fear

SIR JOHN OLDCASTLE   Will you go to the court with that cloak so full of needles?

PRINCE   Cloak, eyelet holes, needles,[5] and all was of mine own devising; and therefore I will wear it.

TOM   I pray you, my lord, what may be the meaning thereof?

PRINCE   Why, man, 'tis a sign that I stand upon thorns till the crown be on my head.

SIR JOHN OLDCASTLE   Or that every needle might be a prick to their hearts that repine at your doings?

PRINCE   Thou sayst true, Jockey. But there's some will say the young Prince will be "a well toward[6] young man," and all this gear,[7] that I had as lief[8] they would break my head with a pot as to say any such thing. But we stand prating here too long. I must needs speak with my father. Therefore, come away!   [*They cross the stage, and knock.*]

          [*Enter a Porter.*]

PORTER   What a rapping keep you at the King's court-gate?

PRINCE   Here's one that must speak with the King.

PORTER   The King is very sick, and none must speak with him.

PRINCE   No? You rascal, do you not know me?

PORTER   You are my lord the young Prince.

PRINCE   Then go and tell my father that I must and will speak with him.   [*Exit Porter.*]

NED [*To Prince*]   Shall I cut off his head?

PRINCE   No, no. Though I would help you in other places, yet I have nothing to do here.[9] What, you are in my father's court.

NED   I will write him in my tables,[10] for so soon as I am made Lord Chief Justice I will put him out of his office.

          The trumpet sounds.

PRINCE   Gog's wounds, sirs, the King comes. Let's all stand aside.   [*They stand aside.*]

     Enter the King, with the Lord of Exeter.

---

5 eyelet holes, needles (Holinshed reports that Prince Henry went to court in 1412 in a gown of blue satin "full of small eyelet holes, at every hole the needle hanging by a silk thread with which it was sewed.")
6 well toward promising   **7 and all this gear** and suchlike nonsense
8 had as lief would just as soon   **9 Though I would . . . here** i.e., though I could get you off on a charge of assault or murder elsewhere, I have no authority of that kind here at my father's court   **10 tables** notebook

KING   And is it true, my lord, that my son is already sent to the Fleet? Now, truly, that man[11] is more fitter to rule the realm than I, for by no means could I rule my son, and he, by one word, hath caused him to be ruled. Oh, my son, my son, no sooner out of one prison but into another?[12] I had thought once whiles I had lived to have seen this noble realm of England flourish by thee, my son, but now I see it goes to ruin and decay.   *He weepeth.*

> *Enters Lord of Oxford.*

OXFORD   An please Your Grace, here is my lord your son that cometh to speak with you. He saith he must and will speak with you.

KING   Who? My son Harry?

OXFORD   Ay, an please Your Majesty.

KING   I know wherefore he cometh. But look that none come with him.

OXFORD   A very disordered company, and such as make very ill rule in Your Majesty's house.

KING   Well, let him come, but look that none come with him.
                              He [Oxford] goeth [to the Prince].

OXFORD   An please Your Grace, my lord the King sends for you.

PRINCE   Come away, sirs, let's go all together.

OXFORD   An please Your Grace, none must go with you.

PRINCE   Why, I must needs have them with me; otherwise I can do my father no countenance.[13] Therefore, come away.

OXFORD   The King your father commands there should none come.

PRINCE   Well, sirs, then begone. And provide me three noise[14] of musicians.   *Exeunt Knights.*[15]

> *Enters[16] the Prince, with a dagger in his hand [to the King, attended].*

KING   Come, my son, come on, i' God's name! I know

---

11 that man i.e., the Lord Chief Justice   **12 one prison . . . another** (The Prince was sent to the Counter for his earlier offense, now to the Fleet.) **13 can do . . . countenance** i.e., will not be able to make a proper show before my father   **14 noise** bands   **15 Knights** i.e., Sir John Oldcastle, Ned, and Tom. (Ned is presumably Ned Poins.)   **16 Enters** (The Prince approaches the King, who is still onstage.)

wherefore thy coming is. Oh, my son, my son, what cause
hath ever been that thou shouldst forsake me and follow this
vile and reprobate company which abuseth youth so manifestly? Oh, my son, thou knowest that these thy doings will
end thy father's days.   *He weeps.*
Ay, so, so, my son, thou fearest not to approach the presence
of thy sick father in that disguised sort. I tell thee, my son,
that there is never a needle in thy cloak but it is a prick to my
heart, and never an eyelet hole but it is a hole to my soul; and
wherefore thou bringest that dagger in thy hand I know not
but by conjecture.   *He weeps.*

PRINCE My conscience accuseth me. Most sovereign lord and
well-beloved Father, to answer first to the last point, that is,
whereas you conjecture that this hand and this dagger shall
be armed against your life: no! Know, my beloved Father, far
be the thoughts of your son—"son," said I? an unworthy
son for so good a father!—but far be the thoughts of any
such pretended[17] mischief. And I most humbly render it to
Your Majesty's hand. [*He gives the King the dagger.*] And
live, my lord and sovereign, forever! And with your dagger-
arm show like vengeance upon the body of—"that your
son," I was about to say, and dare not; ah, woe is me
therefore!—that your vile* slave. 'Tis not the crown that I
come for, sweet Father, because I am unworthy. And those
vile and reprobate companions*—I abandon and utterly
abolish their company forever! Pardon, sweet Father, pardon, the least thing and most desire.[18] And this ruffianly
cloak I here tear from my back and sacrifice it to the devil,
which is master of all mischief. [*He tears off his cloak.*]
Pardon me, sweet Father, pardon me! Good my Lord of
Exeter, speak for me. Pardon me, pardon, good Father! Not a
word? Ah, he will not speak one word! Ah, Harry, now
thrice-unhappy Harry! But what shall I do? I will go take me
into some solitary place and there lament my sinful life, and
when I have done, I will lay me down and die.   *Exit.*

KING Call him again. Call my son again.
                                  [*The Prince is summoned.*]

     [*Enter the Prince.*]

---

17 pretended intended   **18 the least . . . desire** i.e., my least offense as
well as the thing I have most desired (?)

PRINCE And doth my father call me again? Now, Harry, happy be the time that thy father calleth thee again! [*He kneels.*]

KING Stand up, my son, and do not think thy father but at the request of thee, my son, I will pardon thee.[19] And God bless thee and make thee his servant!

PRINCE Thanks, good my lord. And no doubt but this day, even this day, I am born new again.

KING Come, my son and lords, take me by the hands.

Exeunt omnes, [*the King being led*].

[Scene 7]   *Enter Derick* [*shouting at Mistress Cobbler within*].

DERICK Thou art a stinking whore, and a whoreson stinking whore! Dost think I'll take it at thy hands?[1]

Enter John Cobbler, running.

JOHN Derick, Derick, Derick,* hearest 'a?[2] Do, Derick, never while thou livest use[3] that! Why, what will my neighbors say an thou go away so?

DERICK She's an arrant whore, and I'll have the law on you, John.

JOHN Why, what hath she done?

DERICK Marry, mark thou, John. I will prove it, that I will!

JOHN What wilt thou prove?

DERICK That she called me in to dinner—John, mark the tale well, John—and when I was set, she brought me a dish of roots and a piece of barrel-butter[4] therein. And she is a very knave, and thou a drab if* thou take her part.

JOHN Hearest 'a, Derick? Is this the matter? Nay, an it be no worse, we will go home again, and all shall be amended.

---

19 and do not . . . thee (The text is seemingly corrupt, but the King is probably saying, do not think but that at your request I will surely pardon you.)

Scene 7. Location: John Cobbler's house, evidently a public house.
1 take . . . hands take such behavior from you   **2 hearest 'a** do you hear
3 use use such language as   **4 barrel-butter** butter heavily salted for preservation and hence not of the quality that Derick evidently expects

DERICK   Oh, John, hearest 'a, John? Is all well?
JOHN   Ay, all is well.
DERICK   Then I'll go home before, and break all the glass
   windows.   [*Exeunt.*]

[Scene 8]   *Enter the King* [*in his chair*] *with his Lords*
                   [*Exeter and Oxford*].

KING   Come, my lords. I see it boots[1] me not to take any
   physic,[2] for all the physicians in the world cannot cure me;
   no, not one. But, good my lords, remember my last will and
   testament concerning my son, for truly, my lords, I do not
   think but he will prove as valiant and victorious a king as
   ever reigned in England.
BOTH   Let heaven and earth be witness between us if we
   accomplish not thy will to the uttermost!
KING   I give you most unfeigned thanks, good my lords. Draw
   the curtains and depart my chamber awhile, and cause
   some music to rock me asleep.
                   [*The curtains are drawn around his throne.*]
                             He sleepeth. Exeunt Lords.

   Enter the Prince.

PRINCE   Ah, Harry, thrice unhappy, that hath neglect[3] so long
   from visiting of thy sick father! I will go. Nay, but why do I
   not go to the chamber of my sick father to comfort the
   melancholy soul of his body? His soul, said I? Here is his
   body, indeed, but his soul is whereas it needs no body. Now,
   thrice-accursed Harry, that hath offended thy father so
   much! And could not I crave pardon for all? O my dying
   Father! Cursed be the day wherein I was born, and accursed
   be the hour wherein I was begotten! But what shall I do? If
   weeping tears, which come too late, may suffice the negli-
   gence neglected too soon,* I will weep day and night until
   the fountain be dry with weeping.
                             Exit [*taking the crown*].

   Enter Lord[*s*] *of Exeter and Oxford.*

Scene 8. Location: The royal court.
1 boots avails   **2 physic** medicine   **3 neglect** neglected

EXETER   Come easily,[4] my lord, for waking of[5] the King.

KING [*Waking*]   Now, my lords?

OXFORD   How doth Your Grace feel yourself?

KING   Somewhat better after my sleep. But, good my lords, take off my crown. Remove my chair a little back and set me right.

BOTH   An please Your Grace, the crown is taken away.

KING   The crown taken away! Good my Lord of Oxford, go see who hath done this deed.   [*Exit Oxford.*]
No doubt 'tis some vile traitor that hath done it to deprive my son. They that would do it now would seek to scrape and scrawl[6] for it after my death.

> *Enter Lord of Oxford with the Prince [with the crown].*

OXFORD   Here, an please Your Grace, is my lord the young Prince with the crown.

KING   Why, how now, my son? I had thought the last time I had you in schooling[7] I had given you a lesson for all,[8] and do you now begin again? Why, tell me, my son, dost thou think the time so long that thou wouldst have it before the breath be out of my mouth?

PRINCE [*Kneeling*]   Most sovereign lord and well-beloved Father, I came into your chamber to comfort the melancholy soul of your body, and finding you at that time past all recovery and dead, to my thinking—God is my witness! And what should I do but with weeping tears lament the death of you, my Father? And after that, seeing the crown, I took it. And tell me, my Father, who might better take it than I, after your death? But, seeing you live, I most humbly render it into Your Majesty's hands; and the happiest man alive that my father live. [*He gives back the crown.*] And live, my lord and father, forever!

KING   Stand up, my son. [*The Prince arises.*] Thine answer hath sounded well in mine ears, for I must need confess that I was in a very sound sleep and altogether unmindful of thy coming. But come near, my son, and let me put thee in

---

4 easily gently, quietly   **5 for waking of** for fear of waking   **6 scrape and scrawl** claw and scramble   **7 in schooling** as a pupil   **8 for all** for all time

possession whilst I live, that none deprive thee of it after my death.

PRINCE   Well may I take it at Your Majesty's hands, but it shall never touch my head so long as my father lives.

He taketh the crown.

KING   God give thee joy, my son. God bless thee, and make thee his servant, and send thee a prosperous reign! For God knows, my son, how hardly[9] I came by it and how hardly I have maintained it.

PRINCE   Howsoever you came by it I know not; but now I have it from you, and from you I will keep it. And he that seeks to take the crown from my head, let him look that his armor be thicker than mine, or I will pierce him to the heart, were it harder than brass or bullion.

KING   Nobly spoken, and like a king! Now trust me, my lords, I fear not but my son will be as warlike and victorious a prince as ever reigned in England.

BOTH LORDS   His former life shows no less.

KING   Well, my lords, I know not whether it be for sleep, or drawing near of drowsy summer of death, but I am very much given to sleep. Therefore, good my lords and my son, draw the curtains. Depart my chamber and cause some music to rock me asleep.

[*The curtains are drawn. Music sounds.*]
Exeunt omnes. The King dieth.[10]

[Scene 9]   *Enter the Thief.*

THIEF   Ah, God, I am now much like to a bird which hath escaped out of the cage! For so soon as my Lord Chief Justice heard that the old King was dead, he was glad to let me go for fear of my lord the young Prince. But here comes some of his companions. I will see an I can get anything of them for old acquaintance.[1]

9 hardly with difficulty   **10 dieth** (The curtains presumably make it possible for the King to exit after the scene is over without being seen.)

Scene 9. Location: A street where the coronation procession will pass.
1 for old acquaintance for the sake of old acquaintance

Enter Knights, ranging.[2]

TOM   Gog's wounds, the King is dead!

SIR JOHN OLDCASTLE   Dead? Then, Gog's blood, we shall be all kings!

NED   Gog's wounds, I shall be Lord Chief Justice of England.

TOM *[To the Thief]*   Why, how![3] Are you broken out of prison?

NED   Gog's wounds, how the villain stinks!

SIR JOHN OLDCASTLE   Why, what will become of thee now? Fie upon him, how the rascal stinks!

THIEF   Marry, I will go and serve my master[4] again.

TOM   Gog's blood, dost think that he will have any such scabbed knave as thou art? What, man, he is a king now.

NED *[Giving him money]*   Hold thee. Here's a couple of angels[5] for thee. And get thee gone, for the King will not be long before he come this way. And hereafter I will tell the King of thee.   *Exit Thief.*

SIR JOHN OLDCASTLE   Oh, how it did me good to see the King when he was crowned! Methought his seat was like the figure of heaven and his person like unto a god.

NED   But who would have thought that the King would have changed his countenance so?

SIR JOHN OLDCASTLE   Did you not see with what grace he sent his embassage into France to tell the French King that Harry of England hath sent for the crown, and Harry of England will have it?

TOM   But 'twas but a little[6] to make the people believe that he was sorry for his father's death.   *The trumpet sounds.*

NED   Gog's wounds, the King comes! Let's all stand aside.

Enter the King with the Archbishop [of Canterbury] and the Lord of Oxford.

SIR JOHN OLDCASTLE   How do you, my lord?

NED   How now, Harry? Tut, my lord, put away these dumps. You are a king, and all the realm is yours. What, man, do you not remember the old sayings? You know I must be Lord Chief Justice of England. Trust me, my lord, methinks you

---

2 ranging roaming about   **3 how** how now, what's the news   **4 my master** i.e., Prince Henry, now King   **5 angels** gold coins   **6 'twas but a little** i.e., it was only a little device

are very much changed. And 'tis but with a little sorrowing, to make folks believe the death of your father grieves you— and 'tis nothing so.

KING HENRY V   I prithee, Ned, mend thy manners, and be more modester in thy terms, for my unfeigned grief is not to be ruled by thy flattering and dissembling talk. Thou sayst I am changed. So I am, indeed, and so must thou be, and that quickly, or else I must cause thee to be changed.

SIR JOHN OLDCASTLE   Gog's wounds, how like you this? Zounds, 'tis not so sweet as music.

TOM   I trust we have not offended Your Grace no way.

KING HENRY V   Ah, Tom, your former life grieves me and makes me to abandon and abolish your company forever. And therefore, not upon pain of death to approach my presence by ten miles' space. Then, if I hear well of you, it may be I will do somewhat for you. Otherwise, look for no more favor at my hands than at any other man's. And, therefore, begone! We have other matters to talk on.

Exeunt Knights.

[The rest of *Famous Victories* is chiefly concerned with King Henry's exploits in France and his famous victory at Agincourt.]

———————

This selection is based on the first edition of *The Famous Victories of Henry the Fifth, Containing the Honorable Battle of Agincourt; As It Was Played by the Queen's Majesty's Players.* London: Printed by Thomas Creede, 1598. [Designated in textual notes below as Q.]

In the following, departures from the original text appear in boldface; original readings are in roman. (The speech prefixes have been silently regularized.)

p. 147 *executed [Q follows with a slightly varied repetition of the previous five lines beginning with Derick's speech.]   p. 148 *s.d. Exeunt Ned and Tom Exeunt the Theefe [Q]   *s.d. [Exeunt all except] Derick and John Cobbler Enter Dericke and John Cobler [Q]   p. 154 *vile wilde   *companions company   p. 155 *Derick, Derick, Derick Derick, D. D. [Q]   *if it [Q]   p. 156 *too soon to some [Q]

Further Reading

Auden, W. H. "The Prince's Dog." *The Dyer's Hand and Other Essays*. New York: Random House, 1948. Auden inventively examines Falstaff's character, motives, and function within the play, and concludes that "sober reflection in the study may tell us that Falstaff is not, after all, a very admirable person, but Falstaff on the stage gives us no time for sober reflection." Auden denies the damaging irresponsibility many critics have found in Falstaff, declaring him to be "a comic symbol for the supernatural order of charity."

Barber, C. L. "Rule and Misrule in *Henry IV*." *Shakespeare's Festive Comedy*. Princeton, N.J.: Princeton Univ. Press, 1959. In his seminal study of the relation of social and artistic forms, Barber sees Falstaff as a Lord of Misrule burlesquing the sanctities of the historical world. Barber finds, however, that misrule does not threaten the social order, since "it depends utterly on what it mocks." Ultimately "misrule works . . . to consolidate rule," though Falstaff's saturnalian energy always threatens to turn from a "dependent holiday skepticism" to a "dangerously self-sufficient everyday skepticism."

Barish, Jonas A. "The Turning Away of Prince Hal." *Shakespeare Studies* 1 (1965): 18–28. Barish sees Falstaff's rejection as the moment that reveals to us whether we are "moralists or sentimentalists"; we also sense at this moment the antithetical pressures of history and comedy. In rejecting Falstaff, Hal is, in effect, rejecting himself: "to banish plump Jack is to banish what is free and vital and pleasurable in life."

Berger, Harry, Jr. "Sneak's Noise, or Rumor and Detextualization in *2 Henry IV*." *Kenyon Review* n.s. 6.4 (1984): 58–78. Berger explores the tension between "stage-centered" readings, which fix meaning, "detextualizing" language by visualizing it in character and action, and "text-centered" readings, which oppose this fixing, "retextualizing" the language "to recuperate what has been repressed." Focusing on the figure of Rumor, Berger explores the ways in which *2 Henry IV* builds the problematic relationship of text and performance into the play itself as part of "a critical thesis about theater in particular and theatricality in general."

Bradley, A. C. "The Rejection of Falstaff." *Oxford Lectures on Poetry*, 1909. Rpt. New York: St. Martin's Press, 1959. Bradley's influential essay explores the inevitability of Hal's rejection of Falstaff. He recognizes both Falstaff's dangerous attractiveness and Hal's Lancastrian "hardness" that qualifies him for political success but limits his personal appeal. If we enjoy the Falstaff scenes "as surely Shakespeare meant for them to be enjoyed," Bradley argues, we must feel in Falstaff's rejection "a good deal of pain and some resentment."

Burckhardt, Sigurd. " 'Swoll'n with Some Other Grief': Shakespeare's Prince Hal Trilogy." *Shakespearean Meanings*. Princeton, N.J.: Princeton Univ. Press, 1968. Burckhardt argues that the structure of Shakespeare's plays "undercuts Tudor doctrine," exposing its contradictions and inadequacies. The apparently satisfying resolution of *1 Henry IV* dissolves as Falstaff rises from the battlefield, "reminding us that disorder is not slain so neatly and inexpensively as the calculated symmetries of dialectics would have us believe." *2 Henry IV*, even more disillusioned, reveals that the political order of England "has become *secular*. The sanctions it rests on are not divine or cosmic but at best pragmatic."

Calderwood, James L. "*2 Henry IV*: The Embodied Name and the Rejected Mask." *Metadrama in Shakespeare's Henriad: "Richard II" to "Henry V."* Berkeley and Los Angeles: Univ. of California Press, 1979. In *2 Henry IV*, Calderwood sees Falstaff, with his newly gained reputation, entering into "the illusion of historical reality." He abandons the "comic invulnerability" of his former outrageously theatrical existence for a commitment to the historical fiction that ultimately must reveal him to be a disease-ridden old man who must (and can) be repudiated.

Campbell, Lily B. "The Unquiet Time of Henry IV." *Shakespeare's "Histories": Mirrors of Elizabethan Policy*. San Marino, Calif.: Huntington Library, 1947. Campbell considers the historical action of the play in the context of Elizabethan political theory and anxieties about succession. She argues that "the problem of rebellion" is central to the design of *Henry IV* and reflects the realities of sixteenth-century politics as much as the medieval history overtly represented.

Dessen, Alan C. "The Two Phased Structure of *2 Henry IV*." *Shakespeare and the Late Moral Plays*. Lincoln, Nebr., and London: Univ. of Nebraska Press, 1986. Dessen finds in the dramaturgy of the late morality plays of the 1560s and 1570s a structural model for *2 Henry IV*. In plays such as *The Tide Tarrieth No Man* (1576), with a two-phased action in which the public Vice initially controls the action until finally he is superseded by allegorical figures embodying the play's moral norms, Shakespeare finds a prototype for his drama of the "reordering of England."

Greenblatt, Stephen. "Invisible Bullets: Renaissance Authority and Its Subversion." *Glyph* 8 (1981): 40–61. Rev. and rpt. in *Political Shakespeare: New Essays in Cultural Materialism*, ed. Jonathan Dollimore and Alan Sinfield. Ithaca and London: Cornell Univ. Press, 1985. Greenblatt considers the *Henry IV* plays in a provocative account of the operations of Renaissance power. He argues that the subversive challenge to the principles of authority in the play is never really dangerous; indeed, it is not merely contained but actually encouraged by the power structure, since its presence works paradoxically to ratify and reinforce the existing order.

Hunter, G. K. "*Henry IV* and the Elizabethan Two-Part Play." *Review of English Studies* n.s. 5 (1954): 236–248. Rpt. in *Dramatic Identities and Cultural Tradition: Studies in Shakespeare and His Contemporaries*. New York: Barnes and Noble, 1978. Entering into the debate about the relationship of the two parts of *Henry IV*, Hunter argues not that the two plays are continuous but that they have the unity, found also in plays by Christopher Marlowe, John Marston, and George Chapman, "of a dyptich, in which repetition of shape and design focuses attention on what is common to the two parts."

Johnson, Samuel. "*2 Henry IV*." *Johnson on Shakespeare*, ed. Arthur Sherbo. *The Yale Edition of the Works of Samuel Johnson*, vol. 7. New Haven and London: Yale Univ. Press, 1968. Johnson sees Falstaff as dangerous and despicable: "He is a thief, and a glutton, and a coward, and a boaster, always ready to cheat the weak, and prey upon the poor." He is able, however, to endear himself to the Prince "by the most pleasing of all qualities, perpetual gaiety."

Jorgensen, Paul A. "The 'Dastardly Treachery' of Prince John of Lancaster." *PMLA* 76 (1961): 488–492. Jorgensen finds a relationship between the scene of John of Lancaster's arrest of the rebels and the demoralizing war Elizabeth waged against the Irish. Revealing how far the world has fallen from "the happy warriors and outmoded warfare of Agincourt," Prince's John's cynical actions reflect the dispiriting realities of anxious governmental policy in the 1590s.

Kelly, Henry Ansgar. *Divine Providence in the England of Shakespeare's Histories*, pp. 222–232. Cambridge: Harvard Univ. Press, 1970. Examining the play's often noted "providentialism," Kelly finds that the "moral and spiritual sentiments" of Shakespeare's sources are not normative but are distributed in the play according to the partisan uses that can be made of them. He denies that the play presents Henry's difficulties during his reign as "in any way a punishment from God for his sins in acquiring the throne," and concludes that "the crown in *2 Henry IV* is definitely regarded as the rightful possession of the Henrys."

Kernan, Alvin B. "The Henriad: Shakespeare's Major History Plays." In *Modern Shakespearean Criticism: Essays on Style, Dramaturgy, and the Major Plays*, ed. Alvin B. Kernan. New York: Harcourt, Brace, and World, 1970. Kernan traces the movement of the second tetralogy from a sacred, providential conception of history to a secular, pragmatic view, "in which any identity is only a temporary role." Richard II, Henry IV, and Prince Hal mark stages in this transition, and the latter emerges as the modern prince who "never seems to lose sight of the fact he is preparing to be king of England."

Morgann, Maurice. "An Essay on the Dramatic Character of Sir John Falstaff" (1777). In *Eighteenth Century Essays on Shakespeare*, ed. D. Nichol Smith. 2nd edition. Oxford: Clarendon Press, 1963. In an essay that is the earliest sustained account of a Shakespearean character, Morgann sees the complexity of Falstaff's nature as it is presented in the play. He is not the "constitutional coward" that many have seen but a man "of much natural courage and resolution." Morgann, however, recognizes that if Falstaff is endowed with "great natural vigour and alacrity of mind," he also engages "in every debauchery." He has "a mind free of malice or any evil principle; but he never took the trouble of acquiring any good one."

Ornstein, Robert. *"Henry IV Part II." A Kingdom for a Stage: The Achievement of Shakespeare's History Plays.* Cambridge: Harvard Univ. Press, 1972. Ornstein defends the artistic independence and integrity of *2 Henry IV*, finding it a study of dispiriting political realities achieved in a "somber and shadowed monochrome." The play reveals the fragility of human relationships and man's helplessness before the "relentless movement of time." It presents a world of "anti-heroes" for whom "gallantry exists only in memory."

Porter, Joseph A. *"2 Henry IV." The Drama of Speech Acts: Shakespeare's Lancastrian Tetralogy.* Berkeley, Calif.: Univ. of California Press, 1979. Porter examines "the topic of language in the play." Rumor introduces a world of proliferating, private speech that inhibits communication and "eliminates community." In Hal, however, the newly crowned Henry V, "we have a many-tongued monarch who, using a wide range of language purposefully and responsibly, initiates a reign of 'high . . . parliament.' "

Reese, M. M. *"Henry IV." The Cease of Majesty: A Study of Shakespeare's History Plays.* London: Edward Arnold, 1961; New York: St. Martin's Press, 1962. Reese argues that Shakespeare in the two parts of *Henry IV* dramatizes "the education of a prince" and "considers in personal and political terms the sacrifices and disciplines [Hal] will have to accept." Reese considers Falstaff, Hotspur, and Henry IV to be "three tempters" whose defective examples Hal must reject as his youthful impulses are "steeled into disciplined courage and dedicated to honourable ends."

Saccio, Peter. "Henry IV: The King Embattled." *Shakespeare's English Kings: History, Chronicle, and Drama.*

New York: Oxford Univ. Press, 1977. Focusing especially
on the political challenges to Henry's rule, the military
encounters at Shrewsbury and Gaultree Forest, and the
relations between Henry IV and his son, Saccio examines
the historical background of the two parts of *Henry IV*
and traces Shakespeare's transformation of this history
into drama.

Tillyard, E. M. W. "The Second Tetralogy." *Shakespeare's
History Plays*, 1944. Rpt., New York: Barnes and Noble,
1964. In an enormously influential study of Shakespeare's histories, Tillyard argues that the two parts of
Henry IV form a single sequence of ten acts in which Hal
is tested, "Morality-fashion," to prove his worthiness to
rule. *Part One* demonstrates Hal's education in military
virtues, as he tries to mediate between "the excess and
the defect of the military spirit" as they are embodied in
Hotspur and Falstaff; *Part Two* displays his education in
the "civil virtues," as he must choose between Falstaff
and the Lord Chief Justice.

Memorable Lines

A rascally yea-forsooth knave. (FALSTAFF 1.2.35–36)

It is the disease of not listening, the malady of not marking, that I am troubled withal. (FALSTAFF 1.2.120–121)

I am as poor as Job, my lord, but not so patient.
(FALSTAFF 1.2.125–126)

My lord, I was born about three of the clock in the afternoon, with a white head and something a round belly.
(FALSTAFF 1.2.185–187)

A good wit will make use of anything. I will turn diseases to commodity. (FALSTAFF 1.2.246–248)

An habitation giddy and unsure
Hath he that buildeth on the vulgar heart.
(ARCHBISHOP 1.3.89–90)

Away, you scullion, you rampallian, you fustilarian! I'll tickle your catastrophe. (PAGE 2.1.58–59)

He hath eaten me out of house and home. (HOSTESS 2.1.72)

Let the end try the man. (PRINCE 2.2.44)

PRINCE Where sups he? Doth the old boar feed in the old frank?
BARDOLPH At the old place, my lord, in Eastcheap.
(2.2.138–140)

From a god to a bull? A heavy descension! It was Jove's case.
(PRINCE 2.2.165–166)

He a captain? Hang him, rogue! He lives upon moldy stewed prunes and dried cakes. (DOLL 2.4.143–145)

Shall packhorses
And hollow pampered jades of Asia,
Which cannot go but thirty mile a day,
Compare with Caesars, and with Cannibals,
And Troiant Greeks?   (PISTOL   2.4.162–166)

O sleep, O gentle sleep,
Nature's soft nurse, how have I frighted thee.
                             (HENRY IV   3.1.5–6)

Uneasy lies the head that wears a crown.   (HENRY IV   3.1.31)

O God, that one might read the book of fate,
And see the revolution of the times
Make mountains level.   (HENRY IV   3.1.45–47)

There is a history in all men's lives.   (WARWICK   3.1.80)

We have heard the chimes at midnight.   (FALSTAFF   3.2.214)

The second property of your excellent sherris is the warming
of the blood, which, before cold and settled, left the liver
white and pale.   (FALSTAFF   4.3.101–103)

Thy wish was father, Harry, to that thought.
                             (HENRY IV   4.5.92)

. . . commit
The oldest sins the newest kind of ways?
                             (HENRY IV   4.5.125–126)

God knows, my son,
By what bypaths and indirect crook'd ways
I met this crown.   (HENRY IV   4.5.183–185)

. . . busy giddy minds
With foreign quarrels.   (HENRY IV   4.5.213–214)

This new and gorgeous garment, majesty,
Sits not so easy on me as you think.   (HENRY V   5.2.44–45)

I know thee not, old man. Fall to thy prayers.
How ill white hairs becomes a fool and jester!

(HENRY V   5.5.47–48)

When thou dost hear I am as I have been,
Approach me, and thou shalt be as thou wast.

(HENRY V   5.5.60–61)

Contributors

DAVID BEVINGTON, Phyllis Fay Horton Professor of Humanities at the University of Chicago, is editor of *The Complete Works of Shakespeare* (Scott, Foresman, 1980) and of *Medieval Drama* (Houghton Mifflin, 1975). His latest critical study is *Action Is Eloquence: Shakespeare's Language of Gesture* (Harvard University Press, 1984).

DAVID SCOTT KASTAN, Professor of English and Comparative Literature at Columbia University, is the author of *Shakespeare and the Shapes of Time* (University Press of New England, 1982).

JAMES HAMMERSMITH, Associate Professor of English at Auburn University, has published essays on various facets of Renaissance drama, including literary criticism, textual criticism, and printing history.

ROBERT KEAN TURNER, Professor of English at the University of Wisconsin–Milwaukee, is a general editor of the New Variorum Shakespeare (Modern Language Association of America) and a contributing editor to *The Dramatic Works in the Beaumont and Fletcher Canon* (Cambridge University Press, 1966–).

JAMES SHAPIRO, who coedited the bibliographies with David Scott Kastan, is Assistant Professor of English at Columbia University.

❖

JOSEPH PAPP, one of the most important forces in theater today, is the founder and producer of the New York Shakespeare Festival, America's largest and most prolific theatrical institution. Since 1954 Mr. Papp has produced or directed all but one of Shakespeare's plays—in Central Park, in schools, off and on Broadway, and at the Festival's permanent home, The Public Theater. He has also produced such award-winning plays and musical works as *Hair, A Chorus Line, Plenty,* and *The Mystery of Edwin Drood,* among many others.

Shakespeare
ALIVE!

☐ 27081-8 $4.50/$5.50 in Canada

From Joseph Papp, America's foremost theater producer, and writer Elizabeth Kirkland: a captivating tour through the world of William Shakespeare.

Discover the London of Shakespeare's time, a fascinating place to be—full of mayhem and magic, exploration and exploitation, courtiers and foreigners. Stroll through narrow, winding streets crowded with merchants and minstrels, hoist a pint in a rowdy alehouse, and hurry across the river to the open-air Globe Theatre to the latest play written by a young man named Will Shakespeare.

SHAKESPEARE ALIVE! spirits you back to the very heart of that London—as everyday people might have experienced it. Find out how young people fell in love, how workers and artists made ends meet, what people found funny and what they feared most. Go on location with an Elizabethan theater company, learn how plays were produced, where Shakespeare's plots came from and how he transformed them. Hear the music of Shakespeare's language and the words we still use today that were first spoken in his time.

Open this book and elbow your way into the Globe with the groundlings. You'll be joining one of the most democratic audiences the theater has ever known—alewives, apprentices, shoemakers and nobles—in applauding the dazzling wordplay and swordplay brought to you by William Shakespeare.

Look for **SHAKESPEARE ALIVE!** at your local bookstore or use the coupon below: